INTERESTING PEOPLE

INTERESTING PEOPLE

Black American History Makers

George L. Lee

with a foreword by
DR. HELEN E. WILLIAMS

McFarland & Company, Inc., Publishers
Jefferson, North Carolina, and London

ALSO BY GEORGE L. LEE AND FROM MCFARLAND: *Worldwide Interesting People: 162 History Makers of African Descent* (1992; paperback 2012); *Inspiring African Americans: Black History Makers in the United States, 1750–1980* (1991; paperback 2012); *Interesting Athletes: A Newspaper Artist's Look at Blacks in Sports* (1990; paperback 2012)

The present work is a reprint of the library bound edition of Interesting People: Black American History Makers, *first published in 1989 by McFarland.*

LIBRARY OF CONGRESS CATALOGUING-IN-PUBLICATION DATA

Lee, George L., 1906–
    Interesting people : black American history makers / George
L. Lee ; with a foreword by Helen E. Williams.
        p.   cm.
    Includes bibliographical references and index.

    ISBN 978-0-7864-6767-9
    softcover : acid free paper ∞

    1. African Americans—Biography—Juvenile literature.
    2. African Americans—Biography.   3. Blacks—Biography.
    4. Cartoons and comics.
    E185.96 .L37 2012
    920'.009296073—920   88-43542

BRITISH LIBRARY CATALOGUING DATA ARE AVAILABLE

Front cover: *clockwise from top left* Bill Pickett, Dorothy Dandridge (center), Augusta Savage, Ray Charles, Elder Michaux; Back cover: *top* Gen. Daniel (Chappie) James Jr.; *bottom* Dr. Dorothy L. Brown

Manufactured in the United States of America

McFarland & Company, Inc., Publishers
  Box 611, Je⟩erson, North Carolina 28640
  www.mcfarlandpub.com

*Dedicated to
my late wife, Jennie
my son, Richard
my granddaughter, Terri
and my late brother, Bill*

A FULBRIGHT SCHOLAR

DR. HELEN E. WILLIAMS

ASSISTANT PROFESSOR, COLLEGE LIBRARY AND INFORMATION SERVICES AND THE COLLEGE OF EDUCATION, UNIV. OF MARYLAND (1983). SHE HAS HAD A VERY INTERESTING CAREER OF PROFESSIONAL EXPERIENCE IN TEACHING AND LIBRARY SCIENCES AND A BRILLIANT STUDENT. IN 1987 HELEN WAS AWARDED THE PRESTIGIOUS **FULBRIGHT** SCHOLARSHIP AWARD AND WILL TAKE HER TEACHING YEAR (1988-89) AT THE UNIV. OF THE SOUTH PACIFIC IN FIJI. BORN IN TIMMONSVILLE, S.C. THE SECOND DAUGHTER OF FOUR CHILDREN. HER FATHER A BAPTIST MINISTER

Geo Lee

AND FARMER AND MOTHER A MID-WIFE. HELEN AND HER OLDER SISTER BOTH TRAVELED TOGETHER EDUCATIONALLY FROM THE FIRST GRADE THROUGH COLLEGE. HER AWARDS AND HONORS ARE NUMEROUS. LISTED IN WHO'S WHO AMONG BLACK AMERICANS, 1987; 1986 DISTINGUISHED ALUMNI OF THE YEAR CITATION FROM THE NATIONAL ASSN FOR EQUAL OPPORTUNITY IN HIGHER EDUCATION, AMONG THEM. HER WRITINGS OF ARTICLES FOR BOOKS, JOURNALS HAVE BEEN MANY. A VERY BUSY LADY, WHILE AT MORRIS COLLEGE SHE WAS ... VOTED BY HER CLASSMATES - "THE GIRL MOST LIKELY TO SUCCEED". THEY WERE RIGHT!

HELEN WAS ONLY 4 WHEN SHE STARTED FIRST GRADE. ENTERED MORRIS COLLEGE AT 16. GRADUATED 'CUM LAUDE' FOR HER B.A. IN ENGLISH-SOCIAL STUDIES ('54): M.S.L.S IN LIBRARY SCIENCE FROM ATLANTA UNIV. ('60): C.A.S. UNIV. OF ILLINOIS ('68) PH.D UNIV. OF WISC. ('83'. LIB. SCIENCE.

Foreword

George Lee's lifelong pride of heritage and intellectual curiosity have led to the production of this compendium. This book invites and excites readers to examine further the lives and contributions of black people throughout America.

Enlightening biographical sketches with lively descriptions of dramatic events are accompanied by drawings. This format provides, not academic analysis, but helpful information to encourage deeper exploration by general readers. It is intended to stimulate interest in reading; to encourage intellectual curiosity; and to enhance a basic awareness of black history by identifying some of the numerous, significant, and often unsung contributions made by black Americans.

I am grateful to George Lee for this book, which is critically important to thousands of young people who need to understand that genius, achievement, and dedication to noble ideals are not the exclusive province of one segment of the population. This young audience, along with all Mr. Lee's readers, should become immersed in the pride of heritage that inspired this book.

Dr. Helen E. Williams

Contents

Foreword by Helen E.
  Williams vii
Preface xiii

Elizabeth Forth Denison 1
Isabella Baumfree 2
Catherine Harris 3
William W. Brown 4
Frederick Douglas 5
Harriet Tubman 6
Jackie Robinson 6
Rosa Parks 7
Frances E. Harper 7
William E. Scott 7
Mary Fields 8
Fanny L. Jackson Coppin 9
Robert Smalls 10
James T. Rapier 10
John S. Lawson 11
William H. Carney 11
Edmonia Lewis 12
Lewis H. Latimer 13
Nat Love 14
Richard R. Wright 15
Daniel H. Williams 16
Anna Julia Cooper 17
Bill Pickett 18
Ida B. Wells Barnett 19
Doris E. Spears 19

George Washington Carver 20
C.J. Walker 21
Frank Yerby 21
William H. Lewis 22
Edith Sampson 22
Scott Joplin 23
Joel E. Spingarn 24
Ada S. McKinley 25
Robert S. Abbott 26
James Weldon Johnson 27
William Monroe Trotter 28
Bill Robinson 29
Mattie Cunningham Dolby 30
Andrew (Rube) Foster 31
Sara S. Washington 32
Jane Edna Hunter 33
Daisy Lampkin 34
R.J. Salisbury 35
Solomon L. Michaux 36
Arthur W. Mitchell 37
Isaac Murphy 37
James Van Der Zee 38
Sadie Waterford Jones 39
Louis T. Wright 40
Bessie Coleman 41
Augusta Savage 42
Grace Lee Stevens 43
Harriet M. West 44
Jane M. Bolin 44

Contents

Paul R. Williams 45
Charles H. Houston 46
Alberta Hunter 47
Bessie Smith 48
Andy Razaf 49
William Grant Still 50
William O. Walker 51
Marjorie S. Joyner 52
Eslanda Goode Robeson 53
Edith Wilson 54
Martha Barksdale Goldman 55
Jackie (Moms) Mabley 56
Paul Robeson 57
Matthew A. Henson 57
Fredda Witherspoon 58
Sadie Tanner Alexander 59
Irvin C. Mollison 60
Percy L. Julian 61
Martin L. King, Sr. 62
Clayton Bates 63
Jessie "Ma" Houston 64
Thomas A. Dorsey 65
Louis Armstrong 66
Duke Ellington 67
Juanita Hall 68
La Julia Rhea 69
Langston Hughes 70
Charles R. Drew 71
Ralph J. Bunche 72
Henry W. McGee 73
William H. Hastie 74
Count Basie 75
James B. Parsons 76
W.C. Handy 76
James A. Porter 77
Lois Mailou Jones 78
Elizabeth Catlett 79
Charles Alston 79
Thurgood Marshall 80

Ralph Metcalfe 81
Mary Lou Williams 82
Pauli Murray 83
Katherine Dunham 84
Odetta 85
Howlin' Wolf 85
Mahalia Jackson 86
Clarence Mitchell 87
Gordon Parks, Sr. 88
Lionel Hampton 89
Clara Jones 90
Margaret Harris 90
Joe Louis Barrow 91
Emmett Ashford 92
Carolyn Payton 93
Lelia Foley 93
Billie Holiday 94
Muddy Waters 95
Gwendolyn Brooks 96
Adele Chilton Gaillard 97
Alonzo Smith Gaither 98
Thomas Bradley 99
Fannie Lou Hamer 100
Jesse Owens 101
Margaret Bush Wilson 102
Lena Horne 103
Willa Brown 104
Margaret Burroughs 105
Charles White 106
Coleman A. Young 107
Daisy Bates 108
John Steward Sloan 109
Pearl Bailey 110
Nat "King" Cole 111
James Edwards 112
Barbara Watson 113
Nicholas Bros. 114
Charlie Parker 115
Wade Hampton McCree 116

Contents

Della Reese 117
Jane Cooke Wright 118
Dorothy L. Brown 119
Gloria Richardson 120
Daniel James, Jr. 121
Jesse Brown 122
Whitney M. Young, Jr. 123
Dorothy I. Height 124
Alex Haley 125
Leon H. Sullivan 126
Harold Washington 127
Robert L. Kimbrough 128
Dorothy Dandridge 129
Gwendolyn B. Cherry 130
Nathaniel Clifton 131
James Baldwin 132
Charley Pride 133
Sarah Vaughan 134
Lou Gossett, Jr. 135
Vel Phillips 136
Shirley St. Hill Chisholm 137
Malcolm X 138
Benjamin L. Hooks 139
Patricia R. Harris 140
Sidney Poitier 141
Leontyne Price 142
Althea Gibson 143
Ralph David Abernathy 144
Gerald E. Thomas 145
Mary Elizabeth Mahoney 145
Roscoe Robinson 146
The Black Panthers 146
James Earl Jones 147
Lee Elder 148
Frank E. Petersen 149
Constance Baker Motley 150
Coretta Scott King 151
Andrew Young 152
Ray Charles 153

Bill Cosby 154
Charles C. Rogers 155
Hazel W. Johnson 155
Clifford Alexander 156
Quincy Jones 157
Barbara Jordan 158
"Sugar" Ray Robinson 159
James H. Meredith 160
Ruth Love 161
C. Delores Tucker 162
Amayla Kearse 163
Toni Morrison 164
Micki Grant 165
Nikki Giovanni 165
Samella S. Lewis 166
Vinnette Carroll 167
Grace Bumbry 168
Charles Gordone 169
Parren Mitchell 169
Diana Sands 170
Maya Angelou 171
Hank Aaron 172
Diahann Carroll 173
Frank Robinson 174
Shirley Verrett 175
Ernest Green 176
Diana Ross 177
Joe Frazier 178
Elizabeth D. Koontz 179
Azie Taylor Morton 180
Blanche Kelso Bruce 180
Vernon E. Jordan, Jr. 181
Richard Hunt 182
Autherine Lucy 183
Darwin T. Turner 183
Judith Jamison 184
Ernie Davis 185
Willye White 186
Jesse Jackson 187

Contents

Al Green 188

Guion S. Bluford, Jr. 189

Yvonne B. Burke 190

Sam Boynes 191

Oscar Robertson 192

Mary Hatwood Futrell 193

Ronald V. Dellums 194

Marva Collins 195

Faye Wattleton 196

Addie Wyatt 196

Gladys Knight 197

Reggie Jackson 198

Roberta Flack 199

Cicely Tyson 200

Arthur Ashe 201

Jill Brown 202

Otis B. Young 202

Milton L. Olive, III 203

Stevie Wonder 204

Janie Mines 205

Dan Burley 205

About the Author 207

Index 209

Preface

This is a book about interesting people from all walks of life. The drawings are from my black press feature, "Interesting People," begun in 1945. I discontinued the series in 1948 because of the newsprint shortage brought on by World War II. More than twenty years later, in 1970, I revived the series and continued it until my retirement in 1986. All the following pages have appeared in leading black newspapers throughout the United States. The persons depicted are arranged in approximate chronological order according to their life dates.

The purpose of this book is to show that with God's help, good courage, and determination, one can achieve much. May its pages be a source of inspiration, knowledge, and pride for all.

George L. Lee

ELIZABETH FORTH DENISON

1752 - 1866

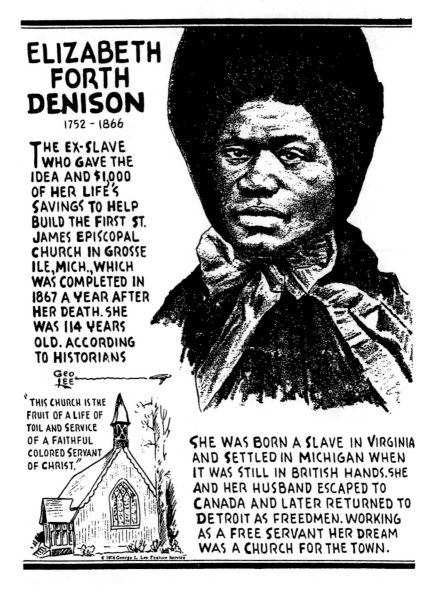

THE EX-SLAVE WHO GAVE THE IDEA AND $1,000 OF HER LIFE'S SAVINGS TO HELP BUILD THE FIRST ST. JAMES EPISCOPAL CHURCH IN GROSSE ILE, MICH., WHICH WAS COMPLETED IN 1867 A YEAR AFTER HER DEATH. SHE WAS 114 YEARS OLD. ACCORDING TO HISTORIANS

Geo Lee

"THIS CHURCH IS THE FRUIT OF A LIFE OF TOIL AND SERVICE OF A FAITHFUL COLORED SERVANT OF CHRIST."

© 1974 George L. Lee Feature Service

SHE WAS BORN A SLAVE IN VIRGINIA AND SETTLED IN MICHIGAN WHEN IT WAS STILL IN BRITISH HANDS. SHE AND HER HUSBAND ESCAPED TO CANADA AND LATER RETURNED TO DETROIT AS FREEDMEN. WORKING AS A FREE SERVANT HER DREAM WAS A CHURCH FOR THE TOWN.

1

WOMEN'S RIGHTS

ISABELLA BAUMFREE
1797 – 1883

BORN A SLAVE ON AN ESTATE IN UPSTATE NEW YORK, BUT GRANTED HER FREEDOM WHEN NEW YORK STATE ABOLISHED SLAVERY IN 1827. WHEN HER MASTER REFUSED TO LET HER GO SHE RAN AWAY. ALTHO ILLITERATE SHE BECAME THE MOST TALKED OF WOMAN IN AMERICA DURING HER TIME. DEEPLY RELIGIOUS, ISABELLA LEFT HER DOMESTIC DUTIES TO PREACH AGAINST INJUSTICE. WITH ORATORY BASED ON HER OWN HARDSHIPS SHE WAS MORE THAN A MATCH FOR HER OPPONENTS. SHE WAS 6 FEET TALL WITH MUSCLES DEVELOPED FROM PLOUGHING AND HARD EXERTION. HER VOICE WAS DEEP AND MANNERS SO FERVENT THAT SHE SEEMED TO BE UNDER A SPELL. NOT ONLY A CHAMPION OF FREEDOM BUT AN ADVOCATE OF WOMEN'S RIGHTS. HER LECTURE CRUSADE TOOK HER TO THE EASTERN STATES, ILL., OHIO, IND., AND MICH. A VISIT TO PRESIDENT LINCOLN WAS A HIGHLIGHT IN HER LIFE. THIS GREAT WOMAN WHO FOUGHT FOR HUMAN RIGHTS CALLED HER-SELF - **SOJOURNER TRUTH!** "AND THE TRUTH SHALL MAKE YOU FREE."

WE MUST UNITE FOR FREEDOM...

"PROCLAIM LIBERTY THROUGHOUT THE LAND UNTO ALL THE INHABITANTS THEREOF"

Geo LEE

2

UNDERGROUND OPERATOR

CATHERINE HARRIS
1809 - 1907

HERE STOOD A STATION OF UNDERGROUND R.R. IN WHICH CATHERINE HARRIS DID HEROIC SERVICE FOR FUGITIVE SLAVES

JAMESTOWN

Geo LEE

1. BORN IN MEADVILLE, PA., ON JUNE 10. HER GRANDFATHER WAS AN AFRICAN BROUGHT TO ENGLAND ON A SLAVE SHIP. HE MARRIED AN ENGLISH WOMAN. THEIR SON CAME TO AMERICA, MARRIED A DUTCH GIRL AND SETTLED AT MEADVILLE. WHEN CATHERINE WAS 7 HER FATHER DIED. AT 19 SHE MET AND MARRIED JOHN HARRIS OF ERIE, PA., THEY SETTLED IN THE VILLAGE OF JAMESTOWN, N.Y. (1831)

2. BEFORE 1835, ANTI-SLAVERY TOOK ROOT IN JAMESTOWN. HER HOUSE BORDERED ON THE PRIMEVAL FOREST AND SWAMP SECTION. IT WAS AN IDEAL PLACE FOR THOSE ESCAPING FROM BONDAGE ON THEIR WAY TO CANADA AND FREEDOM. ONCE A YOUNG MAN SOUGHT REFUGE AT HER "STATION." HE WORE SHOES WHEN HE

3. FLED, BUT THESE WEARING OUT IN HIS FLIGHT, HE WRAPPED HIS FEET IN BURLAP WHICH IN TURN WORE THRU. MRS. HARRIS, ADEPT IN MAKING HEALING SALVES QUICKLY CLEANSED AND MEDICATED HIS PAINFUL FEET. FOR 25 YEARS SHE OPERATED HER UNDERGROUND RAILROAD-STATION-HELPING HER PEOPLE TO FREEDOM. SHE LIVED TO BE 98-YEARS OLD!

© 1971, George L. Lee Feature Service

Catherine Harris is the maternal great-great-grandmother of the author-illustrator of this book, George L. Lee.

FIRST BLACK NOVELIST 1815 1884

WILLIAM W. BROWN

BORN A SLAVE, THE SON OF A WHITE SLAVEHOLDER AND A SLAVE MOTHER, NEAR LEXINGTON, KY. HIS BOYHOOD WAS SPENT IN MISSOURI. AT THE AGE OF 10 HE WAS HIRED OUT TO A CAPTAIN OF A STEAMSHIP, RUNNING BETWEEN ST. LOUIS AND NEW ORLEANS. AT 19 HE ESCAPED AND FLED TO THE GREAT LAKES AREA WHERE HE FOUND WORK ON A LAKE ERIE STEAMER. HE AIDED OTHER FUGITIVE SLAVES TO ESCAPE TO CANADA. HE DILIGENTLY STUDIED READING, WRITING AND ORATORY. HE WROTE HIS

THE ANTI-SLAVERY HARP
A NARRATIVE OF SLAVE LIFE IN THE UNITED STATES
THE NEGRO IN THE AMERICAN REBELLION
THE ESCAPE
THE SOUTH AND ITS PEOPLE
A DRAMA IN FIVE ACTS
THE BLACK MAN

GEO LEE

FIRST MAJOR WORK:"NARRATIVE OF WILLIAM WELLS BROWN, A FUGITIVE SLAVE"(1847). IN 1849 HE WAS INVITED BY THE ANTI-SLAVERY SOCIETY TO VISIT ENGLAND. HE WAS THE FIRST BLACK IN AMERICA TO WRITE A NOVEL–"CLOTEL"(1852); THE FIRST TO WRITE A DRAMA–"THE DOUGH FACE"(1854); THE FIRST TO WRITE A BOOK OF TRAVEL– "THREE YEARS IN EUROPE"(1855).

BEST KNOWN BLACK AUTHOR OF HIS TIME. A CULTURAL GIANT.

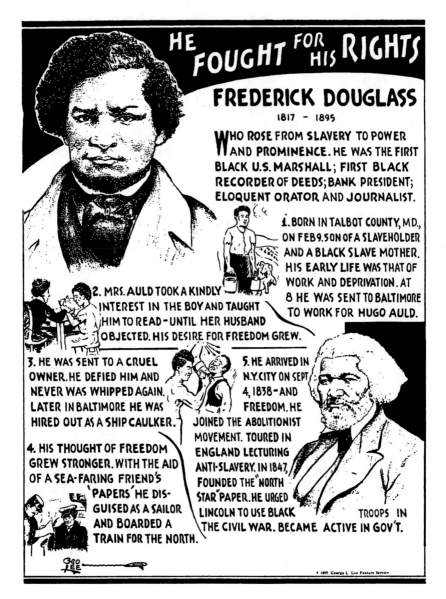

HE FOUGHT FOR HIS RIGHTS

FREDERICK DOUGLASS
1817 – 1895

WHO ROSE FROM SLAVERY TO POWER AND PROMINENCE. HE WAS THE FIRST BLACK U.S. MARSHALL; FIRST BLACK RECORDER OF DEEDS; BANK PRESIDENT; ELOQUENT ORATOR AND JOURNALIST.

1. BORN IN TALBOT COUNTY, MD., ON FEB 9. SON OF A SLAVEHOLDER AND A BLACK SLAVE MOTHER. HIS EARLY LIFE WAS THAT OF WORK AND DEPRIVATION. AT 8 HE WAS SENT TO BALTIMORE TO WORK FOR HUGO AULD.

2. MRS. AULD TOOK A KINDLY INTEREST IN THE BOY AND TAUGHT HIM TO READ – UNTIL HER HUSBAND OBJECTED. HIS DESIRE FOR FREEDOM GREW.

3. HE WAS SENT TO A CRUEL OWNER. HE DEFIED HIM AND NEVER WAS WHIPPED AGAIN. LATER IN BALTIMORE HE WAS HIRED OUT AS A SHIP CAULKER.

4. HIS THOUGHT OF FREEDOM GREW STRONGER. WITH THE AID OF A SEA-FARING FRIEND'S 'PAPERS' HE DISGUISED AS A SAILOR AND BOARDED A TRAIN FOR THE NORTH.

5. HE ARRIVED IN N.Y. CITY ON SEPT 4, 1838 – AND FREEDOM. HE JOINED THE ABOLITIONIST MOVEMENT. TOURED IN ENGLAND LECTURING ANTI-SLAVERY. IN 1847, FOUNDED THE "NORTH STAR" PAPER. HE URGED LINCOLN TO USE BLACK TROOPS IN THE CIVIL WAR. BECAME ACTIVE IN GOV'T.

GEO LEE

5

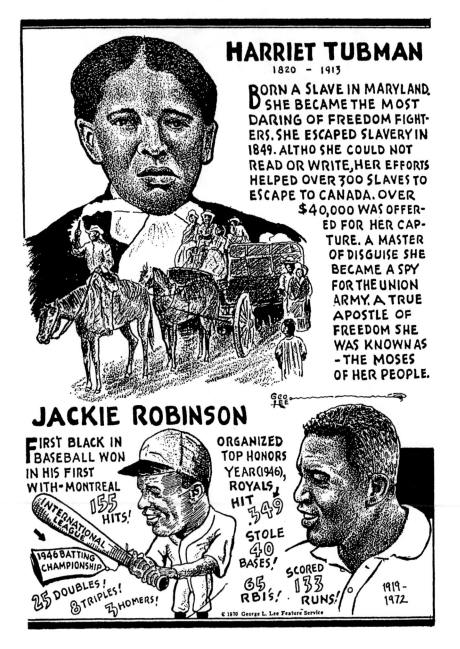

HARRIET TUBMAN
1820 – 1913

BORN A SLAVE IN MARYLAND, SHE BECAME THE MOST DARING OF FREEDOM FIGHTERS. SHE ESCAPED SLAVERY IN 1849. ALTHO SHE COULD NOT READ OR WRITE, HER EFFORTS HELPED OVER 300 SLAVES TO ESCAPE TO CANADA. OVER $40,000 WAS OFFERED FOR HER CAPTURE. A MASTER OF DISGUISE SHE BECAME A SPY FOR THE UNION ARMY. A TRUE APOSTLE OF FREEDOM SHE WAS KNOWN AS – THE MOSES OF HER PEOPLE.

JACKIE ROBINSON

Geo LEE

FIRST BLACK IN BASEBALL WON IN HIS FIRST WITH – MONTREAL

INTERNATIONAL LEAGUE

155 HITS!

1946 BATTING CHAMPIONSHIP

25 DOUBLES! 8 TRIPLES! 3 HOMERS!

ORGANIZED TOP HONORS YEAR (1946), ROYALS, HIT .349

STOLE 40 BASES!

65 RBI's!

SCORED 133 RUNS!

1919 – 1972

© 1970 George L. Lee Feature Service

6

HEROINE OF THE BUS

ROSA PARKS

ON DEC 1, 1955 IN MONTGOMERY, ALA., ROSA PARKS A SEAMSTRESS RIDING A BUS ON HER WAY HOME DECIDED SHE WOULD NOT MOVE - 'TO THE BACK OF THE BUS.' SHE WAS ARRESTED. THUS STARTED A BUS BOYCOTT THAT LASTED 381 DAYS AND ENDED ONLY AFTER A SUPREME COURT DECISION THAT SEGREGATION ON BUSES WAS **ILLEGAL!**

BOYCOTT!

FRANCES E. HARPER 1825 - 1911

FIRST BLACK WOMAN TO PUBLISH A NOVEL IN 1860. THE BOOK RECEIVED WIDE ACCLAIM - "IOLA LEROY; OR, THE SHADOWS LIFTED." A POET, LECTURER AND ABOLITIONIST. SHE BECAME ACTIVE IN THE UNDERGROUND RAILROAD IN 1853. SHE HEADED THE NEGRO WOMEN IN TEMPERANCE. HER BEST KNOWN POEM - 'BURY ME IN A FREELAND.'

WILLIAM E. SCOTT 1884 - 1964

Distinguished Painter

NOTED ARTIST WAS BORN IN INDIANAPOLIS, IND. HE STUDIED AT THE ART INSTITUTE OF CHICAGO AND THE BEAUX ART ACADEMY IN PARIS. FAMOUS FOR HIS MURALS AND PORTRAITS. OVER 200 PUBLIC BUILDINGS DISPLAY HIS MURALS INCLUDING THE RECORDER OF DEEDS BLDG.

1980 GEO L. LEE FEATURE SERVICE

BLACK MARY

GUN-TOTING STAGE COACH DRIVER THE
SECOND WOMAN EVER TO DRIVE A U.S.MAIL
ROUTE. A CRACK SHOT, SHE WORE A 38
STRAPPED UNDER HER APRON....

MARY FIELDS

BORN A SLAVE SOMEWHERE IN TENNESSEE
REPORTEDLY IN 1832. SHE LIVED FOR AWHILE IN
MISSISSIPPI THEN MOVED TO OHIO WHERE SHE
WORKED AT THE URSULINES CONVENT IN
TOLEDO. HERE SHE MET MOTHER AMADEUS
A CATHOLIC NUN. IN 1884 THE NUN WENT
TO MONTANA TO OPEN A SCHOOL FOR
INDIAN GIRLS AT ST. PETER'S MISSION.
WHEN MOTHER AMADEUS TOOK ILL AND
LAY DYING, MARY WENT TO HER AND
NURSED HER BACK TO HEALTH. BLACK
MARY STAYED IN MONTANA AND BECAME
ONE OF THE MOST MEMORABLE CHARAC-
TERS IN ITS HISTORY. TALL AND OVER
200-POUNDS AND EXCEPT FOR AN APRON
AND SKIRT, WORE MEN'S CLOTHES, EVEN
SMOKED CIGARS. SHE DID THE FREIGHTING
FOR THE MISSION FOR 10-YEARS. HER TEMPER
AND FIGHTS WITH THE HIRED MEN FORCED
THE BISHOP TO REMOVE HER FROM THE
CONVENT. SHE WENT TO NEARBY CASCADE TO
LIVE. MOTHER AMADEUS SET HER UP
IN THE RESTAURANT BUSINESS. TOO GOOD-
HEARTED SHE FAILED. LATER MARY WAS
GIVEN A MAIL ROUTE BETWEEN CASCADE
AND THE MISSION. SHE DROVE THE ROUTE FOR
8-YEARS. MARY RENEWED HER FAITH IN THE
CHURCH. HER PASSING IN 1914 WAS MOURNED
BY THE TOWNSPEOPLE. A REAL PIONEER.

Geo.
LEE

© 1973 George L. Lee Feature Service

EDUCATOR

FANNY L. JACKSON COPPIN

WAS BORN A SLAVE IN WASH, D.C., IN 1835 AND LEFT AN ORPHAN AT AN EARLY AGE. HER AUNT BOUGHT HER FREEDOM FOR $125. FANNY WORKED FOR HER SCHOOLING AT STATE NORMAL SCHOOL IN BRISTOL, R.I. LATER TO OBERLIN (OHIO) COLLEGE WHERE SHE GRADUATED IN 1865. SHE ACCEPTED A TEACHER POSITION IN PHILADELPHIA, PA., AT THE "INSTITUTE FOR COLORED YOUTH". (LATER

KNOWN AS THE CHEYNEY TRAINING SCHOOL) IN 1874 BECAME PRINCIPAL AND WAS OUTSTANDING AS AN EDUCATOR UNTIL HER DEATH, JAN 21, 1913. MRS. COPPIN WAS ACTIVE AS ORGANIZER AND LECTURER IN THE BLACK WOMEN'S RIGHTS MOVEMENTS. IN 1832 RICHARD HUMPHREY WHO DIED IN PHILA., AND LEFT $10,000 FOR COLORED YOUTH INSTITUTION (IT WAS FOUNDED IN 1837)... WAS ONCE A SLAVEHOLDER.

© 1977. George L. Lee Feature Service

9

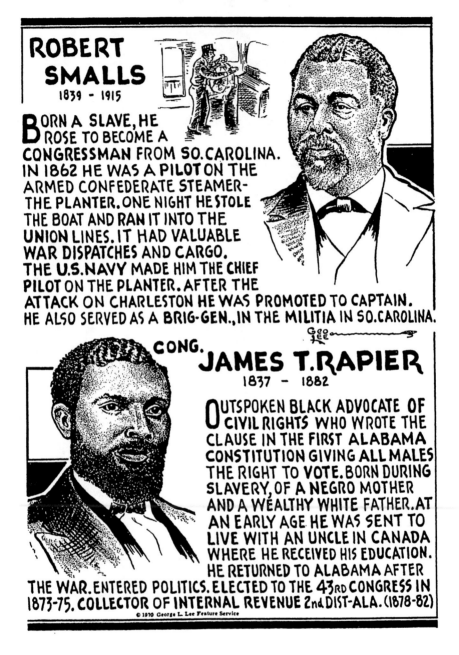

ROBERT SMALLS
1839 - 1915

BORN A SLAVE, HE ROSE TO BECOME A CONGRESSMAN FROM SO. CAROLINA. IN 1862 HE WAS A PILOT ON THE ARMED CONFEDERATE STEAMER- THE PLANTER. ONE NIGHT HE STOLE THE BOAT AND RAN IT INTO THE UNION LINES. IT HAD VALUABLE WAR DISPATCHES AND CARGO. THE U.S. NAVY MADE HIM THE CHIEF PILOT ON THE PLANTER. AFTER THE ATTACK ON CHARLESTON HE WAS PROMOTED TO CAPTAIN. HE ALSO SERVED AS A BRIG-GEN., IN THE MILITIA IN SO. CAROLINA.

CONG. JAMES T. RAPIER
1837 - 1882

OUTSPOKEN BLACK ADVOCATE OF CIVIL RIGHTS WHO WROTE THE CLAUSE IN THE FIRST ALABAMA CONSTITUTION GIVING ALL MALES THE RIGHT TO VOTE. BORN DURING SLAVERY, OF A NEGRO MOTHER AND A WEALTHY WHITE FATHER. AT AN EARLY AGE HE WAS SENT TO LIVE WITH AN UNCLE IN CANADA WHERE HE RECEIVED HIS EDUCATION. HE RETURNED TO ALABAMA AFTER THE WAR. ENTERED POLITICS. ELECTED TO THE 43RD CONGRESS IN 1873-75. COLLECTOR OF INTERNAL REVENUE 2nd DIST-ALA. (1878-82)

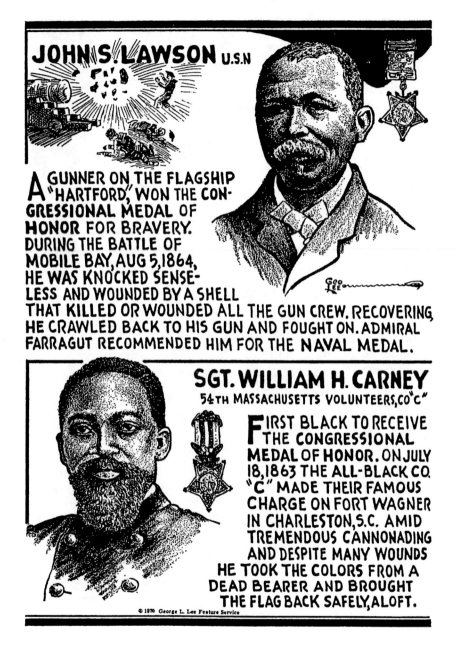

JOHN S. LAWSON U.S.N

A GUNNER ON THE FLAGSHIP "HARTFORD," WON THE CONGRESSIONAL MEDAL OF HONOR FOR BRAVERY. DURING THE BATTLE OF MOBILE BAY, AUG 5,1864, HE WAS KNOCKED SENSELESS AND WOUNDED BY A SHELL THAT KILLED OR WOUNDED ALL THE GUN CREW. RECOVERING, HE CRAWLED BACK TO HIS GUN AND FOUGHT ON. ADMIRAL FARRAGUT RECOMMENDED HIM FOR THE NAVAL MEDAL.

SGT. WILLIAM H. CARNEY
54TH MASSACHUSETTS VOLUNTEERS, CO"C"

FIRST BLACK TO RECEIVE THE CONGRESSIONAL MEDAL OF HONOR. ON JULY 18, 1863 THE ALL-BLACK CO. "C" MADE THEIR FAMOUS CHARGE ON FORT WAGNER IN CHARLESTON, S.C. AMID TREMENDOUS CANNONADING AND DESPITE MANY WOUNDS HE TOOK THE COLORS FROM A DEAD BEARER AND BROUGHT THE FLAG BACK SAFELY, ALOFT.

© 1970 George L. Lee Feature Service

11

EDMONIA LEWIS

BORN 1845

THE FIRST BLACK TO WIN DISTINCTION IN SCULPTURE!

BORN IN NEW YORK, HER MOTHER A FULL-BLOODED CHIPPEWA AND FATHER A FULL-BLOODED NEGRO. THE PARENTS DIED WHEN SHE WAS QUITE YOUNG. AFTER LIVING FOR THREE YEARS WITH THE CHIPPEWAS, HER OLDER BROTHER SOUGHT TO HAVE HER EDUCATED AND ENROLLED HER IN OBERLIN PREP (1859) AND COLLEGE IN OHIO. WHILE THERE SHE BECAME INTERESTED IN SCULPTURE. THEY SETTLED IN BOSTON AND WITH THE HELP OF ABOLITIONIST WILLIAM LLOYD GARRISON SHE STUDIED UNDER EDMUND BRACKETT A NOTED SCULPTOR. HER EXHIBIT OF A BUST OF COL.

Geo LEE

EDMONIA WAS WELL-KNOWN FOR HER BUSTS OF FAMOUS PEOPLE!

LINCOLN

ROBERT G. SHAW IN 1865 MADE IT POSSIBLE FOR EDMONIA TO STUDY IN ROME. SHE SET UP A STUDIO AND WENT ON TO FAME AS A SCULPTRESS. HER BUST OF HENRY W. LONGFELLOW WAS PLACED IN WIDENER LIBRARY AT HARVARD U. (1869). HER BEST-KNOWN WORK WAS "FOREVER FREE." SHE EXHIBITED "THE DEATH OF CLEOPATRA" IN THE 1876 CENTENNIAL EXPOSITION IN PHILADELPHIA, PA.

© 1977, George L. Lee Feature Service

EDISON PIONEER

LEWIS H. LATIMER
1848 – 1928

OF NEW YORK CITY WAS A BRILLIANT DRAFTSMAN AND ELECTRICIAN. IN 1880 HE WAS EMPLOYED BY THE U.S. ELECTRIC CO., AND PRIVATE SECRETARY TO SIR HIRAM MAXIM OF MAXIM GUN FAME. HE WAS SENT TO ENGLAND IN 1881 TO ESTABLISH THE MANUFACTURE OF INCANDESCENT ELECTRIC LAMPS FOR SIR MAXIM. HE RETURNED IN 1882...

JOINED THE THOS. A. EDISON CO., IN 1886 AND INVENTED AND PATENTED THE FIRST ELECTRIC LIGHT BULB WITH A CARBON FILAMENT WHICH EDISON DEVELOPED INTO THE MODERN LAMP. MR. LATIMER WROTE THE FIRST TEXTBOOK ON ELECTRIC LIGHTING SYSTEMS IN THE U.S.

DEADWOOD DICK

NAT LOVE

WAS BORN A SLAVE IN DAVIDSON COUNTY, TENN., IN JUNE 1854. AT THE AGE OF 15 HE HEADED WEST TO DODGE CITY, KANSAS. THE CIVIL WAR WAS OVER AND NAT DECIDED TO GO WEST. HE SOON BECAME A COW- BOY AND TOOK PART IN CATTLE DRIVES ALONG THE FAMOUS CHISHOLM TRAIL. SOMEWHERE ALONG THE DRIVES HE PICKED UP THE NICKNAME OF RED RIVER DICK. ON JULY 4, 1876 HE APPEARED IN A RODEO IN DEADWOOD, SO. DAKOTA. AFTER HIS EXPLO- ITS IN SHOOTIN' AND ROPING AND RIDING...HIS GREAT SKILLS AND DARING, HE WAS NAMED "DEADWOOD DICK". A GOOD INDIAN FIGHTER THE COLORFUL COWBOY WAS TRULY A PART OF WINNING THE WEST. ACCORDING TO HISTORIANS...THE BLACK COWBOYS WERE VERY NUMEROUS. NAT BECAME A LIVING LEG- END AND IN 1907 WROTE HIS AUTOBIOGRAPHY. IN HIS LATTER YEARS WAS A PULLMAN PORTER LIVING IN LOS ANGELES. HE DIED IN 1921.

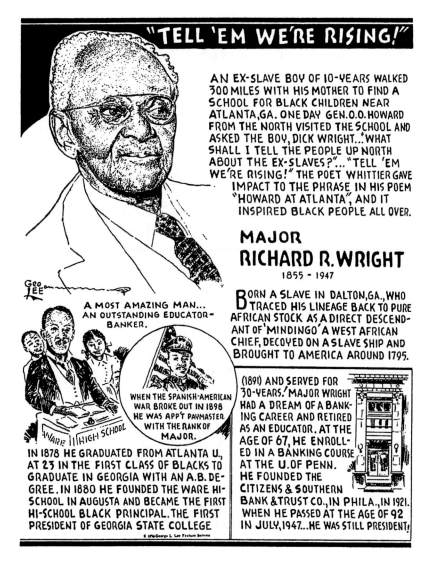

"TELL 'EM WE'RE RISING!"

AN EX-SLAVE BOY OF 10-YEARS WALKED 300 MILES WITH HIS MOTHER TO FIND A SCHOOL FOR BLACK CHILDREN NEAR ATLANTA,GA. ONE DAY GEN.O.O.HOWARD FROM THE NORTH VISITED THE SCHOOL AND ASKED THE BOY, DICK WRIGHT..."WHAT SHALL I TELL THE PEOPLE UP NORTH ABOUT THE EX-SLAVES?"..."TELL 'EM WE'RE RISING!" THE POET WHITTIER GAVE IMPACT TO THE PHRASE IN HIS POEM "HOWARD AT ATLANTA", AND IT INSPIRED BLACK PEOPLE ALL OVER.

MAJOR
RICHARD R. WRIGHT
1855 - 1947

Geo LEE

A MOST AMAZING MAN... AN OUTSTANDING EDUCATOR-BANKER.

BORN A SLAVE IN DALTON,GA.,WHO TRACED HIS LINEAGE BACK TO PURE AFRICAN STOCK AS A DIRECT DESCENDANT OF 'MINDINGO' A WEST AFRICAN CHIEF, DECOYED ON A SLAVE SHIP AND BROUGHT TO AMERICA AROUND 1795.

WHEN THE SPANISH-AMERICAN WAR BROKE OUT IN 1898 HE WAS APP'T PAYMASTER WITH THE RANK OF MAJOR.

WARE HIGH SCHOOL

IN 1878 HE GRADUATED FROM ATLANTA U., AT 23 IN THE FIRST CLASS OF BLACKS TO GRADUATE IN GEORGIA WITH AN A.B. DEGREE. IN 1880 HE FOUNDED THE WARE HI-SCHOOL IN AUGUSTA AND BECAME THE FIRST HI-SCHOOL BLACK PRINCIPAL. THE FIRST PRESIDENT OF GEORGIA STATE COLLEGE

© 1976 George L. Lee Feature Service

(1891) AND SERVED FOR 30-YEARS. MAJOR WRIGHT HAD A DREAM OF A BANK-ING CAREER AND RETIRED AS AN EDUCATOR. AT THE AGE OF 67, HE ENROLL-ED IN A BANKING COURSE AT THE U.OF PENN. HE FOUNDED THE CITIZENS & SOUTHERN BANK &TRUST CO.,IN PHILA.,IN 1921. WHEN HE PASSED AT THE AGE OF 92 IN JULY,1947...HE WAS STILL PRESIDENT!

PIONEERED BLACK MEDICAL TRAINING

DR. DANIEL H. WILLIAMS

DIED 1931

HE LED THE WAY FOR BLACK DOC-TORS AND NURSES. NO HOSPITAL IN CHICAGO WOULD ACCEPT THEM. HE FOUNDED THE PROVIDENT HOSPITAL IN 1891 THE FIRST INTERRACIAL HOSP., IN AMERICA...AND THE FIRST TRAIN-ING SCHOOL FOR BLACK NURSES. BORN ON JAN 18,1856 IN HOLLIDAYS-BURG,PA.,A WHITE FATHER AND A FREE NEGRO MOTHER. AFTER HIS FA-THER DIED THE FAMILY ENDED UP IN JANESVILLE,WIS. HIS INTENSE AMBI-TION...TO BE A SURGEON. BUT NO PRE-MED COURSES IN COLLEGES-THEN. ONE HAD TO SERVE AN APPRENTICE-SHIP WITH A PRACTICING DOCTOR. DAN HAD A BARBERSHOP AND MET SURGEON GEN. HENRY PALMER WHO INVITED

Geo LEE

HE SEWED-UP A HUMAN HEART!

ON THE NIGHT OF JULY 9,1893 A MAN IN A BRAWL WAS STABBED IN THE HEART AND BROUGHT TO PROVIDENT HOSP. DR.DAN OPENED UP THE CHEST AND WITH UNEQUALLED SKILL SEWED UP THE WOUND WITH A FINE CATGUT AND SAVED HIS LIFE.WORLD'S FIRST HEART OPERATION.

HIM TO "READ MEDICINE" IN HIS OFFICE. AFTER 2-YEARS IN 1880 HE ENTERED CHICAGO MEDICAL COLLEGE GRADUATED,1883. INTERNSHIP AT MERCY HOSP.(CHGO). A REMARKABLE CAREER: SO.SIDE DISPENSARY-1884-93; PROVIDENT-1891-93: FREEDMEN'S (D.C.) 1893-98: PROVIDENT 1898-'12: COOK CTY 1900-06:ST.LUKE'S 1912-31: CHARTER MEM-BER AMERICAN COLL.OF SURGERY 1913.

1955 DEC 1. LEE FEATURE OFFICE

16

PIONEER TEACHER

ANNA JULIA COOPER

A LIFELONG QUEST FOR HIGHER EDUCATION FOR BLACKS. A PIONEER WHO LIVED FROM SLAVERY INTO THE CIVIL RIGHTS MOVEMENT. FOUGHT FOR WOMEN'S RIGHTS. BORN IN 1858 IN RALEIGH, N.C. AND HISTORIANS PRESUMED, FATHERED BY HER MASTER, DR. HAYWOOD. AS A CHILD WAS SENT TO RALEIGH'S ST. AUGUSTINES NORMAL SCHOOL AND COLLEGIATE INST., A SCHOOL TO PREPARE BLACK TEACHERS. AT 19, MARRIED HER GREEK STUDIES TEACHER GEORGE A.C. COOPER, HE DIED TWO YEARS LATER (1879). ANNA BECAME A FULL-TIME TEACHER. EAGER FOR HIGHER EDUCATION SHE ENROLLED AT OBERLIN COLLEGE (OHIO) IN 1881. ONE OF THE FIRST BLACK WOMEN TO EARN A BACHELOR'S DEGREE AT A MAJOR COLLEGE (1884). HEADED SCIENCE AND MODERN LANG. DEPT. AT WILBERFORCE COLL...FOR THIS WORK, OBERLIN AWARDED HER A MASTER'S. SHE TAUGHT AT "M" STREET PREPARATORY SCHOOL A BLACK SCHOOL IN WASH, D.C...BECAME PRINCIPAL IN 1902...BUT HER HIGHER CURRICULUM...THE D.C. BOARD FIRED HER (1906). LATER AND BACK IN THE D.C. SYSTEM AND IN HER 60's SHE WENT TO PARIS AND EARNED A DOCTORATE AT SORBONNE UNIV. DIED 1964...106 YRS!

1984 Geo L. Lee Feature Service

THE BLACK KING OF THE RODEO COWBOYS ON HIS HORSE "SPRADLEY."

BILL PICKETT

DIED IN 1932

BORN IN TEXAS AROUND 1860. HE WAS REARED IN THE RANGE COUNTRY AND GREW UP IN THE SADDLE. HIS MOTHER A CHOCTAW INDIAN, HIS FATHER BLACK. ON THE RANGE BILL NOTICED THAT A BULL DOG FOLLOWED THE HERD AND WHEN AN UNRULY STEER WENT ASTRAY...THE DOG COULD CONTROL THE STEER BY BITING IT'S LIP.' THE DARING COWBOY TRIED BITING THE STEER'S LIP AND AT THE SAME TIME GRASPING THE HORNS AND TWISTING IT'S NECK ...THUS FORCING THE STEER TO THE GROUND. THE "ART OF BULLDOGGING" WAS BORN. BY HIS DARING EXPLOITS... HE WAS SIGNED BY THE MILLERS 101 RANCH WILD WEST SHOWS...AND FOR YEARS HE WAS THE STAR ATTRACTION. BILLED AS THE "WORLD CHAMPION BULLDOGGER!

JUMPING FROM A RUNNING HORSE ON THE STEER MADE HIS ACT VERY EXCITING!

GEO LEE

© 1975 George L. Lee Feature Service

FOUGHT FOR CIVIL RIGHTS

IDA B. WELLS BARNETT
1862-1931

BORN IN HOLLYSPRINGS, MISS., LEFT AN ORPHAN AT 14 WITH 7 YOUNGER BROTHERS AND SISTERS TO CARE FOR. SHE TAUGHT SCHOOL, LATER AN EDITOR AND PUBLISHER OF "FREESPEECH" IN MEMPHIS, TENN. HER FIGHT AGAINST LYNCHING WAS SO FEARLESS THAT HER PLANT WAS BURNED AND SHE WAS FORCED TO FLEE FOR HER LIFE. IN NEW YORK SHE CONTINUED HER ANTI-LYNCHING EDITORIALS THRU THE BLACK NEW YORK AGE NEWSPAPER. SHE TOOK HER CAUSE TO ENGLAND IN 1893-94. IN 1895 MISS. WELLS MARRIED FERDINAND L. BARNETT, THE PUBLISHER OF CHICAGO'S FIRST BLACK NEWSPAPER, THE "CHICAGO CONSERVATOR". THEY FOUGHT TIRELESSLY FOR EQUAL RIGHTS IN AMERICA. SHE ORGANIZED CIVIC AND WELFARE GROUPS. A COURAGEOUS WOMAN WITH VISION!

MRS. DORIS E. SPEARS

OF LOS ANGELES, CALIF., IN 1944 WAS THE FIRST WOMAN DEPUTY SHERIFF...APPOINTED IN THE STATE OF CALIFORNIA, TO THE LOS ANGELES COUNTY SHERIFF'S STAFF. —ONCE A STUDENT OF THE LOS ANGELES CITY COLLEGE.

HEY!

WHAT A MINUTE BIG BOY!

Geo LEE

© 1954 George L. Lee Feature Service

19

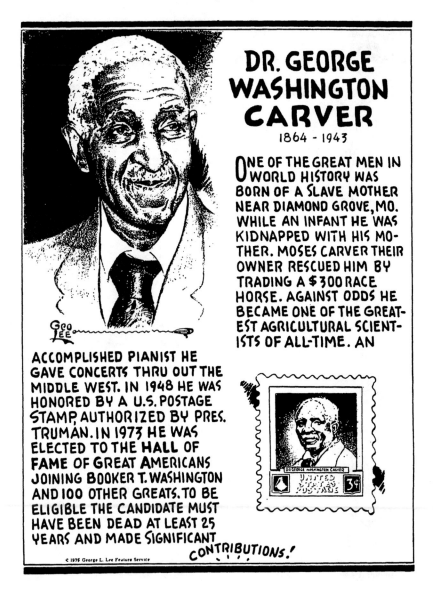

DR. GEORGE WASHINGTON CARVER

1864 - 1943

ONE OF THE GREAT MEN IN WORLD HISTORY WAS BORN OF A SLAVE MOTHER NEAR DIAMOND GROVE, MO. WHILE AN INFANT HE WAS KIDNAPPED WITH HIS MOTHER. MOSES CARVER THEIR OWNER RESCUED HIM BY TRADING A $300 RACE HORSE. AGAINST ODDS HE BECAME ONE OF THE GREATEST AGRICULTURAL SCIENTISTS OF ALL-TIME. AN ACCOMPLISHED PIANIST HE GAVE CONCERTS THRU OUT THE MIDDLE WEST. IN 1948 HE WAS HONORED BY A U.S. POSTAGE STAMP, AUTHORIZED BY PRES. TRUMAN. IN 1973 HE WAS ELECTED TO THE **HALL** OF **FAME** OF **GREAT AMERICANS** JOINING BOOKER T. WASHINGTON AND 100 OTHER GREATS. TO BE ELIGIBLE THE CANDIDATE MUST HAVE BEEN DEAD AT LEAST 25 YEARS AND MADE SIGNIFICANT CONTRIBUTIONS!

Geo Lee

DR. GEORGE WASHINGTON CARVER
UNITED STATES POSTAGE 3¢

© 1975 George L. Lee Feature Service

MADAME C.J. WALKER
1867 - 1919

FOUNDER OF THE MME.C. J.WALKER MFG CO, THE OLDEST NEGRO COSMETICS CO. BORN IN A CABIN IN DELTA, LA., SHE STARTED HER BUSINESS WITH $2 AND AN ORIGINAL FORMULA FOR STRAIGHTENING HAIR – AND BECAME THE FIRST BLACK WOMAN MILLIONAIRE !

FRANK YERBY
OF AUGUSTA, GA.

NOVELIST, SOLD HIS FIRST NOVEL "THE FOXES OF HARROW" AFTER HE HAD WRITTEN ONLY 27 PAGES. HE WROTE THE BEST SELLER WHILE WORKING 12 HRS A DAY IN A LONG ISLAND WAR PLANT DURING WORLD WAR II. HIS MANY ROMANTIC HISTORICAL NOVELS HAVE SOLD 20 MILLION COPIES. THE EX-TEACHER LIVES IN EUROPE.

WILLIAM H. LEWIS

FIRST BLACK, APPOINTED ASS'T U.S. ATTORNEY GENERAL BY PRES. WILLIAM H. TAFT IN 1911. BORN IN BERKELEY, VA., (1868) HE ATTENDED VIRGINIA NORMAL AND COLLEGIATE INSTITUTE... THEN TO AMHERST COLLEGE, IN MASS. AN OUTSTANDING FOOTBALL CENTER AND CAPT., OF THE AMHERST TEAM. ENTERED HARVARD WHERE HE WAS NAMED ALL-AMERICAN BY WALTER CAMP IN 1892 AND 1893. LATER NAMED AS ALL-TIME, ALL-AMERICAN CENTER. HE WAS LINE COACH AT HARVARD FOR MANY YEARS. AUTHOR OF SPORTS BOOK: "HOW TO PLAY FOOTBALL".

GEO LEE

JUDGE EDITH SAMPSON

FIRST BLACK WOMAN EVER ELECTED TO THE BENCH IN THE U.S...THE CIRCUIT COURT OF COOK COUNTY (CHGO) IN 1962. FIRST U.S. BLACK UN DELEGATE APPOINTED, 1950 BY PRES. TRUMAN. BORN IN MEADVILLE, PA., SHE STUDIED FOR THE SOCIAL SERVICE BEFORE TURNING TO LAW. IT TOOK MANY YEARS OF NIGHT CLASSES AT JOHN MARSHALL LAW SCHOOL IN CHICAGO... WORKING DAYS...TO EARN HER DEGREE. SHE WAS THE FIRST WOMAN EVER TO EARN A MASTER'S IN LAW AT LOYOLA U. A BRILLIANT WOMAN OF MANY "FIRSTS".

KING OF RAGTIME'

SCOTT JOPLIN
1868 - 1917

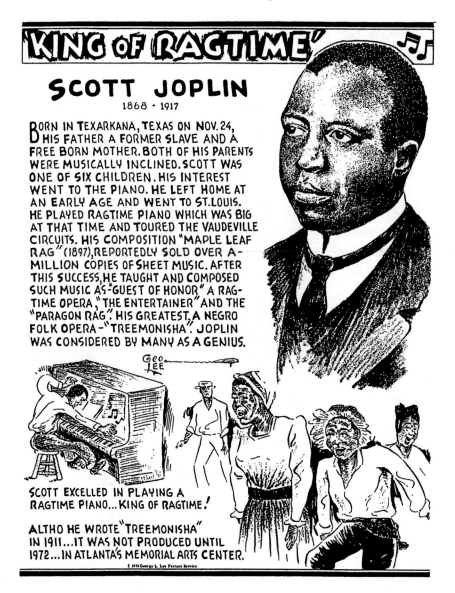

BORN IN TEXARKANA, TEXAS ON NOV. 24, HIS FATHER A FORMER SLAVE AND A FREE BORN MOTHER. BOTH OF HIS PARENTS WERE MUSICALLY INCLINED. SCOTT WAS ONE OF SIX CHILDREN. HIS INTEREST WENT TO THE PIANO. HE LEFT HOME AT AN EARLY AGE AND WENT TO ST. LOUIS. HE PLAYED RAGTIME PIANO WHICH WAS BIG AT THAT TIME AND TOURED THE VAUDEVILLE CIRCUITS. HIS COMPOSITION "MAPLE LEAF RAG" (1897), REPORTEDLY SOLD OVER A MILLION COPIES OF SHEET MUSIC. AFTER THIS SUCCESS, HE TAUGHT AND COMPOSED SUCH MUSIC AS "GUEST OF HONOR" A RAGTIME OPERA, "THE ENTERTAINER" AND THE "PARAGON RAG". HIS GREATEST, A NEGRO FOLK OPERA - "TREEMONISHA". JOPLIN WAS CONSIDERED BY MANY AS A GENIUS.

SCOTT EXCELLED IN PLAYING A RAGTIME PIANO... KING OF RAGTIME!

ALTHO HE WROTE "TREEMONISHA" IN 1911... IT WAS NOT PRODUCED UNTIL 1972... IN ATLANTA'S MEMORIAL ARTS CENTER.

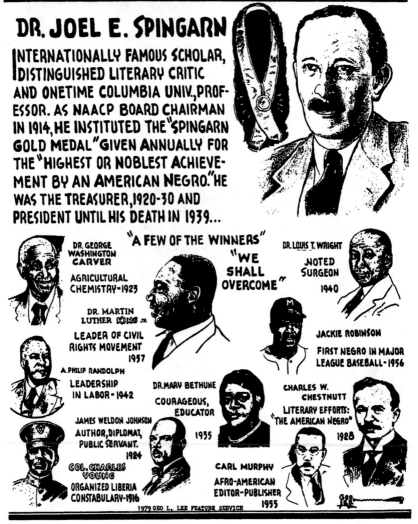

The SPINGARN MEDAL

DR. JOEL E. SPINGARN

INTERNATIONALLY FAMOUS SCHOLAR, DISTINGUISHED LITERARY CRITIC AND ONETIME COLUMBIA UNIV., PROFESSOR. AS NAACP BOARD CHAIRMAN IN 1914, HE INSTITUTED THE "SPINGARN GOLD MEDAL" GIVEN ANNUALLY FOR THE "HIGHEST OR NOBLEST ACHIEVEMENT BY AN AMERICAN NEGRO." HE WAS THE TREASURER, 1920-30 AND PRESIDENT UNTIL HIS DEATH IN 1939...

"A FEW OF THE WINNERS"

"WE SHALL OVERCOME"

DR. GEORGE WASHINGTON CARVER
AGRICULTURAL CHEMISTRY-1923

DR. LOUIS T. WRIGHT
NOTED SURGEON
1940

DR. MARTIN LUTHER KING JR
LEADER OF CIVIL RIGHTS MOVEMENT
1957

JACKIE ROBINSON
FIRST NEGRO IN MAJOR LEAGUE BASEBALL-1956

A. PHILIP RANDOLPH
LEADERSHIP IN LABOR - 1942

DR. MARY BETHUNE
COURAGEOUS, EDUCATOR
1935

CHARLES W. CHESTNUTT
LITERARY EFFORTS: "THE AMERICAN NEGRO"
1928

JAMES WELDON JOHNSON
AUTHOR, DIPLOMAT, PUBLIC SERVANT.
1924

COL. CHARLES YOUNG
ORGANIZED LIBERIA CONSTABULARY-1916

CARL MURPHY
AFRO-AMERICAN EDITOR-PUBLISHER
1955

1979 GEO L. LEE FEATURE SERVICE

24

McKINLEY HOUSE

ADA S. McKINLEY
1868 - 1952

WHO DEVOTED HER LIFE TO WORK FOR THE POOR. A SOCIAL WORKER GIVING HER UNTIRING EFFORTS, TIME AND MONEY TO HELP HER PEOPLE. SHE FOUNDED THE "SOUTHSIDE SETTLEMENT HOUSE" IN 1919, IN CHICAGO...THE FIRST FOR BLACKS WITH A BLACK STAFF. DURING WORLD WAR I BLACKS FLOCKED TO CHICAGO LOOKING FOR WORK. HER AIM WAS TO AID THOSE IN NEED...SHE DID! SLOWLY SHE PROGRESSED...BY 1949 WITH THE HELP OF THE COMMUNITY FUND AND OTHERS A NEW HOME WAS FOUND AND RE-NAMED "McKINLEY HOUSE."

Geo Lee

A SMALL WOMAN IN SIZE WITH A BIG HEART...PLEASANT...FRIENDLY... THE GREAT WOMAN WAS BORN IN TEXAS. ATTENDED PRAIRIE VIEW COLLEGE. TAUGHT SCHOOL IN AUSTIN, TEX...WENT TO CHICAGO. AFTER LOSING HER FAMILY BY DEATH, ADA S. McKINLEY WAS INSPIRED TO HELP OTHERS. SHE PASSED AT AGE 84 LEAVING A LEGACY OF LOVE, KINDNESS AND A HELPING HAND!

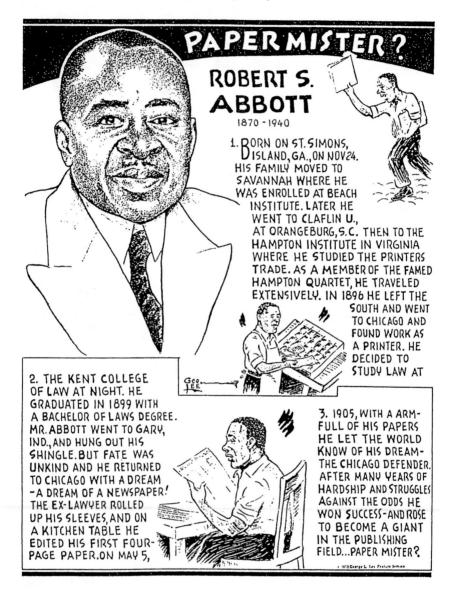

PAPER MISTER?

ROBERT S. ABBOTT
1870-1940

1. BORN ON ST. SIMONS, ISLAND, GA., ON NOV 24. HIS FAMILY MOVED TO SAVANNAH WHERE HE WAS ENROLLED AT BEACH INSTITUTE. LATER HE WENT TO CLAFLIN U., AT ORANGEBURG, S.C. THEN TO THE HAMPTON INSTITUTE IN VIRGINIA WHERE HE STUDIED THE PRINTERS TRADE. AS A MEMBER OF THE FAMED HAMPTON QUARTET, HE TRAVELED EXTENSIVELY. IN 1896 HE LEFT THE SOUTH AND WENT TO CHICAGO AND FOUND WORK AS A PRINTER. HE DECIDED TO STUDY LAW AT

2. THE KENT COLLEGE OF LAW AT NIGHT. HE GRADUATED IN 1899 WITH A BACHELOR OF LAWS DEGREE. MR. ABBOTT WENT TO GARY, IND., AND HUNG OUT HIS SHINGLE. BUT FATE WAS UNKIND AND HE RETURNED TO CHICAGO WITH A DREAM —A DREAM OF A NEWSPAPER! THE EX-LAWYER ROLLED UP HIS SLEEVES, AND ON A KITCHEN TABLE HE EDITED HIS FIRST FOUR-PAGE PAPER. ON MAY 5,

3. 1905, WITH A ARM-FULL OF HIS PAPERS HE LET THE WORLD KNOW OF HIS DREAM- THE CHICAGO DEFENDER. AFTER MANY YEARS OF HARDSHIP AND STRUGGLES AGAINST THE ODDS HE WON SUCCESS-AND ROSE TO BECOME A GIANT IN THE PUBLISHING FIELD...PAPER MISTER?

26

"LIFT EV'RY VOICE AND SING"

JAMES WELDON JOHNSON

1871
1938

ONE OF BLACK AMERICA'S MEN OF LETTERS. HIS CONTRIBUTIONS TO THE CULTURAL AND SOCIAL ADVANCEMENT OF BLACKS WERE OUTSTANDING. HIS FAMOUS POEM, "LIFT EV'RY VOICE AND SING" WAS SET TO MUSIC BY HIS BROTHER, J. ROSAMOND JOHNSON (1900) AND BECAME THE NEGRO NATIONAL ANTHEM. BORN IN JACKSONVILLE, FLA., THE SON OF A HEAD WAITER. AFTER HIGH SCHOOL, HE GRADUATED FROM ATLANTA U., IN 1894. RETURNING HOME HE TAUGHT SCHOOL. BECAME PRINCIPAL OF THE STANTON SCHOOL. STUDIED LAW AND WAS THE FIRST BLACK ADMITTED

HE WROTE MANY BOOKS-PROSE AND POEMS-TO NAME A FEW...

MY SPARE TIME IS VALUABLE!

(1912)

- THE AUTOBIOGRAPY OF AN EX-COLORED MAN
- ALONG THIS WAY (1931)
- NEGRO AMERICAN, WHAT NOW? (1934)
- GOD'S TROMBONES (1927)
- EDITOR, NEW YORK AGE (1914)
- FOUNDED, FIRST NEGRO DAILY PAPER - THE DAILY AMERICAN

MR. JOHNSON JOINED THE NAACP IN 1916; EXEC. SECRETARY-1920; RECEIVED NAACP's 1925 SPINGARN MEDAL FOR HIGH ACHIEVEMENT AS AUTHOR, DIPLOMAT AND PUBLIC SERVANT

Geo LEE

TO THE FLORIDA BAR. WITH HIS BROTHER THEY WROTE OVER 200 SONGS ON BROADWAY (1901-06). PRES. TEDDY ROOSEVELT APPOINTED HIM U.S. CONSUL TO VENEZUELA AND NICARAGUA (1906-12). HIS SPARE TIME CREATIVE EFFORTS DID MUCH FOR HIS SUCCESS IN AIDING BLACK AMERICA.

1982 GEO L. LEE FEATURE SERVICE

27

PROTEST PIONEER

1872
1934

WILLIAM MONROE TROTTER

WHO DEMANDED EQUAL RIGHTS FOR BLACKS WITHOUT COMPROMISE WAS NOT FROM THE GHETTO BUT BORN AND RAISED IN THE ELITE SUBURBS OF BOSTON, OF WELL-TO-DO-PARENTS. A BRILLIANT STUDENT HE GRADUATED FROM HARVARD UNIV., IN 1895 ...MAGNA CUM LAUDE, RECEIVING HIS M.A.DEGREE IN 1896. A PHI BETA KAPPA, HE SETTLED DOWN AS A REAL ESTATE BROKER. BUT SOON REALIZED THE NEEDS OF THE

Geo
LEE

THE FIERY EDITOR DEMANDED FULL RIGHTS FOR THE NEGRO. IMMEDIATELY!

BLACK MASSES AND THEIR RIGHTS. IN 1901 HE FOUNDED A PROTEST NEWSPAPER THE "BOSTON GUARDIAN." IN 1905 WITH W.E.B DUBOIS HE HELPED TO ORGANIZE THE NIAGARA MOVEMENT A PROTEST GROUP WHICH LATER BECAME THE "NAACP" IN 1909. TROTTER BELIEVED IN A NO-COMPROMISE POLICY SO HE FORMED THE NAT'L EQUAL RIGHTS LEAGUE...BUT HE COULDN'T BUCK THE CIVIL WRONGS.

28

1878 1949

'BOJANGLES'

BILL ROBINSON

DEAN OF THE TAP-DANCERS WAS BORN IN RICHMOND, VA. HE STARTED HIS GREAT DANCING CAREER AT 8, BUT DIDN'T GET ON THE SUCCESS LADDER UNTIL 1916. IT HAPPENED IN CHICAGO...SO THE STORY GOES. COOPER AND ROBINSON HAD BEEN A TEAM FOR 6-YEARS BUT THEY COULDN'T GET ALONG OFF THE STAGE. THEY SPLIT, BUT THE ORPHEUM THEATER CIRCUIT WOULDN'T BOOK BILL AS A SINGLE. HE GOT A JOB AT THE MARIGOLD GARDENS AT $76-

EVERY-THING IS, "KOPASETIC"

A-WEEK. HE CREATED HIS FAMOUS STAIR-STEPS NUMBER AND STAYED 69-WEEKS AT $225 PER. THE ORPHEUM LURED HIM BACK. 'BOJANGLES' WENT ON TO BECOME THE WORLD'S GREATEST. IN 1936 HE DREW $3500 A-WEEK AT THE COTTON CLUB (N.Y.). HE DANCED WITH SHIRLEY TEMPLE IN THE MOVIES...AND STARRED IN MUSICALS. THE SELF-TAUGHT DANCER EARNED 3-MILLION DOLLARS IN 60-YEARS OF SHO-BIZ!

WHAT'S KOPASETIC?

IT MEANS EVERY-THING IS FINE AN' DANDY.

Geo Lee

© 1976 George L. Lee Feature Service

MATTIE CUNNINGHAM DOLBY

1878
•
1956

FIRST WOMAN MINISTER IN THE CHURCH OF THE BRETHREN.

BORN IN HOWARD COUNTY, IND., AND RAISED BY PARENTS OF THE CHURCH OF THE BRETHREN. HER FATHER DID NOT APPROVE OF GIRLS GOING TO COLLEGE, BUT WITH HER BROTHER JOE SHE ENROLLED IN MANCHESTER COLLEGE, (INDIANA). MATTIE WORKED IN THE KITCHENS TO PAY HER WAY. AFTER COLLEGE SHE WORKED AS A MISSIONARY IN PALESTINE, ARK., IN 1903. DUE TO MALARIA IN 1907 SHE RETURN- ED TO OHIO. DURING THE YEAR SHE MARRIED NEWTON DOLBY, MOVED TO

AUNT MATTIE AS SHE WAS KNOWN TO ALL TOOK IN WASHIN' AND IRONING TO PROVIDE FOR HER 6-CHILDREN AFTER HER HUSBAND DIED IN 1926.

Geo
LEE

ILLINOIS THEN TO INDIANA WHERE SHE BECAME A DEACON IN A FRANK- FORT CHURCH. ON DEC 30, 1911 SHE WAS INSTALLED AS THE FIRST WOM- AN MINISTER IN THE CHURCH OF THE BRETHREN. IN 1917 THE CHURCH AD- MINISTRATION CHANGED AND PREJU- DICE AROSE, MATTIE WAS FORCED TO LEAVE. LATER SHE MINISTERED IN THE METHODIST AND THE CHURCH OF GOD. TRULY A WOMAN OF GOD.

BLACK BASEBALL FOUNDER

ANDREW(RUBE)FOSTER

1879.
1930.

Geo LEE

THE DRIVING FORCE BEHIND THE FOUNDING OF BLACK BASEBALL. THE FIRST GREAT BLACK PITCHER, A GOOD FIELD MANAGER,TEAM CO-OWNER AND THE FOUNDER AND TOP EXECUTIVE OF THE NEGRO NATIONAL LEAGUE(1921). RUBE WAS BORN IN CALVERT,TEXAS NEAR WACO, THE SON OF A MINISTER. IN GRADE SCHOOL HE ORGANIZED THE BASEBALL TEAM. AFTER THE 8th GRADE HE LEFT SCHOOL TO SEEK A CAREER IN BASEBALL. BY AGE 18 HE WAS A STAR PITCHER WITH THE BLACK WACO YELLOW JACKETS. IN 1902 WENT TO CHICAGO AND THE UNION GIANTS. IN 1903 TO THE CUBAN X GIANTS A VERY GOOD EASTERN TEAM. RUBE WAS GREAT AND THE PHILA.,GIANTS SIGNED HIM. HE BECAME A PLAYING MANAGER IN 1910 WITH THE CHICAGO LELAND GIANTS. IN 1911 FORMED THE AMERICAN GIANTS AS CO-OWNER.RUBE ORGANIZED THE NEGRO NATIONAL LEAGUE IN 1921... 8-TEAMS.RUBE FOSTER MADE BLACK BASEBALL!

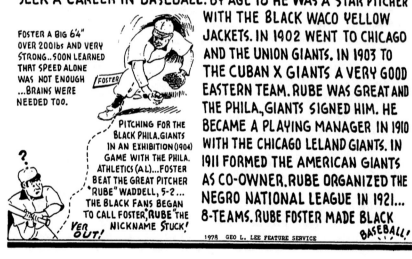

FOSTER A BIG 6'4" OVER 200lbs AND VERY STRONG..SOON LEARNED THAT SPEED ALONE WAS NOT ENOUGH ...BRAINS WERE NEEDED TOO.

FOSTER

PITCHING FOR THE BLACK PHILA.GIANTS IN AN EXHIBITION(1904) GAME WITH THE PHILA. ATHLETICS(AL)...FOSTER BEAT THE GREAT PITCHER "RUBE" WADDELL, 5-2... THE BLACK FANS BEGAN TO CALL FOSTER "RUBE" THE NICKNAME STUCK!

YER OUT!

?

1978   GEO L. LEE FEATURE SERVICE

TOP BUSINESS WOMAN

MADAME SARA S. WASHINGTON
1881 – 1953

ONE OF BLACK AMERICA'S TOP WOMEN PIONEERS IN BUSINESS. BORN IN BUCKLEY, VA., NEAR NORFOLK. SHE RECEIVED HER EARLY EDUCATION AT THE MISSION SCHOOL AND HIGHER EDUCATION AT THE NORTHWESTERN COLLEGE AND COLUMBIA UNIV., N.Y. HER FIRST BUSINESS VENTURE, A BEAUTY SHOP IN PHILADELPHIA. IN 1918 SHE WENT TO ATLANTIC CITY AND OPENED A BEAUTY SHOP AND A SCHOOL FOR BEAUTICIANS.

IN A ONE-ROOM STRUCTURE SHE STARTED PREPARING HAIR PRODUCTS IN 1920 UNDER THE NAME OF APEX HAIR PRODUCTS. IT WAS A SUCCESS. MODERN MACHINERY WAS INSTALLED AND MME. WASHINGTON PREPARED BEAUTY CREAMS, PERFUME, ROUGE AND VARIOUS SKIN FRESHENERS MADE FOR THE BLACK WOMAN. THE APEX BEAUTY COLLEGES WERE FOUNDED ALONG WITH THE APEX NEWS, A TRADE PAPER. THE GROWTH OF HER BUSINESS WAS TREMENDOUS. SHE WAS ONE OF THE FIRST BLACK MILLIONAIRES!

SORRY MADAM.

HALP IM BURNING

STUDENT

HMMM

BEAUTIFUL MADAM.

32

DISTINGUISHED LEADER

JANE EDNA HUNTER

1882.
1971 •

ROSE FROM A HUMBLE BEGIN-
NING TO FAME AS A GREAT
LEADER AND AN INSPIRATION
TO AMERICA'S BLACK WOMEN.
BORN ON THE WOODBURN FARM
IN PENDLETON, S.C., OF POOR SHARE-
CROPPER PARENTS. AT 10 SHE WAS
HIRED OUT TO WORK IN WHITE
FAMILIES. HER EARLY EDUCATION
WAS VERY DIFFICULT. WITH THE
HELP OF FRIENDS SHE GRAD-
UATED FROM HIGH SCHOOL.
STUDIED NURSING AND TOOK
POST GRADUATE AT HAMPTON
INSTITUTE, VA., WENT TO CLEVELAND,

JANE WALKED 12-MILES
TO THE COUNTY SCHOOL....
BUT HER EFFORTS PAID OFF
AND SHE BECAME A
CRUSADER FOR HUMAN
RIGHTS.

HER AUTOBIOGRAPHY "A
NICKEL AND A PRAYER" (1940)
TELLS OF HER GREAT ACHIEVEMENTS.
A CIVIC LEADER WHO GAINED
FAME AS A PHILANTHROPIST.....

1979 GEO L. LEE FEATURE SERVICE

OH., TO NURSE BUT SOON REALIZED A
GREAT NEED FOR A HOME FOR NEEDY
GIRLS. JANE BEGAN A NEW CAREER...
SOCIAL SERVICE. IN 1911 SHE FOUNDED
THE PHILLIS WHEATLEY ASSN, SUCCESS
FOLLOWED. IN 1922, ENTERED BALDWIN
LAW SCHOOL...PASSED THE OHIO STATE
BAR IN 1925. MISS HUNTER FOUNDED THE
PHILLIS WHEATLEY FOUNDATION A SCHOL-
ARSHIP FUND FOR BLACK STUDENTS!

33

NAACP PIONEER - TOP FUND RAISER

1883
1965

Geo
LEE

MRS. DAISY LAMPKIN

DURING HER YEARS OF INTENSE ACTIVITY IN THE NAACP, THOUSANDS OF NEW MEMBERS JOINED, NEW BRANCHES OPENED AND GOOD WILL WAS HIGH. SHE WAS NOTED FOR HER TREMENDOUS FUND RAISING SUCCESS AND THE ADVANCEMENT OF BLACK WOMEN. BORN IN WASH, D.C., AND EDUCATED IN THE PUBLIC SCHOOLS. HER PUBLIC CAREER BEGAN IN PITTSBURGH, PA., IN 1912 BY SPEAKING TO BLACK WOMEN GROUPS. ORGANIZED THE LUCY STONE LEAGUE IN 1915 AND BECAME INVOLVED IN THE SUFFRAGE MOVEMENT. IN 1928 BECAME ACTIVE IN STATE (PA) POLITICS AND WAS THE FIRST BLACK WOMAN ELECTED AS A DELEGATE-AT-LARGE FROM PENNSYLVANIA TO THE GOP CONVENTION. IN 1929 SHE JOINED THE PITTSBURGH COURIER STAFF AND ROSE TO VICE-PRESIDENT. MRS. LAMPKIN BECAME ACTIVE IN THE NAACP AND WAS REGIONAL FIELD SECRETARY (1930-35); NATIONAL FIELD SECRETARY (1935-47). SHE RETIRED AND WAS ELECTED TO THE NATIONAL BOARD OF DIRECTORS.

SHE RECEIVED THE FIRST ELEANOR ROOSEVELT - MARY McLEOD BETHUNE WORLD CITIZENSHIP AWARD (1964) FOR HER DYNAMIC LEADERSHIP TO ADVANCE THE STATUS OF BLACK WOMEN........"

THE DELTA SIGMA THETA SORORITY MADE HER AN HONORARY SOROR(1947) THE FIRST SINCE MARY BETHUNE IN 1925.

1982 ОЮ L. LEE FEATURE SERVICE

FIRST STEAMBOAT CAPTAIN

R.J. SALISBURY

WHO LEFT HIS FARM HOME IN THE BACKWOODS OF NORTH CAROLINA AT THE AGE OF 16 TO BATTLE JIM CROW. HE HIRED OUT AS A SHIP'S COOK ON THE TAR RIVER. EAGER TO LEARN ABOUT NAVIGATION HE WATCHED EVERY MOVE BY THE PILOT AND MADE NOTES OF THE LANDMARKS AND BUOYS ON THE RIVER COURSE. HE BECAME A WHEELMAN. AFTER RIOTS IN WILMINGTON AND THE PASSING OF JIM CROW LAWS, HE ASKED HIS EMPLOYER FOR PERMISSION TO APPLY FOR A PILOT'S LICENSE. THE EXAMINATION TOOK PLACE AT THE U.S. STEAMBOAT INSPECTORS IN NORFOLK, VA., ON DEC 19, 1900. HE QUALIFIED, AFTER DIFFICULTY IN GETTING HIS LICENSE OFFICIALLY SIGNED AND ENGINEERS TO SAIL WITH HIM. ON MAY 16, 1904 HE WAS GIVEN CHARGE OF THE STEAMER "SHILOH". FIRST BLACK STEAMBOAT CAPTAIN.

CAPT. SALISBURY PLIED TAR RIVER BETWEEN TARBORO AND WASHINGTON, N.C. UNTIL 1908. DURING HIS CAREER HE WAS A REPORTER, RAILWAY POSTAL CLERK AND AUTHOR.

1979 GEO L. LEE FEATURE SERVICE

"HAPPY AM I"

ELDER MICHAUX

THE FAMED RADIO PREACHER WHO STARTED HIS SUNDAY BROADCASTS OVER STATION WJSV IN WASH.,D.C.,IN 1927, USED HIS SONG"HAPPY AM I", AS HIS THEME. BORN IN NEWPORT NEWS,VA.,THE SON OF A SALOON-KEEPER. BEFORE TURNING TO RELIGION HE WAS A SUCCESSFUL FISH PEDDLER.INFLUENCED BY HIS WIFE MARY, A HOME MISSIONARY, HE STARTED PREACHING IN HOPEWELL, VA., IN 1917. IN THE 1920s, 30s, AND 40s, HE ESTABLISHED MANY CONGREGATIONS. HE FOUNDED THE GOSPEL SPREADING ASSN. OF THE CHURCH OF GOD. KNOWN AS THE "HELPER OF THE POOR", HE FED AND HOUSED HUNDREDS DURING THE DEPRESSION. IN 1938 HE HELD "BAPTISM CEREMONIES" IN THE GRIFFITH BALL PARK, IN WASH.,D.C. HE ONCE BAPTIZED 105 CONVERTS BEFORE AN AUDIENCE OF 20,000. WITH FHA LOANS HE BUILT LOW-COST HOUSING. ELDER SOLOMON LIGHTFOOT MICHAUX, DIED AT 84 IN 1968.

Geo LEE

© 1977, George L. Lee Feature Service

36

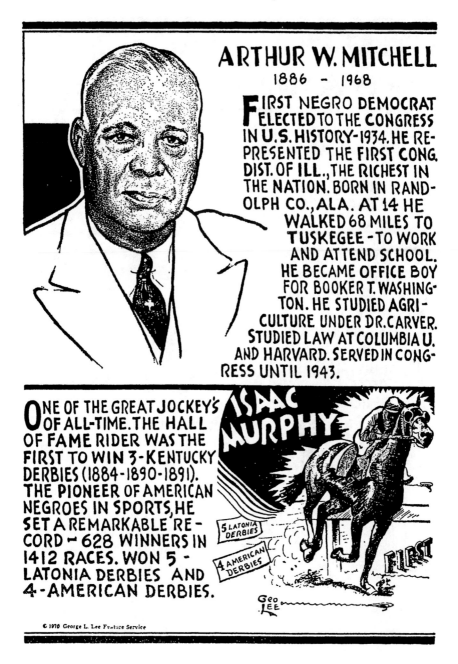

ARTHUR W. MITCHELL
1886 – 1968

FIRST NEGRO DEMOCRAT ELECTED TO THE CONGRESS IN U.S. HISTORY-1934. HE REPRESENTED THE FIRST CONG. DIST. OF ILL., THE RICHEST IN THE NATION. BORN IN RANDOLPH CO., ALA. AT 14 HE WALKED 68 MILES TO TUSKEGEE - TO WORK AND ATTEND SCHOOL. HE BECAME OFFICE BOY FOR BOOKER T. WASHINGTON. HE STUDIED AGRICULTURE UNDER DR. CARVER. STUDIED LAW AT COLUMBIA U. AND HARVARD. SERVED IN CONGRESS UNTIL 1943.

ISAAC MURPHY

ONE OF THE GREAT JOCKEY'S OF ALL-TIME. THE HALL OF FAME RIDER WAS THE FIRST TO WIN 3-KENTUCKY DERBIES (1884-1890-1891). THE PIONEER OF AMERICAN NEGROES IN SPORTS, HE SET A REMARKABLE RECORD – 628 WINNERS IN 1412 RACES. WON 5 - LATONIA DERBIES AND 4-AMERICAN DERBIES.

5 LATONIA DERBIES

4 AMERICAN DERBIES

FIRST

Geo LEE

HARLEM'S PICTURE TAKIN' MAN

JAMES VAN DER ZEE
1886 – 1983

ONE OF THE FINEST BLACK PHOTO-GRAPHERS OF HIS TIME. HIS CAMERA RECORDED THE LIVES AND EVENTS OF BLACK AMERICANA. THE GREATS, THE NEAR GREATS, THE GOOD LIFE AND POVERTY. HE CAPTURED THE PRIDE AND HUMANITY OF HARLEM'S BLACK RENAISSANCE. BORN IN LENOX, MASS., AND NOW (1980) NEARING 94 YEARS. HE BECAME INTERESTED IN TAK-ING PICTURES AT 12. TURNED PROFESSIONAL IN NEW YORK. HIS GENIUS CAME THROUGH THE LENS OF HIS CAMERA FOR 70 YEARS. RECOGNITION CAME LATE... WHEN HIS REMARKABLE COLLECTION

MADAME C. J. WALKER

JACK JOHNSON

GEO LEE

HOLD IT!

BILL ROBINSON

MARCUS GARVEY

IN 1969 HE PUBLISHED HIS COLLECTION IN A BOOK... "THE WORLD OF JAMES VAN DER ZEE." AND GAINED NATIONAL ATTENTION!

1980 GEO L. LEE FEATURE SERVICE

WAS DISCOVERED IN 1967. A FELLOW OF THE METROPOLITAN MUSEUM OF ART (N.Y). HIS WORK IS PART OF THE PERMANENT COLLECTION... ALSO LISTED IN IN "WHO'S WHO IN THE EAST", BY THE AMERICAN SOCIETY OF MAGAZINE PHOTOGRAPHERS.

NEVER TOO LATE FOR GOOD

SADIE WATERFORD JONES

AT 85 YEARS YOUNG FOUNDED THE "SADIE WATERFORD JONES MANOR" A $500.000 HALFWAY HOUSE FOR GIRLS IN CRESTWOOD A CHICAGO SOUTH SUBURB IN 1974. HER DREAM BEGAN IN THE 1940's WHILE WORKING FOR THE ILL. COMMISSION FOR DELINQUENCY PREVENTION. AS A CASE-WORKER SHE BECAME AWARE OF THE GREAT NEED FOR BLACK GIRLS TO HAVE COUNSELING AND GUIDANCE IN A HOME ATMOSPHERE. BORN ON AUG 13, 1889. EARLY CHILDHOOD SPENT IN OKLA., INDIAN TERR. GRADUATE OF LANGSTON U. (OKLA) 1911. STUDIED

1889 - 1986

Geo LEE

TEACHING METHODS AT U OF CHICAGO AND TAUGHT SCHOOL. BECAME INTER-ESTED IN COMMUNITY AND SOCIAL WORK. EXCELLED IN FUND RAISING AND ORGANIZATION. IN 1950 FOUND-ED THE BEATRICE CAFFREY YOUTH SERVICE (CHGO). HER UNTIRING EFF-ORTS MADE HER DREAM COME TRUE. AT 95 WAS STILL VERY ACTIVE!

1984 GEO L. LEE FEATURE SERVICE

BRAIN SURGEON

1891-
1952

DR. LOUIS T. WRIGHT

OUTSTANDING IN THE FIELD OF SURGERY IN THE TREATMENT OF SKULL FRACTURES AND BRAIN INJURIES. BORN IN LA GRANGE, GA., HE GRADUATED FROM CLARK UNIV., IN 1911 (ATLANTA). AND THE HARVARD MEDICAL SCHOOL IN 1915. SERVED IN THE U.S. ARMY MEDICAL CORPS IN 1917 DURING WORLD WAR I. WHILE THERE HE DISCOVERED THE TECHNIQUE FOR GIVING A SMALL-POX INJECTION. DR. WRIGHT INVENTED THE BRACE USED IN THE TRANSPORTATION AND HANDLING OF PATIENTS WITH

Geo LEE

NECK INJURIES. OPENED HIS PRACTICE IN N.Y.C. JOINED THE STAFF OF THE HARLEM HOSPITAL (1919). BECAME NYC POLICE SURGEON IN 1928. ROSE TO HEAD THE SURGICAL DEPT., OF HARLEM HOSPITAL. ONLY BLACK FELLOW IN THE ACS IN 1945. THE 1940 WINNER OF NAACP's "SPINGARN MEDAL". WROTE 15 SCIENTIFIC PAPERS ON BRAIN SURGERY.

© 1976, George L. Lee Feature Service

FIRST BLACK WOMAN AVIATRIX

BESSIE COLEMAN

1892
1926

ONE OF THE FIRST WOMEN IN THE U.S. TO ENTER THE FIELD OF AVIATION...THE FIRST BLACK WOMAN TO RECEIVE A PILOT'S LICENSE. BORN IN ATLANTA, TEXAS AND RAISED IN WAXAHACHIE. AFTER HIGH SCHOOL SHE LEFT FOR CHICAGO SEEKING WORK. BESSIE BECAME INTERESTED IN AVIATION AFTER WORLD WAR I. SHE SOUGHT TO ENROLL IN A FLYING SCHOOL BUT BEING A WOMAN AND BLACK WAS REJECTED. DETERMINED SHE WAS ADVISED TO GO TO EUROPE. TAUGHT BY FRENCH AND GERMAN AVIATORS SHE QUALIFIED FOR A INTERNATIONAL PILOT'S LICENSE. RETURNING TO

OH MY!

BESSIE'S DARING FEATS WERE THRILLING TO SPECTATORS.

1978 GEO L. LEE FEATURE SERVICE

CHICAGO SHE WENT INTO THE FIELD OF "EXHIBITION FLYING" (1922), IN A TEST-FLIGHT JUST BEFORE A SHOW IN JACKSONVILLE, FLA., HER PLANE WENT INTO A NOSEDIVE THEN...SUDDENLY THE PLANE FLIPPED OVER...SHE FELL OUT AT 5,300 FEET AND MET HER UNTIMELY DEATH... APRIL 10, 1926. A TEST-PILOT WAS AT THE CONTROLS!

AUGUSTA SAVAGE
1892 – 1962

SCULPTRESS AND ART TEACHER WELL-KNOWN FOR HER OUTSTANDING WORKS. IN 1929 SHE WAS AWARDED A ROSENWALD FUND GRANT AND WENT TO PARIS TO STUDY AT THE GRAND CHAUMIERE. SHE ALSO RECEIVED A GRANT FROM THE CARNEGIE FOUNDATION. MISS SAVAGE WAS THE FIRST DIRECTOR OF HARLEM COMMUNITY ART. HER BETTER

KNOWN WORK, "LIFT EVERY VOICE AND SING" WAS MADE FOR THE N.Y. WORLD'S FAIR IN 1939. HER WORKS WERE SHOWN AT THE ANDERSON GALLERIES (N.Y.)- STATE MUSEUM (N.J) AND THE SOCIETE DES ARTISTES FRANCAIS BEAUX ARTS (PARIS). HER "GAMIN" A POPULAR CHILDREN PIECE IS IN THE SCHOMBURG COLLECTION.

AMAZIN' GRACE

1893 1975

GRACE LEE STEVENS

PROMINENT WOMEN'S CLUB LEADER WAS BORN IN SPRINGFIELD, ILL. RAISED AND EDUCATED IN CHICAGO AND THE MOTHER OF SEVEN. SHE WAS APPOINTED AS A NATIONAL ORGANIZER OF WANDS (WOMENS ARMY FOR NATIONAL DEFENSE) DURING WORLD WAR II. IN 1946 SHE WAS CITED BY THE U.S. TREASURY DEPT., FOR HER UNTIRING EFFORTS WITH THE RED CROSS, USO AND WAR BOND SALES. IN HER HONOR A FEDERATED CLUB WAS ORGANIZED..." THE GRACE LEE STEVENS CIVIC AND CHARITY CLUB "AND NAMED HER PRESIDENT. SHE ORGANIZED 10 SUCH CLUBS. HER COMMUNITY AND CHURCH SERVICE WAS REWARDING. IN 1959 SHE RECEIVED THE CHICAGO CONFERENCE FOR BROTHERHOOD AWARD... AND THE GOOD AMERICAN AWARD FROM THE CHICAGO COMMITTEE OF 100 FOR HER EFFORTS IN PUBLIC RELATIONS. IN 1971 HER BIOGRAPHY WAS RECORDED IN **WHO'S WHO IN AMERICA.** A BEAUTIFUL HUMAN BEING!

TRAVELED TO THE WEST COAST TO URGE WOMEN TO JOIN WANDS.

AMERICA NEEDS YOU!

© 1976 George L. Lee Feature Service

43

THEY WERE FIRST

MAJ. HARRIET M. WEST
OF WASHINGTON, D.C.

ON AUG 21, 1943 SHE BECAME THE FIRST BLACK WOMAN TO ATTAIN THE RANK OF MAJOR IN THE WACS. A NATIVE OF KANSAS CITY, MO., SHE GRADUATED FROM KANSAS STATE COLLEGE. A FOUNDER OF THE IOTA PHI LAMDA, A NATIONAL BUSINESS AND PROFESSIONAL SORORITY. ONCE ADMINISTRATIVE ASS'T TO MARY McLEOD BETHUNE, DIRECTOR OF NEGRO AFFAIRS OF THE NAT'L YOUTH ADMIN.

JUSTICE JANE M. BOLIN
A NATIVE OF POUGHKEEPSIE, N.Y.

BECAME AMERICA'S FIRST BLACK WOMAN JUDGE ON JULY 22, 1939 WHEN SHE WAS APPOINTED BY MAYOR FIORELLO LaGUARDIA TO THE COURT OF DOMESTIC RELATIONS IN NEW YORK CITY. JUSTICE BOLIN A GRADUATE OF WELLESLEY COLLEGE AND THE YALE LAW SCHOOL.

© 1972 George L. Lee Feature Service

OUTSTANDING ARCHITECT

Geo
LEE

PAUL R. WILLIAMS

ONE OF AMERICA'S DISTINGUISHED ARCHITECTS, INTERNATIONALLY FAMOUS FOR DESIGNS OF BEAUTIFUL CALIFORNIA MANSIONS FOR MOVIE STARS ALSO BUILDINGS, SCHOOLS, AIRPORTS AND PUBLIC HOUSING. BORN IN LOS ANGELES ON FEB 18, 1894. IN HIGH SCHOOL HE DECIDED TO BECOME AN ARCHITECT. HIS STUDENT ADVISOR TOLD HIM A NEGRO COULD NEVER BE A SUCCESS. HE TOOK THE ADVICE AS A PERSONAL CHALLENGE... WORKED HIS WAY THROUGH THE UNIV. OF CALIF.,

THEN THE BEAUX ARTS INSTITUTE OF DESIGN, WINNING THE BEAUX ARTS MEDAL. HIS TALENT DEFIED THE COLOR-LINE. HE DESIGNED NAVAL-BASES DURING WORLD WAR II. A "FELLOW" IN THE AMERICAN INSTI. OF ARCHITECTS. PRES. LOS ANGELES ART COMM. WINNER OF NAACP's 38th SPINGARN MEDAL FOR ACHIEVEMENT (1953). ONE OF THE GREAT ARCHITECTS OF HIS TIME! MR. WILLIAMS DIED JAN 1980.

MR. WILLIAMS BECAME FAMOUS DESIGNING HOMES FOR MOVIE STARS AND BEAUTIFUL BUILDINGS!

1980 GEO L. LEE FEATURE SERVICE

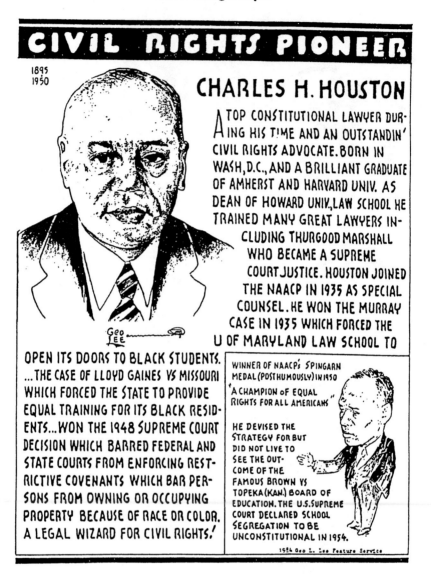

CIVIL RIGHTS PIONEER

1895
1950

CHARLES H. HOUSTON

A TOP CONSTITUTIONAL LAWYER DURING HIS TIME AND AN OUTSTANDIN' CIVIL RIGHTS ADVOCATE. BORN IN WASH, D.C., AND A BRILLIANT GRADUATE OF AMHERST AND HARVARD UNIV. AS DEAN OF HOWARD UNIV, LAW SCHOOL HE TRAINED MANY GREAT LAWYERS INCLUDING THURGOOD MARSHALL WHO BECAME A SUPREME COURT JUSTICE. HOUSTON JOINED THE NAACP IN 1935 AS SPECIAL COUNSEL. HE WON THE MURRAY CASE IN 1935 WHICH FORCED THE U OF MARYLAND LAW SCHOOL TO OPEN ITS DOORS TO BLACK STUDENTS. ...THE CASE OF LLOYD GAINES VS MISSOURI WHICH FORCED THE STATE TO PROVIDE EQUAL TRAINING FOR ITS BLACK RESIDENTS...WON THE 1948 SUPREME COURT DECISION WHICH BARRED FEDERAL AND STATE COURTS FROM ENFORCING RESTRICTIVE COVENANTS WHICH BAR PERSONS FROM OWNING OR OCCUPYING PROPERTY BECAUSE OF RACE OR COLOR. A LEGAL WIZARD FOR CIVIL RIGHTS!

Geo LEE

WINNER OF NAACP'S SPINGARN MEDAL (POSTHUMOUSLY) IN 1950
"A CHAMPION OF EQUAL RIGHTS FOR ALL AMERICANS"

HE DEVISED THE STRATEGY FOR BUT DID NOT LIVE TO SEE THE OUTCOME OF THE FAMOUS BROWN VS TOPEKA (KAN.) BOARD OF EDUCATION. THE U.S.SUPREME COURT DECLARED SCHOOL SEGREGATION TO BE UNCONSTITUTIONAL IN 1954.

1954 Geo L. Lee Feature Service

SINGIN' THE BLUES AT 83!

ALBERTA HUNTER

FAMOUS BLUES SINGER WHO INTRODUCED "THE DRAFTING BLUES" IN WORLD WAR I AND FOR GEN. EISENHOWER'S CONVENTION OF ALLIED GENERALS IN WORLD WAR II. ONE OF THE FIRST RECORDING STARS IN THE EARLY 20's.

SANG WITH JOE OLIVER AND THE GREAT MUSICIANS OF THE DAY. BECAME THE TOAST OF EUROPE. BORN IN MEMPHIS IN 1895 SHE LEFT HOME AT 12 TO SING IN CHICAGO FOR $10 A-WEEK. AN AMAZIN' CAREER STARTED...LATER SANG AT THE PANAMA AND DREAM-LAND. INTRODUCED THE "ST. LOUIS BLUES" TO CHICAGO. WROTE THE "DOWNHEARTED BLUES" WHICH BECAME BESSIE SMITH'S FIRST BIG RECORD. WHEN BESSIE LEFT THE BROADWAY SHOW, "HOW COME?" ALBERTA REPLACED HER IN 1923. PLAYED IN "SHOW BOAT" WITH ROBESON IN 1928 IN LONDON. SANG WITH THE USO DURING WW II AND KOREAN. RETIRED 1954... IN 1957 A PRACTICAL NURSE FOR 20-YEARS. RETIRED 1977...RE-DISCOVERED AS A BLUES SINGER AT 82...AT THE COOKERY (N.Y.). RECORDED AN ALBUM AT 83!

GEO LEE

1979 GEO L. LEE FEATURE SERVICE

47

SINGING THE BLUES ♪

1895
1937

BESSIE SMITH

THE EMPRESS OF THE BLUES WAS BORN IN BITTER POVERTY IN CHATTANOOGA, TENN. HER CAREER STARTED AT A VERY EARLY AGE. RECORDED HER FIRST DISC IN 1923, FOR COLUMBIA..."DOWN-HEARTED BLUES" AND SOLD OVER A-MILLION COPIES. BESSIE BECAME AN OVERNIGHT STAR. DURING HER PEAK YEARS SHE COULD COMMAND $2,000-PER WEEK. SHE MADE A LOT OF MONEY

Geo Lee

MY HOW THAT GAL CAN SING!

MA RAINEY, THE FIRST NATIONALLY FAMOUS BLUES SINGER DISCO-VERED 13-YEAR OLD BESSIE AND PUT HER IN HER MINSTREL SHOW. BESSIE SANG HER WAY INTO THE WORLD'S GREATEST BLUES SINGER. HER TOP RECORDING (1929) "NOBODY KNOWS YOU WHEN YOU'RE DOWN AND OUT."

AND SPENT IT. BESSIE MADE BLACK HISTORY! SHE PUT THE BLUES ON A PEDESTAL. HER GREATNESS LEFT HER MARK ON SUCH GREATS AS... MAHALIA JACKSON, BILLIE HOLIDAY, DINAH WASHINGTON, JANIS JOPLIN. SHE RECORDED 160 SONGS...BUT THE DEPRESSION IN 1933 SLOWED HER CAREER. IN 1937 A CAR ACCIDENT OUTSIDE OF CLARKSDALE, MISS., PROVED FATAL WHEN THE HOSPITALS REFUSED HER ADMITTANCE.....

1979 GEO L. LEE FEATURE SERVICE

WHEEL CHAIR COMPOSER

ANDY RAZAF

1895 – 1973

WHO ENTERED THE SONG-WRITERS HALL OF FAME IN MAY, 1972...STARTED HIS CAREER IN THE 1920's. DURING THE 1930's HE WROTE THE LYRICS FOR SUCH BIG HITS, AS "HONEYSUCKLE ROSE," AIN'T MISBEHAVIN'," AND "STOMPIN' AT THE SAVOY" WITH GREATS... W. C. HANDY, FATS WALLER AND EUBIE BLAKE. HE WROTE HIS FIRST BIG HIT..."S'POSIN" IN 1928 WHICH WAS FEATURED BY RUDY VALLEE. HE CONTRIBUTED TO MORE THAN 1000 SONGS. IN 1950 HE HAD A STROKE WHICH LEFT HIM PARALIZED FROM THE WAIST DOWN, BUT HE CONTINUED HIS GREAT TALENT AS A SONGWRITER.

Geo Lee

© 1975 George L. Lee Feature Service

49

♪ A BRILLIANT COMPOSER ♪

WILLIAM GRANT STILL

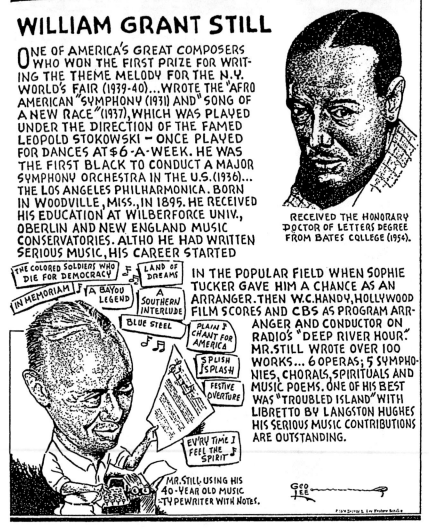

ONE OF AMERICA'S GREAT COMPOSERS WHO WON THE FIRST PRIZE FOR WRITING THE THEME MELODY FOR THE N.Y. WORLD'S FAIR (1939-40)...WROTE THE "AFRO AMERICAN" SYMPHONY (1931) AND "SONG OF A NEW RACE" (1937), WHICH WAS PLAYED UNDER THE DIRECTION OF THE FAMED LEOPOLD STOKOWSKI — ONCE PLAYED FOR DANCES AT $6-A-WEEK. HE WAS THE FIRST BLACK TO CONDUCT A MAJOR SYMPHONY ORCHESTRA IN THE U.S. (1936)... THE LOS ANGELES PHILHARMONICA. BORN IN WOODVILLE, MISS., IN 1895. HE RECEIVED HIS EDUCATION AT WILBERFORCE UNIV., OBERLIN AND NEW ENGLAND MUSIC CONSERVATORIES. ALTHO HE HAD WRITTEN SERIOUS MUSIC, HIS CAREER STARTED

RECEIVED THE HONORARY DOCTOR OF LETTERS DEGREE FROM BATES COLLEGE (1954).

THE COLORED SOLDIERS WHO DIE FOR DEMOCRACY

LAND OF DREAMS

IN MEMORIAM ♪ A BAYOU LEGEND

A SOUTHERN INTERLUDE

BLUE STEEL

PLAIN ♪ CHANT FOR AMERICA

SPLISH ♪ SPLASH

FESTIVE OVERTURE

EV'RY TIME I FEEL THE ♪ SPIRIT

MR. STILL USING HIS 40-YEAR OLD MUSIC TYPEWRITER WITH NOTES.

IN THE POPULAR FIELD WHEN SOPHIE TUCKER GAVE HIM A CHANCE AS AN ARRANGER. THEN W.C.HANDY, HOLLYWOOD FILM SCORES AND CBS AS PROGRAM ARRANGER AND CONDUCTOR ON RADIO'S "DEEP RIVER HOUR." MR. STILL WROTE OVER 100 WORKS... 6 OPERAS; 5 SYMPHONIES, CHORALS, SPIRITUALS AND MUSIC POEMS. ONE OF HIS BEST WAS "TROUBLED ISLAND" WITH LIBRETTO BY LANGSTON HUGHES HIS SERIOUS MUSIC CONTRIBUTIONS ARE OUTSTANDING.

GEO LEE

50

DEAN OF BLACK JOURNALISM

WILLIAM O. WALKER

1896
1981

OUTSTANDING PUBLISHER, POLITICALLY ASTUTE AND A HUMANITARIAN. FOR HIS NEVER-ENDING EFFORTS HE WAS INDUCTED INTO THE OHIO HALL OF FAME (1979). BORN IN SELMA, ALA., WHERE HE RECEIVED HIS EARLY EDUCATION. A GRADUATE OF WILBERFORCE U., IN BUSINESS (1916). FROM OBERLIN BUSINESS COLLEGE (OHIO) 1918. HIS NEWSPAPER CAREER BEGAN AS A REPORTER FOR THE PITTSBURGH COURIER...THEN CITY EDITOR ON THE NORFOLK JOURNAL. IN 1921 HE AIDED IN FOUNDING THE WASHINGTON TRIBUNE (D.C.) AS MANAGING EDITOR UNTIL 1930. HE WENT TO CLEVELAND IN 1932 AND

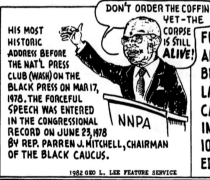

HIS MOST HISTORIC ADDRESS BEFORE THE NAT'L PRESS CLUB (WASH) ON THE BLACK PRESS ON MAR 17, 1978. THE FORCEFUL SPEECH WAS ENTERED IN THE CONGRESSIONAL RECORD ON JUNE 23, 1978 BY REP. PARREN J. MITCHELL, CHAIRMAN OF THE BLACK CAUCUS.

1982 GEO L. LEE FEATURE SERVICE

FOUNDED THE CALL & POST NEWSPAPER AND BECAME A DRIVING FORCE IN THE BLACK PRESS. ELECTED TO THE CLEVELAND CITY COUNCIL (1939). FIRST BLACK CABINET MEMBER OF OHIO AS DIR. OF INDUSTRIAL RELATIONS (1963). A NATIONALLY KNOWN AND HIGHLY RESPECTED REPUBLICAN. TRULY A GIANT!

CIVIC LEADER · HUMANITARIAN

DR. MARJORIE S. JOYNER

PIONEER ORGANIZER, TRAVELER AND COMMUNITY LEADER. IN 1980 SHE WON THE U.S. COMMUNITY SERVICES ADMINISTRATION AWARD - FOR HER EFFORTS ON THE BEHALF OF THE POOR AND NEEDY. AT 86 SHE IS STILL THE CHAIRPERSON OF THE CHICAGO DEFENDER CHARITIES. IN 1929 SHE HELPED TO ORGANIZE THE FIRST BUD BILLIKEN ANNUAL PARADE AND PICNIC. BORN IN MONTERAY, VA., OCT 23, 1896 THE 7th GIRL IN A FAMILY OF 11. SHE ATTENDED PUBLIC SCHOOLS IN DAYTON, OH., AND CHICAGO. THEN THE BETHUNE-COOKMAN COLLEGE.

Geo Lee

JOYNER STUDIED BEAUTY CULTURE. AT MOLER COLLEGE IN CHICAGO. SHE TRAINED OTHERS IN BLACK HAIR CARE. JOINED MME. C.J. WALKER CO AND IN 1924 WAS MADE A NATIONAL SUPERVISOR. SHE ORGANIZED OVER 100 BEAUTY SCHOOLS. RETIRED IN 1961. ALSO FOUNDED THE UNITED BEAUTY SCHOOL OWNERS AND TEACHERS ASSN.

AT AGE 77, EARNED HER BACHELOR OF SCIENCE DEGREE. RECEIVED AN HONORARY DOCTORATE DEGREE IN 1971. BOTH FROM BETHUNE-COOKMAN COLLEGE. SHE FOUNDED THE ALPHA CHI PI OMEGA SORORITY AND FRATERNITY FOR BEAUTICIANS (1945).

1983 Geo L. Lee Feature Service

52

1897 1965 ESLANDA GOODE ROBESON

WIFE OF PAUL ROBESON, ONE OF AMERICA'S GREAT BLACK PERSONALITIES. MRS. ROBESON HAD AN INTERESTING LIFE-SCIENTIST -AUTHOR AND ANTHROPOLOGIST.

ESLANDA, A HARLEM GIRL MET PAUL AT COLUMBIA UNIVERSITY IN 1919. SHE WAS A BRILLIANT CHEMISTRY STUDENT (FIRST BLACK ANALYTICAL CHEMIST) AND HE WAS STUDYING LAW. IN 1920 SHE INSISTED ON

-AS SHE APPEARED IN THE RED CROSS IN 1944...

PAUL TO TAKE AN ACTING ROLE IN A YMCA PRODUCTION. IN 1921 THEY WERE MARRIED AND SHE BECAME HIS MANAGER UNTIL SHE PASSED IN 1965. MRS. ROBESON EMERGED A CELEBRITY IN HER OWN RIGHT. THEY WENT TO LONDON IN 1925. WHERE SHE STUDIED ANTHROPOLOGY AT THE LONDON U. AND RECEIVED HER PH.D FROM HARTFORD (CONN.) THEOLOGICAL SEMINARY. IN 1936 WITH HER SON, PAUL, JR THEY TRAVELED THRU AFRICA FOR 4-MONTHS. NINE YEARS OF WRITING PUT HER EXPERIENCES IN A BOOK -"AFRICAN JOURNEY." HER FIRST BOOK "PAUL ROBESON, NEGRO." DURING THE 1950'S SERVED AS A CORRESPONDENT ATTACHED TO THE UNITED NATIONS. A BRILLIANT WOMAN!

Geo LEE

© 1978 George L. Lee Feature Service

A LEGEND IN HER TIME

ONCE ACTED IN A BOGART FILM, "TO HAVE AND HAVE NOT."..SANG IN SISSLE AND BLAKE'S FAMED "SHUFFLE ALONG".

EDITH WILSON

STARTED HER BLUES SINGING CAREER IN 1920 THAT CARRIED HER TO THE HEIGHTS. SHE TOURED EUROPE, LONDON PARIS, BERLIN. A NATIVE OF LOUISVILLE, KY., BEGAN SHOW BIZ AS A TEENAGER IN A SINGING TRIO. MADE HER FIRST RECORDING FOR COLUMBIA (1921). A GREAT CABARET AND STAGE CAREER BEGAN. EDITH APPEARED WITH FLOR-ENCE MILLS IN "PLANTATION REVUE", AND "BLACKBIRDS"...WITH BILL ROBINSON IN "MEMPHIS BOUND". THE FAMOUS COTTON CLUB WITH DUKE, "HOT CHOCOLATES" WITH CAB...

SANG WITH FATS AND LOUIS... AND BIG BANDS. JOINED RADIO'S AMOS 'N ANDY - SHOW AS KING-FISH'S MOTHER-IN-LAW. IN 1948 LEFT RADIO TO BECOME AUNT JEMIMA FOR THE QUAKER OATS CO., AS A TRAVELING PITCHWOMAN TO SELL PANCAKE MIX, AND STAYED 18-YEARS. IN 1971 BEGAN A SECOND SINGING CAREER AND MADE AN LP ALBUM - "HE MAY BE YOUR MAN." EDITH WAS STILL APPEARING IN 1978 AFTER NEARLY 60-YEARS OF SHO-BIZ!

"HE MAY BE YOUR MAN BUT HE COMES TO SEE ME SOMETIMES"

WHAT DID I DO TO BE SO BLACK AND BLUE?

1897 1981

Geo LEE

1978 GEO L. LEE FEATURE SERVICE

54

MARTHA BARKSDALE GOLDMAN

A PIONEER AND PERHAPS THE FIRST BLACK WOMAN TO WORK IN A SECRETARIAL CAPACITY FOR THE FEDERAL GOVERNMENT IN WASH, D.C. BORN IN WINCHESTER, MASS., SHE WAS THE FIRST BLACK WOMAN GRADUATE OF THE WINCHESTER HI-SCHOOL (1912). A GRADUATE OF THE FAMED BRYANT STRATTON SECRE-TARIAL SCHOOL IN BOSTON. BECAME A COURT REPORTER.... WORKED IN THE OFFICES OF THE STATE TREA-SURER IN THE STATE HOUSE (MASS). IN 1918 MARTHA WENT TO WASH, D.C. AND BEGAN HER CAREER IN THE BUREAU OF STANDARDS; DEPT. OF AGRICULTURE AND THE TREA-SURY DEPT. SERVED AS SECRETARY TO DR. H. A. HUNT OF THE FEDERAL CREDIT ADM. DURING WORLD WAR II WAS VERY ACTIVE IN "DEFENSE BOND" SALES. ACTIVE IN THE NAT'L COUNCIL OF NEGRO WOMEN, YWCA AND SHILOH BAPTIST CHURCH IN WASH, D.C., WHERE SHE ESTABLISHED A "BARKSDALE GOLD-MAN" SCHOLARSHIP FUND. A VERY INTERESTING PERSON. DIED JUNE 3, '73.

1978 GEO L. LEE FEATURE SERVICE

MARTHA BARKSDALE LED THE WAY.

FUNNY LADY

JACKIE (MOMS) MABLEY

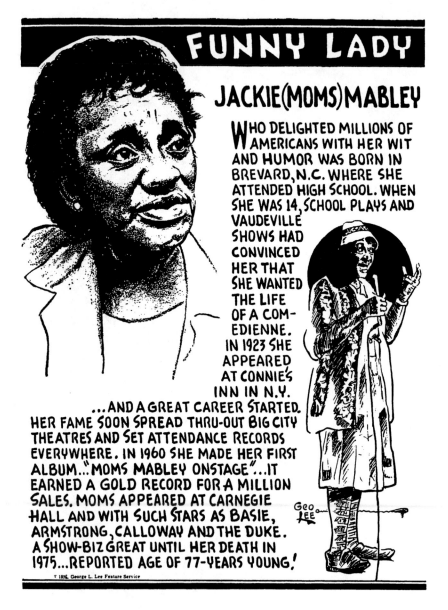

WHO DELIGHTED MILLIONS OF AMERICANS WITH HER WIT AND HUMOR WAS BORN IN BREVARD, N.C. WHERE SHE ATTENDED HIGH SCHOOL. WHEN SHE WAS 14, SCHOOL PLAYS AND VAUDEVILLE SHOWS HAD CONVINCED HER THAT SHE WANTED THE LIFE OF A COMEDIENNE. IN 1923 SHE APPEARED AT CONNIE'S INN IN N.Y. ...AND A GREAT CAREER STARTED. HER FAME SOON SPREAD THRU-OUT BIG CITY THEATRES AND SET ATTENDANCE RECORDS EVERYWHERE. IN 1960 SHE MADE HER FIRST ALBUM..."MOMS MABLEY ONSTAGE"...IT EARNED A GOLD RECORD FOR A MILLION SALES. MOMS APPEARED AT CARNEGIE HALL AND WITH SUCH STARS AS BASIE, ARMSTRONG, CALLOWAY AND THE DUKE. A SHOW-BIZ GREAT UNTIL HER DEATH IN 1975...REPORTED AGE OF 77-YEARS YOUNG!

Geo Lee

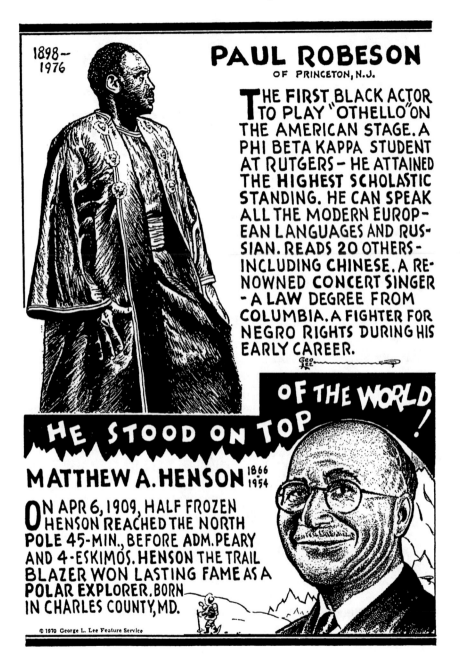

1898–1976

PAUL ROBESON
OF PRINCETON, N.J.

THE FIRST BLACK ACTOR TO PLAY "OTHELLO" ON THE AMERICAN STAGE. A PHI BETA KAPPA STUDENT AT RUTGERS – HE ATTAINED THE HIGHEST SCHOLASTIC STANDING. HE CAN SPEAK ALL THE MODERN EUROPEAN LANGUAGES AND RUSSIAN. READS 20 OTHERS – INCLUDING CHINESE. A RENOWNED CONCERT SINGER – A LAW DEGREE FROM COLUMBIA. A FIGHTER FOR NEGRO RIGHTS DURING HIS EARLY CAREER.

HE STOOD ON TOP OF THE WORLD!

MATTHEW A. HENSON
1866–1954

ON APR 6, 1909, HALF FROZEN HENSON REACHED THE NORTH POLE 45-MIN., BEFORE ADM. PEARY AND 4-ESKIMOS. HENSON THE TRAIL BLAZER WON LASTING FAME AS A POLAR EXPLORER. BORN IN CHARLES COUNTY, MD.

© 1970 George L. Lee Feature Service

NATIONAL SORORITY PRESIDENT

DR. FREDDA WITHERSPOON

AN EXTREMELY BUSY AND VERY INTERESTING PERSON....THE NATIONAL PRESIDENT OF THE IOTA PHI LAMBDA SORORITY, INC., WHICH WAS FOUNDED IN 1929 TO UNITE BUSINESS AND PROFESSIONAL WOMEN. HER EDUCATION STARTED IN HOUSTON, TEX., GRADUATED FROM HI-SCHOOL WITH HONORS AT 14 AND BISHOP COLLEGE IN DALLAS AT 18. EARNED 3 MASTER'S DEGREES-SOCIAL WORK PSYCHOLOGY, GUIDANCE AND COUNSELING FROM U OF CHICAGO, WASHINGTON UNIV., ST.LOUIS UNIV....

Geo Lee

DR. WITHERSPOON IS LISTED IN~ WHO'S WHO AMONG AMERICAN WOMEN WHO'S WHO IN THE MIDWEST OUTSTANDING EDUCATORS OF AMERICA BIOGRAPHY OF INTERNA., SCHOLARS TWO THOUSAND WOMEN OF ACHIEVEMENT COMMUNITY LEADERS AND NOTEWORTHY AMERICANS WHO'S WHO AMONG BLACK AMERICANS

GREAT! / RIGHT ON / MY MY

A PH.D FROM ST.LOUIS U. VERY ACTIVE IN COMMUNITY SERVICE... THE FIRST BLACK PRESIDENT OF THE ST.LOUIS YWCA. DR.WITHERSPOON IS THE CURRENT-PRES.(1979) OF THE MISSOURI STATE NAACP...ALSO PROF. OF GUIDANCE AND COUNSELING OF JUNIOR COLLEGE (ST.LOUIS), FIELD INS-TRUCTOR (ST.LOUIS CTY), AND SOCIAL WORK STUDENTS AT WASH., UNIV. STUDIES LAW, TO NAME ONLY A FEW.

1979 GEO L. LEE FEATURE SERVICE

In 1970, Dr. Witherspoon received Iota Phi Lambda's highest national accolade, the Lola M. Parker Achievement Award.

FIRST BLACK WOMAN PH.D. IN U.S.

SADIE TANNER ALEXANDER

NOTED LAWYER AND HUMANITARIAN IS A NATIVE OF PHILADELPHIA (1898). THE WIDOW OF JUDGE RAYMOND PACE ALEXANDER. SHE EARNED HER B.S. IN EDUCATION, A MASTERS (1918) AND A DOCTORATE IN ECONOMICS (1921) AT THE U OF PENN...THE FIRST BLACK WOMAN PH.D IN NATION. FIRST BLACK WOMAN GRADUATE OF THE U OF PENN., LAW SCHOOL (1927); THE FIRST TO BE ADMITTED TO THE PHILA., BAR. SERVED AS ASS'T CITY SOLICITOR AND A PRACTICING ATTORNEY FOR OVER 50-YEARS! A MEMBER OF PRES. TRUMAN'S COMMISSION ON CIVIL RIGHTS AND ALSO ON PRES. J.F.K's COMMITTEE. FIRST NAT'L PRES., OF DELTA SIGMA THETA SORORITY. SEC'Y OF THE NAT'L URBAN LEAGUE EXEC. BOARD FOR 25-YEARS. A CHAMPION OF HUMAN RIGHTS. MRS. ALEXANDER WAS NAMED BY PRES. CARTER TO CHAIR THE 1981 WHITE HOUSE CONFERENCE ON AGING. SHE WAS 82!

1980 GEO L. LEE FEATURE SERVICE

"DISTINGUISHED DAUGHTER OF PENNSYLVANIA (1970). MARY CHURCH TERRELL AWARD FOR-DISTINGUISHED LEADERSHIP AND SERVICE" -DELTA SIGMA THETA SOR. (1971) LISTED AMONG 200 MOST IMPORTANT BLACKS IN THE LAST 200 YEARS (1976) - BY EBONY + JET...... THEY HELPED SHAPE BLACK AMERICA!

Geo LEE

FIRST BLACK FEDERAL JUDGE in U.S.

IRVIN C. MOLLISON

1899
1962

A SUCCESSFUL CHICAGO ATTORNEY WITH A WIDE REPUTATION AS AN EXPONENT OF CIVIL LIBERTIES WAS APPOINTED BY PRES. TRUMAN ON OCT 3, 1945 AS A JUDGE OF THE U.S. CUSTOMS COURT AND BECAME THE FIRST BLACK WITHIN THE CONTINENTAL U.S. BORN IN VICKS-BURG, MISS. EDUCATED AT OBERLIN COLLEGE AND LEGAL TRAINING AT U OF CHICAGO, A PHI BETA KAPPA GRADUATE... ADMITTED TO THE ILL-INOIS BAR IN 1923. LICENSED TO PRACTICE BEFORE THE U.S. SUPREME COURT, CIRCUIT COURT OF APPEALS, AND FEDERAL DIST. COURT. GAINED NATIONAL ATTENTION AS ONE OF THE ATTORNEYS WHO WON THE SUP-REME COURT CASE AGAINST THE RES-TRICTIVE COVENANT CLAUSE IN CHI-CAGO AND ALLOWED BLACKS TO BUY PROPERTY IN PREVIOUSLY RESTRICT-ED AREAS. VERY ACTIVE IN NAACP CIVIL RIGHTS CASES. HIS FATHER, WILLIS MOLLISON WAS SUPT. OF ED-UCATION OF ISSAQUENNA COUNTY, MISS., IN 1882 BEFORE OLE MISS, HAD SEPARATE SCHOOLS.

Geo LEE

NOV 3, 1945

HISTORY WAS MADE IN NYC WHEN ATT. MOLLISON WAS SWORN IN AS JUDGE OF U.S. CUSTOMS COURT IN BROOKLYN FOR A LIFE TENURE AT $10,000-YEARLY.

1984 Geo L. Lee Feature Service

RESEARCH CHEMIST

DR. PERCY L. JULIAN

THE BRILLIANT SCIENTIST WHO ENTERED DEPAUW UNIV., AS A "SUB-FRESHMAN" AND GRADUATED IN 1920 WITH THE HIGHEST HONORS, THE PHI BETA KAPPA KEY AND DELIVERED THE VALEDICTORIAN ADDRESS. HE EARNED HIS MASTERS DEGREE AT HARVARD IN 1923 AND PH.D. AT THE UNIV. OF VIENNA IN 1931. HE WAS BORN IN MONTGOMERY, ALA., IN 1899. HE TAUGHT AT HOWARD AND W.VIRGINIA U. DR. JULIAN JOINED THE GLIDDEN CO., IN 1936, A PAINT COMPANY IN CHICAGO. DURING WORLD WAR II HE PRODUCED A FIRE-FIGHTING FOAM FROM SOYBEAN PROTEIN THAT SAVED

DIED 1975

GREAT HONOR

HEY DOC! WHERE DO YOU WANT THE BEANS?

SOYBEANS

DR. JULIAN WON THE 1947 SPINGARN MEDAL - NAACP'S HIGHEST AWARD.

Geo LEE

© 1975 George L. Lee Feature Service

THOUSANDS OF LIVES IN THE ARMY AND NAVY. HIS CONTRIBUTIONS TO MANKIND HAVE BEEN TREMENDOUS, HE DEVELOPED CORTISONE AT LOW-COST FOR ARTHRITIS SUFFERERS, DRUGS TO AID RHEUMATIC FEVER, GLAUCOMA, BIRTH CONTROL PILLS AND COUNTLESS OTHER USES. THE RESEARCH OF THE SOYBEAN SOON ESTABLISHED THE JULIAN LABORATORIES AND ITS SUBSIDIARIES.

61

"DADDY" KING - MAN OF FAITH

REV. DR. MARTIN L. KING Sr

WHO HAS SHOWN HIS STRENGTH IN COURAGE AND FAITH IN HIS LOSS OF HIS SONS, MARTIN JR., A.D. KING, HIS WIFE AND GRANDDAUGHTER. "DADDY" KING LED HIS SONS TO GREATNESS AND TRUTH. BORN ON DEC 19, 1899 OF SHARECROPPER PARENTS, THE SECOND OF NINE, NEAR STOCKBRIDGE, GA. EARLY IN LIFE HE SAW THE HATE AND INJUSTICE OF MAN'S INHUMANITY TO MAN. TO OVERCOME HIS BITTERNESS HE TURNED TO GOD AND PREACHIN'. AT 15, A LICENSED PREACHER...BUT NO EDUCATION. HE LEFT FOR ATLANTA, WORKING ODD JOBS AND PREACHING. ALTHOUGH NEARLY 21 HE TOOK A TEST AT THE BRYANT PREPARATORY

AMONG HIS HONORARY DEGREES: DOCTOR OF DIVINITY" FROM MOREHOUSE, MORRIS BROWN COLLEGES AND ALLEN U. "DOCTOR OF HUMANITIES". FROM WILBERFORCE U., VA. SEMINARY, BETHUNE-COOKMAN. "DOCTOR OF LETTERS" FROM UNIV OF HAITI. "CLERGYMAN OF THE YEAR" (1975), BY THE COUNCIL OF CHRISTIANS AND JEWS. "THE ORDER OF THE LION "SENEGAL, W. AFRICA'S HIGHEST HONOR TO A FOREIGNER (1975).

INSTITUTE AND PLACED IN THE 5th-GRADE. DETERMINED, HE STUDIED HIS WAY TO MOREHOUSE COLLEGE AND A THEOLOGY DEGREE (1926). MARRIED, IN COLLEGE TO ALBERTA WILLIAMS, DAUGHTER OF REV. A.D. WILLIAMS, PASTOR OF EBENEZER BAPTIST CHURCH WHO..... PASSED IN 1931. KING BECAME PASTOR OF EBENEZER AND STAYED 44 YEARS!

1981 GEO L. LEE FEATURE SERVICE

At 75, he stepped down as minister of his 4,000-member church, but continued as pastor emeritus. Daddy King died November 11, 1984, still a man of great faith.

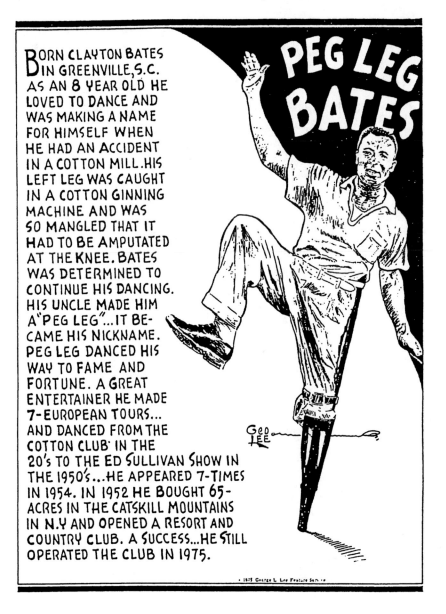

BORN CLAYTON BATES IN GREENVILLE, S.C. AS AN 8 YEAR OLD HE LOVED TO DANCE AND WAS MAKING A NAME FOR HIMSELF WHEN HE HAD AN ACCIDENT IN A COTTON MILL. HIS LEFT LEG WAS CAUGHT IN A COTTON GINNING MACHINE AND WAS SO MANGLED THAT IT HAD TO BE AMPUTATED AT THE KNEE. BATES WAS DETERMINED TO CONTINUE HIS DANCING. HIS UNCLE MADE HIM A "PEG LEG"...IT BE-CAME HIS NICKNAME. PEG LEG DANCED HIS WAY TO FAME AND FORTUNE. A GREAT ENTERTAINER HE MADE 7-EUROPEAN TOURS... AND DANCED FROM THE COTTON CLUB IN THE 20's TO THE ED SULLIVAN SHOW IN THE 1950's...HE APPEARED 7-TIMES IN 1954. IN 1952 HE BOUGHT 65-ACRES IN THE CATSKILL MOUNTAINS IN N.Y AND OPENED A RESORT AND COUNTRY CLUB. A SUCCESS...HE STILL OPERATED THE CLUB IN 1975.

PEG LEG BATES

Geo Lee

© 1975 George L. Lee Feature Service

PRISON MISSION PIONEER

REV. JESSIE "MA" HOUSTON

1899
1980

KNOWN TO THOUSANDS OF PRISON INMATES AS "MA", BECAUSE SHE TOUCHED SO MANY WITH KINDNESS, HOPE AND COUNSEL. AN ORDAINED MINISTER SHE HEADED THE PRISON OUTPOST OF OPERATION BREADBASKET WHICH LATER BECAME "PUSH", SHE CONTINUED HER GOOD WORK AND SERVED ON THE GOVERNOR'S COR-RECTIONAL ADVISORY PANEL OF ILLINOIS. BORN IN BLACKMAN, LA., AND REARED IN ARKANSAS. STRICK-EN WITH POLIO AT AN EARLY AGE SHE SPENT MUCH OF HER CHILD-HOOD IN WHEELCHAIRS AND ON CRUTHES. IN 1925 SHE AND HER HUS-BAND MOVED TO CHICAGO AND SHE BEGAN HER WRITING TO LONELY

Geo
Lee

JESSIE "MA" HOUSTON
COMMUNITY CORRECTIONAL
CENTER

IN MEMORY OF HER CRUSADE TO HELP OTHERS A CENTER WAS NAMED IN HER HONOR (SEPT 10,'80). HER PHYSICAL HANDICAP DID NOT DETER HER DEVOTION TO MINISTERING TO PRISONERS

SERVICEMEN ALTHOUGH A SEMI-INVALID. WHEN ONE OF THEM WAS PUT IN JAIL SHE VISITED HIM...THUS HER PRISON MISSION STARTED AND LASTED OVER 50-YEARS. "MA" HOUSTON WAS A WELCOME SIGHT IN MANY ILLINOIS PRISONS SPREADING HOPE AND COURAGE TO THE INMATES. SHE WAS THE "FIRST" WOMAN ALLOWED TO MINISTER TO PRISONERS ON DEATH ROW IN ILLINOIS

1983 GEO L. LEE FEATURE SERVICE

TAKE MY HAND

PRECIOUS LORD

THOMAS A. DORSEY

BORN IN GEORGIA IN 1899. HE PLAYED THE PIANO AT AN EARLY AGE. IN HIS TEENS HE BEGAN TO COMPOSE AND ARRANGE JAZZ AND BLUES, SOON WAS POPULAR AS "GEORGIA TOM." HE WENT TO CHICAGO AND WORKED IN STEEL MILLS TO EARN MONEY TO ATTEND THE CHICAGO MUSICAL COLLEGE. IN 1920, FORMED HIS OWN BAND AND WROTE BLUES FOR SUCH GREATS AS, MA RAINEY. IN 1921 HE JOINED THE PILGRIM BAPTIST CHURCH AND BEGAN TO BLEND TRADITIONAL BLACK CHURCH MUSIC WITH HIS BLUES...GOSPEL MUSIC WAS BORN. DORSEY'S FIRST WAS, "I DO, DON'T YOU." HIS GOSPEL HAS BEEN SUNG BY THE BEST...MAHALIA JACKSON, TENNESSEE ERNIE FORD, CLARA WARD, EDDIE ARNOLD AND MANY OTHERS. TRAGEDY STRUCK HIS FAMILY IN 1932 AND HE WROTE HIS GREATEST "TAKE MY HAND, PRECIOUS LORD..." 1977, DORSEY STILL DIRECTED THE PILGRIM GOSPEL CHORUS. DEAN OF GOSPEL MUSICAL RESEARCH, HE GAVE UP THE "BLUES" FOR THE LORD.

COMPOSER OF OVER 900 SONGS. HIS MUSIC HAS BEEN FELT AROUND THE WORLD.

Geo Lee

© 1977, George L. Lee Feature Service

In 1985, the 86-year-old Dorsey was recognized as "The Father of Gospel Music" during Chicago's first Gospel Music Festival. Dorsey no longer plays or composes.

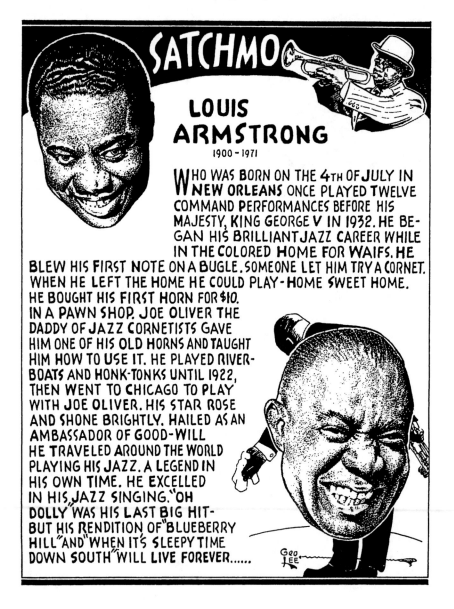

SATCHMO

LOUIS ARMSTRONG
1900 - 1971

WHO WAS BORN ON THE 4TH OF JULY IN NEW ORLEANS ONCE PLAYED TWELVE COMMAND PERFORMANCES BEFORE HIS MAJESTY, KING GEORGE V IN 1932. HE BEGAN HIS BRILLIANT JAZZ CAREER WHILE IN THE COLORED HOME FOR WAIFS. HE BLEW HIS FIRST NOTE ON A BUGLE. SOMEONE LET HIM TRY A CORNET. WHEN HE LEFT THE HOME HE COULD PLAY - HOME SWEET HOME. HE BOUGHT HIS FIRST HORN FOR $10. IN A PAWN SHOP. JOE OLIVER THE DADDY OF JAZZ CORNETISTS GAVE HIM ONE OF HIS OLD HORNS AND TAUGHT HIM HOW TO USE IT. HE PLAYED RIVERBOATS AND HONK-TONKS UNTIL 1922, THEN WENT TO CHICAGO TO PLAY WITH JOE OLIVER. HIS STAR ROSE AND SHONE BRIGHTLY. HAILED AS AN AMBASSADOR OF GOOD-WILL HE TRAVELED AROUND THE WORLD PLAYING HIS JAZZ. A LEGEND IN HIS OWN TIME. HE EXCELLED IN HIS JAZZ SINGING. "OH DOLLY" WAS HIS LAST BIG HIT - BUT HIS RENDITION OF "BLUEBERRY HILL" AND "WHEN IT'S SLEEPY TIME DOWN SOUTH" WILL LIVE FOREVER......

Geo
Lee

TAKE THE A-TRAIN

DUKE ELLINGTON

WHILE WORKING AS A SODA-JERKER AT THE AGE OF 15, HE WROTE HIS FIRST SONG, "SODA FOUNTAIN RAG". BOTH PARENTS PLAYED THE PIANO AND AT THE AGE OF 7, HE STARTED TAKING LESSONS. HIS TEACHER SOON GAVE UP ON HIM, BECAUSE HE WOULDN'T PRACTICE SCALES. BORN IN WASH. D.C. ON APRIL 29, 1899. HE ORGANIZED A SMALL BAND IN NEW YORK 1922, THEY GOT THEIR FIRST BIG BREAK IN 1927, BROADCASTING OVER NATIONAL RADIO FROM THE COTTON CLUB IN HARLEM. DUKE A BRILLIANT PIANIST

MOOD INDIGO • BLACK, BROWN AND BEIGE • JUMP FOR JOY • SOPHISTICATED LADY • CARAVAN

DUKE HAS WRITTEN OVER 2,000 SONGS. HIS HIT SONG "SOLITUDE" WAS WRITTEN IN 20-MINUTES. • DO NOTHING TILL YOU HEAR FROM ME • I GOT IT BAD • MY PEOPLE

ROSE TO THE TOP OF THE MUSIC WORLD THRU HIS CREATIVE ABILITY. HE IS A RARE COMBINATION OF ARRANGER, LEADER AND COMPOSER. ALTHO HE NEVER FINISHED HIGH SCHOOL HE HAS RECEIVED 10 HONORARY DOCTORATE DEGREES. HONORED BY 4-U.S. PRESIDENTS, POPE PIUS XII, QUEEN ELIZABETH AMONG THE MANY. NOW 74, HE RECENTLY RECEIVED FRANCE'S HIGHEST HONOR-THE FRENCH LEGION OF HONOR. THE FIRST JAZZ MUSICIAN.

WE LOVE YOU MADLY!

DIED 1974

© 1976 George L. Lee Feature Service

67

BLOODY MARY - HAPPY TALK

JUANITA HALL
1901 – 1968

ROSE TO BROADWAY FAME IN 1950 WHEN SHE CREATED THE ROLE OF "BLOODY MARY", IN THE HIT MUSICAL "SOUTH PACIFIC". AS "BLOODY MARY" THE TONKINESE WOMAN WHO CHEWED BETEL NUTS, SOLD GRASS SKIRTS TO THE SEABEES AND SANG SUCH HIT SONGS AS - HAPPY TALK AND BALI HAI AND NEARLY STOLE THE SHOW. BORN IN KEYPORT, N.J., THE SINGER AND

ACTRESS PLAYED HER FIRST MAJOR ROLE ON BROADWAY IN 1928 IN SHOW BOAT. IN 1930 SANG IN THE CHORUS OF GREEN PASTURES. THEN TO THE HALL JOHNSON CHOIR AS SOLOIST AND ASS'T DIRECTOR. IN THE 40'S PLAYED ON BROADWAY IN ST. LOUIS WOMAN, DEEP ARE THE ROOTS AND THE PIRATE. IN 1958 PLAYED MADAM LIANG IN THE "FLOWER DRUM SONG." A BLACK STAR WHO SHONE BRIGHTLY IN..... CHINESE ROLES.

68

FIRST TO INTEGRATE U.S. OPERA

AS SHE
APPEARED
IN 1980

GEO
LEE

LA JULIA RHEA

ON DEC 26, 1937 SHE SANG IN THE CHICAGO CITY OPERA COMPANY'S PRODUCTION OF VERDI'S "AIDA" AND MUSICAL HISTORY WAS BEGUN AT THE CHICAGO CIVIC OPERA HOUSE. A SOPRANO, HER DRAMATIC VOICE MADE HER TITLE ROLE SUPERB. BORN IN CABBAGE PATCH ON THE OUTSKIRTS OF LOUISVILLE, KY., AND RAISED IN CHICAGO. A LITTLE GIRL WHO WANTED TO BE AN OPERA STAR. SHE FIRST SANG IN THE PROVIDENCE BAPTIST CHOIR. GRADUATED FROM THE

CHICAGO MUSICAL COLLEGE. MADE HER DEBUT IN RECITAL AT KIMBALL HALL, CHICAGO IN 1929. TOURED AS SOLOIST OF THE CECIL MACK CHOIR IN "RHAPSODY IN BLACK" WITH ETHEL WATERS IN 1932. WON A MAJOR BOWES AUDITION IN 1935. STUDIED WITH ROSA RAISA FAMED OPERA STAR. SANG WITH THE AMERICAN NEGRO LIGHT OPERA ASSOC. MRS. RHEA OPENED THE DOOR FOR BLACK OPERA SINGERS. SHE RESIDES IN ROBBINS, ILL.

LA JULIA SINGING THE TITLE ROLE IN "AIDA."

SANG JOSEPHINE IN "TROPICAL PINAFORE" IN 1940.

1980 GEO L. LEE FEATURE SERVICE

69

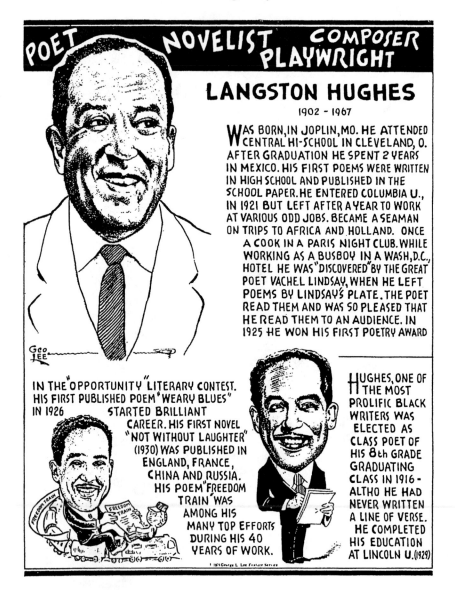

POET NOVELIST COMPOSER PLAYWRIGHT

LANGSTON HUGHES
1902 – 1967

WAS BORN, IN JOPLIN, MO. HE ATTENDED CENTRAL HI-SCHOOL IN CLEVELAND, O. AFTER GRADUATION HE SPENT 2 YEARS IN MEXICO. HIS FIRST POEMS WERE WRITTEN IN HIGH SCHOOL AND PUBLISHED IN THE SCHOOL PAPER. HE ENTERED COLUMBIA U., IN 1921 BUT LEFT AFTER A YEAR TO WORK AT VARIOUS ODD JOBS. BECAME A SEAMAN ON TRIPS TO AFRICA AND HOLLAND. ONCE A COOK IN A PARIS NIGHT CLUB. WHILE WORKING AS A BUSBOY IN A WASH, D.C., HOTEL HE WAS "DISCOVERED" BY THE GREAT POET VACHEL LINDSAY, WHEN HE LEFT POEMS BY LINDSAY'S PLATE. THE POET READ THEM AND WAS SO PLEASED THAT HE READ THEM TO AN AUDIENCE. IN 1925 HE WON HIS FIRST POETRY AWARD

Geo LEE

IN THE "OPPORTUNITY" LITERARY CONTEST. HIS FIRST PUBLISHED POEM "WEARY BLUES" IN 1926 STARTED BRILLIANT CAREER. HIS FIRST NOVEL "NOT WITHOUT LAUGHTER" (1930) WAS PUBLISHED IN ENGLAND, FRANCE, CHINA AND RUSSIA. HIS POEM "FREEDOM TRAIN" WAS AMONG HIS MANY TOP EFFORTS DURING HIS 40 YEARS OF WORK.

HUGHES, ONE OF THE MOST PROLIFIC BLACK WRITERS WAS ELECTED AS CLASS POET OF HIS 8th GRADE GRADUATING CLASS IN 1916 – ALTHO HE HAD NEVER WRITTEN A LINE OF VERSE. HE COMPLETED HIS EDUCATION AT LINCOLN U. (1929)

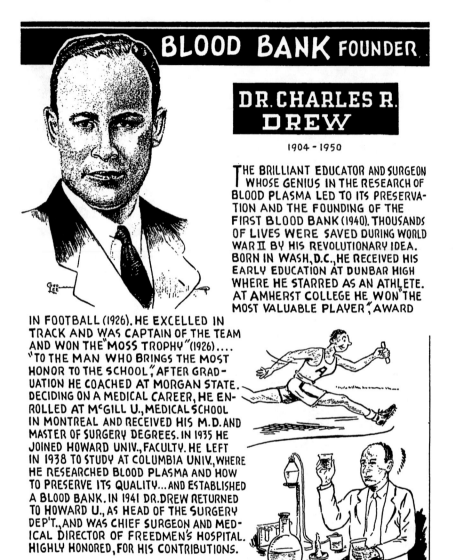

BLOOD BANK FOUNDER

DR. CHARLES R. DREW

1904 – 1950

THE BRILLIANT EDUCATOR AND SURGEON WHOSE GENIUS IN THE RESEARCH OF BLOOD PLASMA LED TO ITS PRESERVATION AND THE FOUNDING OF THE FIRST BLOOD BANK (1940). THOUSANDS OF LIVES WERE SAVED DURING WORLD WAR II BY HIS REVOLUTIONARY IDEA. BORN IN WASH., D.C., HE RECEIVED HIS EARLY EDUCATION AT DUNBAR HIGH WHERE HE STARRED AS AN ATHLETE. AT AMHERST COLLEGE HE WON THE "MOST VALUABLE PLAYER," AWARD IN FOOTBALL (1926). HE EXCELLED IN TRACK AND WAS CAPTAIN OF THE TEAM AND WON THE "MOSS TROPHY" (1926)....."TO THE MAN WHO BRINGS THE MOST HONOR TO THE SCHOOL," AFTER GRADUATION HE COACHED AT MORGAN STATE. DECIDING ON A MEDICAL CAREER, HE ENROLLED AT McGILL U., MEDICAL SCHOOL IN MONTREAL AND RECEIVED HIS M.D. AND MASTER OF SURGERY DEGREES. IN 1935 HE JOINED HOWARD UNIV., FACULTY. HE LEFT IN 1938 TO STUDY AT COLUMBIA UNIV., WHERE HE RESEARCHED BLOOD PLASMA AND HOW TO PRESERVE ITS QUALITY... AND ESTABLISHED A BLOOD BANK. IN 1941 DR. DREW RETURNED TO HOWARD U., AS HEAD OF THE SURGERY DEP'T., AND WAS CHIEF SURGEON AND MEDICAL DIRECTOR OF FREEDMEN'S HOSPITAL. HIGHLY HONORED, FOR HIS CONTRIBUTIONS.

* 1976 George L. Lee Feature Service

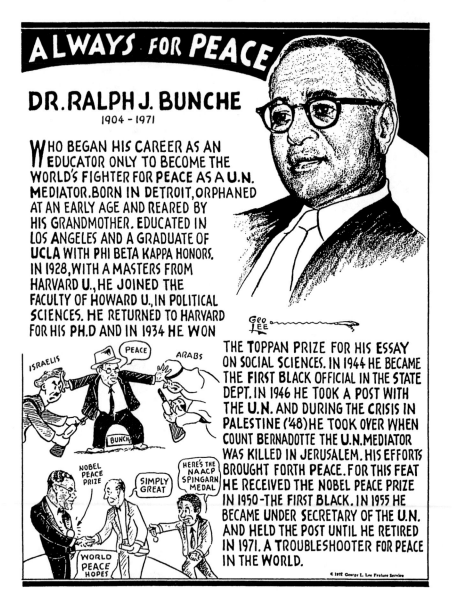

ALWAYS FOR PEACE

DR. RALPH J. BUNCHE
1904 - 1971

WHO BEGAN HIS CAREER AS AN EDUCATOR ONLY TO BECOME THE WORLD'S FIGHTER FOR PEACE AS A U.N. MEDIATOR. BORN IN DETROIT, ORPHANED AT AN EARLY AGE AND REARED BY HIS GRANDMOTHER. EDUCATED IN LOS ANGELES AND A GRADUATE OF UCLA WITH PHI BETA KAPPA HONORS. IN 1928, WITH A MASTERS FROM HARVARD U., HE JOINED THE FACULTY OF HOWARD U., IN POLITICAL SCIENCES. HE RETURNED TO HARVARD FOR HIS PH.D AND IN 1934 HE WON THE TOPPAN PRIZE FOR HIS ESSAY ON SOCIAL SCIENCES. IN 1944 HE BECAME THE FIRST BLACK OFFICIAL IN THE STATE DEPT. IN 1946 HE TOOK A POST WITH THE U.N. AND DURING THE CRISIS IN PALESTINE ('48) HE TOOK OVER WHEN COUNT BERNADOTTE THE U.N. MEDIATOR WAS KILLED IN JERUSALEM. HIS EFFORTS BROUGHT FORTH PEACE. FOR THIS FEAT HE RECEIVED THE NOBEL PEACE PRIZE IN 1950 - THE FIRST BLACK. IN 1955 HE BECAME UNDER SECRETARY OF THE U.N. AND HELD THE POST UNTIL HE RETIRED IN 1971. A TROUBLESHOOTER FOR PEACE IN THE WORLD.

© 1972 George L. Lee Feature Service

CHICAGO'S FIRST BLACK POSTMASTER

GEO LEE

HENRY W. McGEE

THE FIRST CAREER MAIL EMPLOYEE EVER APPOINTED HEAD OF A LARGE POST OFFICE, IN 1966. A NATIVE OF HILLBORO, TEX., HIS POSTAL CAREER STARTED IN CHICAGO IN 1929 AS A SUB-CLERK. IN 1935 HE BECAME A REGULAR. HE ATTENDED CRANE JR COLLEGE FOR TWO YEARS THEN ENROLLED AT IIT (ILL INSTITUTE OF TECHNOLOGY) AND EARNED A DEGREE IN PERSONNEL MANAGEMENT DESPITE WORKING AND BRINGING UP A FAMILY. GRADUATING IN 1949, HIS PROGRESS WAS RAPID. A SUPERVISOR IN 1949; GEN. FOREMAN 1952; STATION SUPT., 1956; ATTAINED.... M.A DEGREE FROM U OF CHICAGO, 1961; REGIONAL DIR. OF PERSONNEL FOR ILL., AND MICH., 1961. POSTMASTER IN 1966; BECAME HEAD OF THE CHICAGO AREA OF 251 POST OFFICES, IN 1972. RETIRED 1973 AFTER 44-YEARS OF SERVICE

1979 GEO L. LEE FEATURE SERVICE .

STARTED AS A SUB-CLERK.

HIS CONTRIBUTIONS IN CIVIC AND COMMUNITY AFFAIRS WERE TREMENDOUS AMONG THEM-THE JOINT NEGRO APPEAL.

FIRST BLACK FEDERAL JUDGE

WILLIAM H. HASTIE

1904, 1976

AN OUTSTANDING SCHOLAR, DISTIN-GUISHED JURIST, MEMBER OF THE AMERICAN ACADEMY OF ARTS AND SCIENCES WAS BORN IN KNOXVILLE, TENN. RAISED IN WASH, D.C. AN HONOR GRADUATE OF AMHERST COLLEGE HE EARNED A LL.B IN LAW AND A PH.D IN JURISTIC SCIENCE FROM THE HARVARD LAW SCHOOL (1930-33). JOINED THE FACULTY OF HOWARD LAW SCHOOL (1930-37). ASS'T. SOLICITOR, DEPT OF INTER-IOR (1933-37); FIRST BLACK FEDERAL JUDGE OVER THE U.S. VIRGIN ISLANDS IN 1937 AND THE YOUNGEST U.S. FEDERAL JUDGE AT 32. DEAN OF HOWARD LAW SCHOOL (1939); SERVED AS CIVILIAN AIDE TO THE SEC'Y OF WAR (1940-42), RESIGNED OVER DISCRIMINATORY PRAC-TICES IN THE ARMED FORCES. WINNER OF THE NAACP'S 1943 "SPINGARN AWARD". FIRST BLACK GOVERNOR OF THE VIRGIN ISLANDS (1946). JUDGE OF THE 3rd U.S. CIRCUIT COURT OF APPEALS, THE FIRST BLACK (1949). CHIEF JUDGE, 1968!

"ONE OF THE ABLEST JUDGES EVER TO SIT ON OUR COURTS......"
CHIEF JUSTICE
WARREN E. BURGER.

VIRGIN ISLANDS

Geo. Lee

1980 GEO L. LEE FEATURE SERVICE

74

ONE O'CLOCK JUMP

COUNT BASIE

BORN IN RED BANK, N.J. ON AUG 21, 1904. CHRISTENED WILLIAM HE STARTED HIS PIANO LESSONS FROM HIS MOTHER AT THE AGE OF FIVE. LATER TRAVELED TO HARLEM AND STUDIED UNDER THE GREAT FATS WALLER AND JAMES P. JOHNSON. IN 1928 HE JOINED WALTER PAIGE'S BLUE DEVILS... PLAYED WITH BENNIE MOTEN, AFTER MOTEN DIED IN 1935 BASIE RE-

—AS HE APPEARED IN 1958.

GEO LEE

ORGANIZED THE BAND AND THE GREAT BASIE STYLE HAS BEEN GOING ON EVER SINCE. IN 1957 HIS BAND WAS THE FIRST FROM THE U.S. TO PLAY A ROYAL COMMAND PERFORMANCE FOR THE QUEEN OF ENGLAND. ELECTED TO DOWN BEAT'S HALL OF FAME IN 1958. RECEIVED AN HONORARY DOCTORATE OF MUSIC FROM THE PHILA., MUSIC ACADEMY IN 1974. THE JAZZ IMMORTAL WAS STILL PLAYING HIS EXCITING STYLE OF CHORD PROGRESSIONS IN 1976.

EVERY TUB
JUMPIN' AT THE WOODSIDE
ALRIGHT, OK YOU WIN
EVERY DAY
THE COMEBACK
RED BANK BOOGIE
SWINGIN' THE BLUES
APRIL IN PARIS

A FEW OF THE MANY SONGS MADE POPULAR BY THE COUNT.

© 1976 George L. Lee Feature Service

Count Basie died on April 26, 1984.

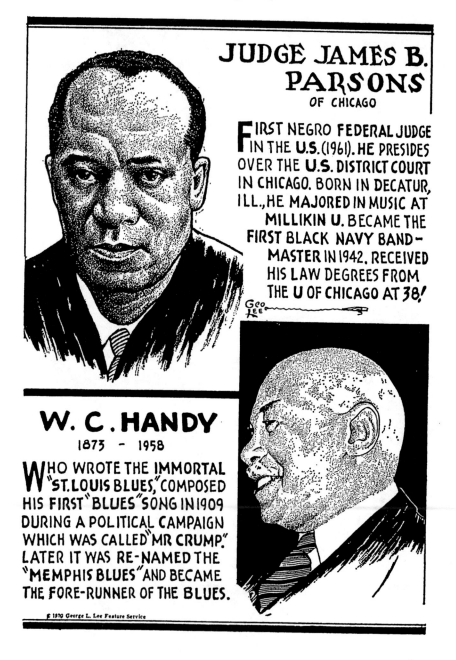

JUDGE JAMES B. PARSONS
OF CHICAGO

FIRST NEGRO FEDERAL JUDGE IN THE U.S. (1961). HE PRESIDES OVER THE U.S. DISTRICT COURT IN CHICAGO. BORN IN DECATUR, ILL., HE MAJORED IN MUSIC AT MILLIKIN U. BECAME THE FIRST BLACK NAVY BAND-MASTER IN 1942. RECEIVED HIS LAW DEGREES FROM THE U OF CHICAGO AT 38!

W. C. HANDY
1873 - 1958

WHO WROTE THE IMMORTAL "ST. LOUIS BLUES," COMPOSED HIS FIRST "BLUES" SONG IN 1909 DURING A POLITICAL CAMPAIGN WHICH WAS CALLED "MR CRUMP." LATER IT WAS RE-NAMED THE "MEMPHIS BLUES" AND BECAME THE FORE-RUNNER OF THE BLUES.

WORLD-RENOWNED PAINTER

JAMES A. PORTER

OUTSTANDING ARTIST, LECTURER, TEACHER AND AUTHOR. ONE OF 25 TEACHERS IN THE U.S. TO RECEIVE THE NATIONAL GALLERY OF ART MEDAL HONORARIUM FOR DISTINGUISHED ACHIEVEMENT IN ART EDUCATION. A CUM LAUDE ART GRADUATE FROM HOWARD U., IN 1927 AND IMMEDIATELY APPOINTED TO THE ART DEPARTMENT. HE WAS A PROFESSOR AND HEAD OF HOWARD'S ART DEPT., FOR OVER 40 YEARS. PORTER STUDIED AT COLUMBIA U., AT THE SORBONNE (PARIS) AND THE BELGIUM-AMERICAN ART SEMINAR. HE TRAVELED ON FELLOWSHIPS TO W. AFRICA, EGYPT, CUBA, HAITI, AND EUROPEAN ART CENTERS. IN 1943 PUBLISHED "MODERN NEGRO ART". HE HAD 10 ONE-MAN SHOWS AND NUMEROUS EXHIBITIONS. A MEMBER OF MANY ART ASSOCIATIONS. A BRILLIANT PAINTER AND ART CRITIC. HE DIED AT 64 (1968).

1979 GEO L. LEE FEATURE SERVICE

ALSO AN EXCELLENT WRITER AND LECTURER

77

LOIS MAILOU JONES

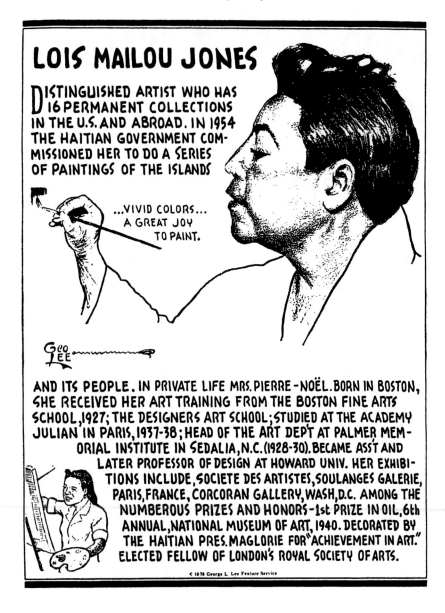

DISTINGUISHED ARTIST WHO HAS 16 PERMANENT COLLECTIONS IN THE U.S. AND ABROAD. IN 1954 THE HAITIAN GOVERNMENT COMMISSIONED HER TO DO A SERIES OF PAINTINGS OF THE ISLANDS

...VIVID COLORS...
A GREAT JOY
TO PAINT.

AND ITS PEOPLE. IN PRIVATE LIFE MRS. PIERRE-NOËL. BORN IN BOSTON, SHE RECEIVED HER ART TRAINING FROM THE BOSTON FINE ARTS SCHOOL, 1927; THE DESIGNERS ART SCHOOL; STUDIED AT THE ACADEMY JULIAN IN PARIS, 1937-38; HEAD OF THE ART DEP'T AT PALMER MEMORIAL INSTITUTE IN SEDALIA, N.C. (1928-30). BECAME ASS'T AND LATER PROFESSOR OF DESIGN AT HOWARD UNIV. HER EXHIBITIONS INCLUDE, SOCIETE DES ARTISTES, SOULANGES GALERIE, PARIS, FRANCE, CORCORAN GALLERY, WASH, D.C. AMONG THE NUMBEROUS PRIZES AND HONORS—1st PRIZE IN OIL, 6th ANNUAL, NATIONAL MUSEUM OF ART, 1940. DECORATED BY THE HAITIAN PRES. MAGLORIE FOR "ACHIEVEMENT IN ART." ELECTED FELLOW OF LONDON'S ROYAL SOCIETY OF ARTS.

ELIZABETH CATLETT

FIRST WOMAN PROFESSOR OF SCULP-TURE AT THE NATIONAL UNIV., OF MEXICO. A NATIVE OF WASH,D.C.,SHE HAS LIVED IN MEXICO FOR MANY YEARS.THE VERY FINE SCULPTOR AND ARTIST RECEIVED HER TRAINING AT HOWARD U.,WHERE SHE GRADUATED CUM LAUDE. SHE WAS THE FIRST TO EARN A MAS-TERS DEGREE IN FINE ARTS EVER AWARDED BY THE IOWA STATE U. HER WORKS APPEAR IN COLLECTIONS OF MUSEUM OF MODERN ART IN MEXICO; LIBRARY OF CONGRESS; UNIVERSITIES OF IOWA, HOWARD AND ATLANTA; MUSEUM OF MODERN ART IN N.Y. AND BROCKMAN GALLERY IN LOS ANGELES.

CHARLES ALSTON

NOTED AMERICAN ARTIST, SCULPTOR, MURALIST AND TEACHER WAS BORN IN CHARLOTTE, N.C.(1907). HE EARNED A B.A. AND M.A. DEGREES FROM COLUMBIA U.(N.Y) RECEIVED FELLOW-SHIPS FROM DOW (COLUMBIA) AND ROSENWALD IN PAINTING (1939-41). HIS WORKS APPEAR IN THE WHITNEY MUSEUM,METROPOLITAN MUSEUM,IBM, BUTLER INSTIT., OF AMERICAN ARTS,THE NAACP AMONG MANY. A PLACE IN THE SUN!

SUPREME COURT JUSTICE — FIRST

THURGOOD MARSHALL

BORN IN BALTIMORE, MD., IN 1908. HIS FATHER A COUNTRY CLUB STEWARD AND MOTHER, A SCHOOL TEACHER. HIS GRANDFATHER WAS ONCE A SLAVE. HE RECEIVED HIS HIGHER EDUCATION AT LINCOLN U., WHERE HE GRADUATED CUM LAUDE IN 1929. THEN...HOWARD'S LAW SCHOOL, GRADUATING MAGNA CUM LAUDE IN 1933. NAACP PRESIDENT ARTHUR SPINGARN ASKED HIM TO BE ASS'T COUNSEL TO CHAS. HOUSTON. HIS FIRST MAJOR CASE WON THE NEGRO THE RIGHT TO ENROLL AT THE U OF MARYLAND LAW SCHOOL (1935). HE BECAME SPECIAL COUNSEL WHEN HOUSTON LEFT IN 1938. THE HISTORIC SCHOOL DESEGREGATION

Geo LEE

CASE HEADED BY MARSHALL, UPSET THE NATION WHEN A FAVORABLE DECISION WAS HANDED DOWN ON MAY 17, 1954. HE WAS APPOINTED JUDGE OF U.S. CIRCUIT COURT OF APPEALS (N.Y.) IN 1961; U.S. SOLICITOR GENERAL (1965) AND A U.S. SUPREME COURT JUSTICE (1967). THE FIRST BLACK.

"MR CIVIL RIGHTS", AS HE WAS KNOWN AS THE CHIEF COUNSEL FOR THE NAACP WAS AWARDED THE 1946 SPINGARN MEDAL...FOR HIS OUTSTANDING ACHIEVEMENTS IN THE FIELD OF CIVIL RIGHTS. ONLY 37, HE BECAME THE 31st RECIPIENT. TRULY A BRILLIANT LEGAL MIND AND A GREAT AMERICAN...

© 1975 George L. Lee Feature Service

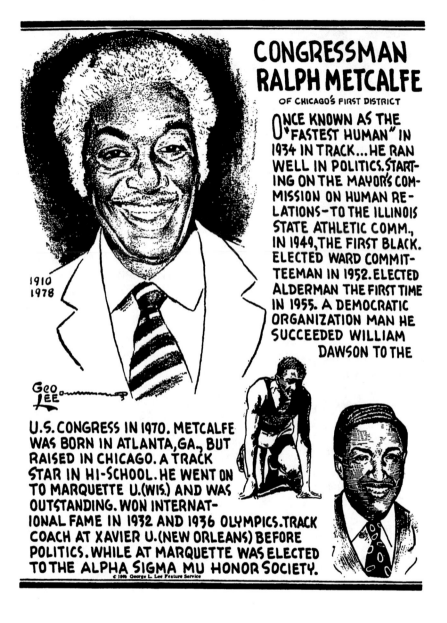

CONGRESSMAN RALPH METCALFE
OF CHICAGO'S FIRST DISTRICT

ONCE KNOWN AS THE "FASTEST HUMAN" IN 1934 IN TRACK...HE RAN WELL IN POLITICS. STARTING ON THE MAYOR'S COMMISSION ON HUMAN RELATIONS—TO THE ILLINOIS STATE ATHLETIC COMM., IN 1949, THE FIRST BLACK. ELECTED WARD COMMITTEEMAN IN 1952. ELECTED ALDERMAN THE FIRST TIME IN 1955. A DEMOCRATIC ORGANIZATION MAN HE SUCCEEDED WILLIAM DAWSON TO THE

1910
1978

Geo LEE

U.S. CONGRESS IN 1970. METCALFE WAS BORN IN ATLANTA, GA., BUT RAISED IN CHICAGO. A TRACK STAR IN HI-SCHOOL. HE WENT ON TO MARQUETTE U.(WIS.) AND WAS OUTSTANDING. WON INTERNATIONAL FAME IN 1932 AND 1936 OLYMPICS. TRACK COACH AT XAVIER U. (NEW ORLEANS) BEFORE POLITICS. WHILE AT MARQUETTE WAS ELECTED TO THE ALPHA SIGMA MU HONOR SOCIETY.

© 1986 George L. Lee Feature Service

81

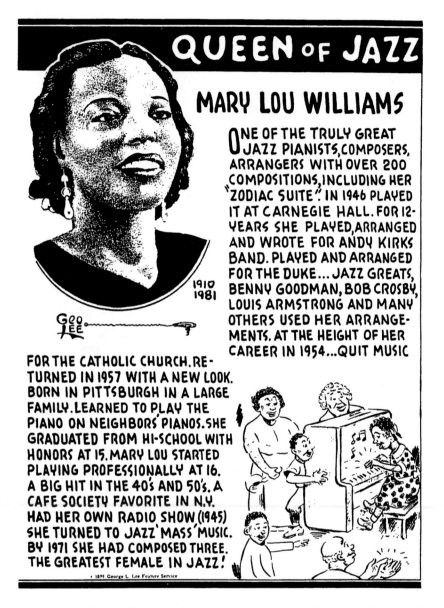

QUEEN OF JAZZ

MARY LOU WILLIAMS

ONE OF THE TRULY GREAT JAZZ PIANISTS, COMPOSERS, ARRANGERS WITH OVER 200 COMPOSITIONS, INCLUDING HER "ZODIAC SUITE". IN 1946 PLAYED IT AT CARNEGIE HALL. FOR 12-YEARS SHE PLAYED, ARRANGED AND WROTE FOR ANDY KIRKS BAND. PLAYED AND ARRANGED FOR THE DUKE... JAZZ GREATS, BENNY GOODMAN, BOB CROSBY, LOUIS ARMSTRONG AND MANY OTHERS USED HER ARRANGEMENTS. AT THE HEIGHT OF HER CAREER IN 1954...QUIT MUSIC

1910
1981

Geo Lee

FOR THE CATHOLIC CHURCH. RETURNED IN 1957 WITH A NEW LOOK. BORN IN PITTSBURGH IN A LARGE FAMILY. LEARNED TO PLAY THE PIANO ON NEIGHBORS' PIANOS. SHE GRADUATED FROM HI-SCHOOL WITH HONORS AT 15. MARY LOU STARTED PLAYING PROFESSIONALLY AT 16. A BIG HIT IN THE 40's AND 50's. A CAFE SOCIETY FAVORITE IN N.Y. HAD HER OWN RADIO SHOW (1945) SHE TURNED TO JAZZ 'MASS' MUSIC. BY 1971 SHE HAD COMPOSED THREE. THE GREATEST FEMALE IN JAZZ!

· 1975 George L. Lee Feature Service

Mary Lou Williams died in Durham, N.C., in 1981. At the time of her death she had been artist-in-residence at Duke University for four years.

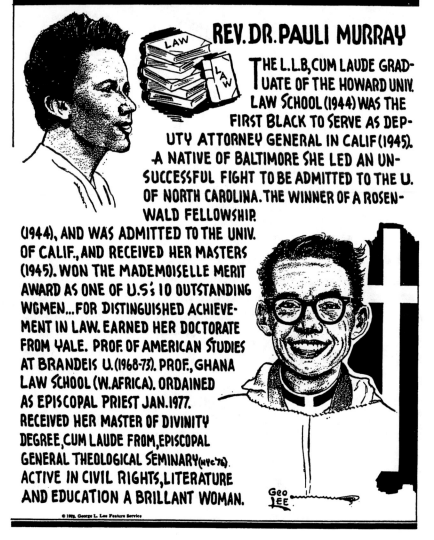

FROM PORTIA TO PRIEST

REV. DR. PAULI MURRAY

THE L.L.B, CUM LAUDE GRADUATE OF THE HOWARD UNIV. LAW SCHOOL (1944) WAS THE FIRST BLACK TO SERVE AS DEPUTY ATTORNEY GENERAL IN CALIF (1945). A NATIVE OF BALTIMORE SHE LED AN UNSUCCESSFUL FIGHT TO BE ADMITTED TO THE U. OF NORTH CAROLINA. THE WINNER OF A ROSENWALD FELLOWSHIP (1944), AND WAS ADMITTED TO THE UNIV. OF CALIF., AND RECEIVED HER MASTERS (1945). WON THE MADEMOISELLE MERIT AWARD AS ONE OF U.S's 10 OUTSTANDING WOMEN...FOR DISTINGUISHED ACHIEVEMENT IN LAW. EARNED HER DOCTORATE FROM YALE. PROF. OF AMERICAN STUDIES AT BRANDEIS U. (1968-73). PROF., GHANA LAW SCHOOL (W. AFRICA). ORDAINED AS EPISCOPAL PRIEST JAN. 1977. RECEIVED HER MASTER OF DIVINITY DEGREE, CUM LAUDE FROM, EPISCOPAL GENERAL THEOLOGICAL SEMINARY (NYC 76). ACTIVE IN CIVIL RIGHTS, LITERATURE AND EDUCATION A BRILLANT WOMAN.

Geo LEE

© 1978, George L. Lee Feature Service

Pauli Murray died in 1985 at the age of 75.

A LIVING LEGEND

KATHERINE DUNHAM

HIGHLY ACCLAIMED DANCER - TEACHER, CHOREOGRAPHER, ANTHROPOLOGIST AND HUMANITARIAN. IN 1983 RECEIVED THE HIGHEST HAITIAN AWARD FOR A NON-NATIONAL AND HONORED BY THE KENNEDY CENTER. IN 1979 THE ALBERT SCHWEITZER MUSIC AWARD FOR HER CONTRIBUTIONS. A NATIVE OF JOLIET, IL.,

AS A YOUNG DANCER

SHE STARTED DANCING AT 9. EDUCATED AT THE U. OF CHICAGO... SHE PAID BY GIVING DANCE LESSONS.

IN 1936 SHE WON A TRAVEL FELLOWSHIP TO THE WEST INDIES WHERE SHE STUDIED BLACK CULTURE. A BRILLIANT CHOREOGRAPHER HER DANCERS WERE KNOWN THE WORLD OVER. IN 1959 SHE WENT TO HAITI AND OPENED A CLINIC FOR THE UNDERPRIVILEGED ON HER ESTATE AND BECAME A "GOOD SAMARITAN." RETURNED TO U.S. IN 1962 AND CONTINUED HER DANCE TROUPE TOUR. IN 1971 BECAME DIRECTOR OF PERFORMING ARTS AT SOUTHERN ILL., UNIV. A REMARKABLE TALENT MISS. DUNHAM IS TRULY A LIVING LEGEND!

1984 Geo L. Lee Feature Service

ODETTA

WHOSE FULL NAME IS ODETTA FELIOUS GORDON WAS BORN IN BIRMINGHAM, ALA., AND GREW UP IN LOS ANGELES. HER VOICE WAS ORIGINALLY TRAINED FOR OPERA AND SHE PAID FOR HER LESSONS BY WORKING IN A BUTTON FACTORY. ONE NIGHT AT A PARTY SHE HEARD A GROUP OF PERFORMERS SING FOLK SONGS...SHE FELL IN LOVE WITH THE MUSIC. THUS BEGAN A CAREER THAT TOOK HER TO TV, CONCERT CIRCUIT, NIGHT CLUBS AND CARNEGIE HALL (1960). "EXCITING" IS THE VOICE OF ODETTA...INTERNATIONALLY FAMOUS.

HOWLIN' WOLF

1910. 1976.

THE FATHER OF ROCK MUSIC, THE SINGER OF HARD TIME BLUES AND MIGHTY JOYS WAS GIVEN AN HONORARY DOCTOR OF ARTS DEGREE AT COLUMBIA COLLEGE (1972)...ALTHO HE NEVER WENT ANY HIGHER THAN THE 7th GRADE. BORN CHESTER BURNETT ON A COTTON PLANTATION IN MISS., HE WENT TO CHICAGO IN 1952 AND MADE GOOD. HIS STYLE INSPIRED THE ROLLING STONES.!

Geo Lee

© 1976 George L. Lee Feature Service

85

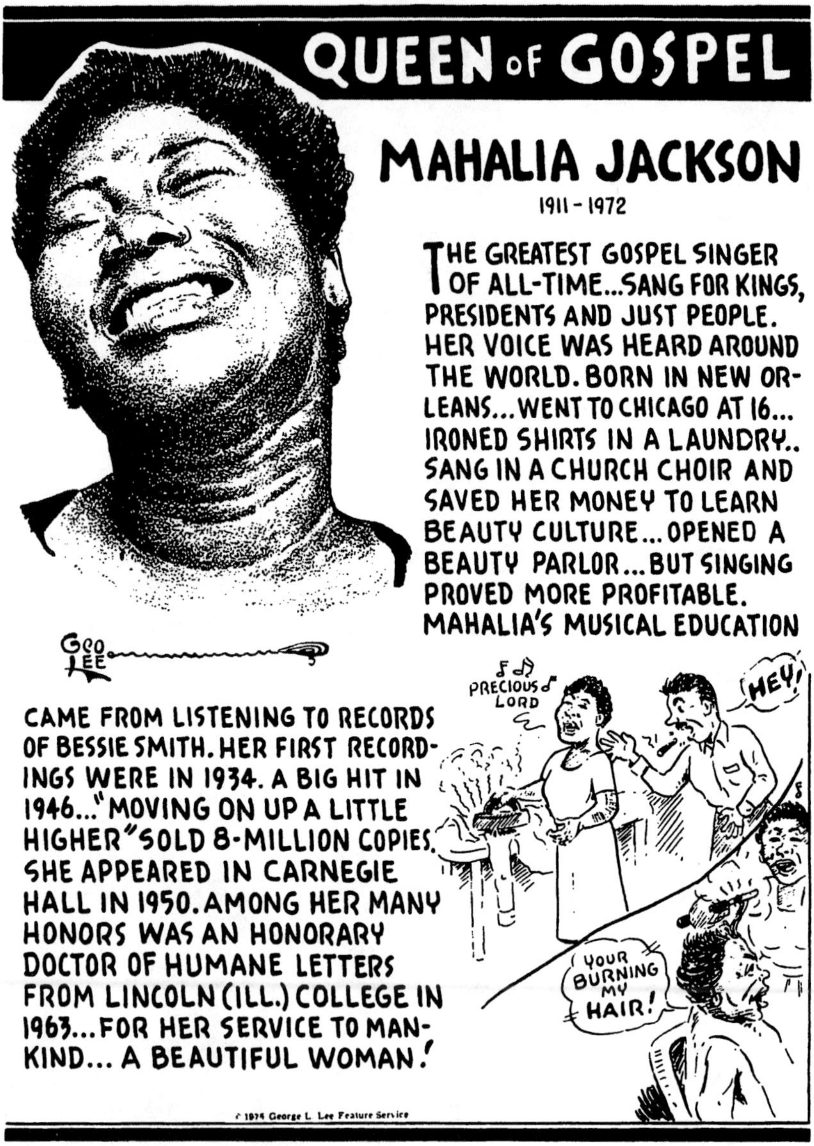

QUEEN of GOSPEL

MAHALIA JACKSON
1911 – 1972

THE GREATEST GOSPEL SINGER OF ALL-TIME...SANG FOR KINGS, PRESIDENTS AND JUST PEOPLE. HER VOICE WAS HEARD AROUND THE WORLD. BORN IN NEW ORLEANS...WENT TO CHICAGO AT 16... IRONED SHIRTS IN A LAUNDRY.. SANG IN A CHURCH CHOIR AND SAVED HER MONEY TO LEARN BEAUTY CULTURE...OPENED A BEAUTY PARLOR...BUT SINGING PROVED MORE PROFITABLE. MAHALIA'S MUSICAL EDUCATION

GEO LEE

CAME FROM LISTENING TO RECORDS OF BESSIE SMITH. HER FIRST RECORDINGS WERE IN 1934. A BIG HIT IN 1946..."MOVING ON UP A LITTLE HIGHER" SOLD 8-MILLION COPIES. SHE APPEARED IN CARNEGIE HALL IN 1950. AMONG HER MANY HONORS WAS AN HONORARY DOCTOR OF HUMANE LETTERS FROM LINCOLN (ILL.) COLLEGE IN 1963...FOR HER SERVICE TO MANKIND... A BEAUTIFUL WOMAN!

PRECIOUS LORD

HEY!

YOUR BURNING MY HAIR!

The "101st SENATOR"

CLARENCE MITCHELL

HIS SKILL IN INFLUENCING CIVIL RIGHTS LEGISLATION ON CAPITOL HILL EARNED HIM THE TITLE, THE "101st SENATOR". THE HIGHLY RESPECTED CIVIL-RIGHTS LOBBYIST WAS BORN IN BALTIMORE ON MAR 4, 1911. A GRADUATE OF LINCOLN (PA) UNIV. HE DID GRADUATE WORK AT ATLANTA U., AND UNIV. OF MINNESOTA. MITCHELL RECEIVED HIS LLB AND JD DEGREES FROM THE UNIV., OF MARYLAND LAW SCHOOL. HIS CAREER STARTED AS A REPORTER FOR THE BALTIMORE AFRO-AMERICAN. HE JOINED THE NAACP AS LABOR SECRETARY IN THE 1940's. NAMED DIRECTOR OF THE WASHINGTON BUREAU AND BECAME THE NATION'S TOP CIVIL RIGHTS LOBBYIST. IN 1950. HE URGED CONGRESS TO PASS THE 1957 CIVIL RIGHTS ACT, CREATING THE U.S. COMM., ON CIVIL RIGHTS. HIS EFFORTS IN THE PASSAGE OF THE FAIR HOUSING ACT IN 1968 WON HIM THE "SPINGARN MEDAL" IN 1969... NAACP's HIGHEST HONOR.

A FEW OF HIS EFFORTS -
- PASSAGE OF THE CIVIL RIGHTS ACT OF 1964
- PASSAGE, VOTING RIGHTS ACT OF 1965
- IN 1970 HE LED THE FIGHT TO EXTEND THE VOTING RIGHTS ACT's BAN AGAINST LITERACY TESTS FOR 5-YEARS
- IN 1972, THE PASSAGE OF ENFORCEMENT POWERS FOR THE EQUAL EMPLOYMENT OPPORTUNITY COMMISSION

AFTER MANY YEARS OF BRILLIANT SERVICE HE RESIGNED IN 1979.

1982 GEO L. LEE FEATURE SERVICE

In 1980, Clarence Mitchell was awarded the "Medal of Freedom" by President Carter for his contributions in civil rights. Mitchell died in 1984.

PHOTO-JOURNALIST, DIRECTOR, AUTHOR

GORDON PARKS SR

A MAN OF MANY TALENTS. ONE OF THE NATIONS FOREMOST PHOTO-JOURNALISTS. BORN IN FORT SCOTT, KAN., ON NOV 30, 1912, THE YOUNGEST OF 15. HIS MOTHER INSPIRED HIM TO ACHIEVE AGAINST THE ODDS. AFTER SHE PASSED HE LIVED WITH A SISTER IN ST. PAUL, MINN. DUE TO CONDITIONS HE HAD TO DROP-OUT OF HI-SCHOOL. A KEEN EAR FOR MUSIC HE LEARNED TO PLAY THE PIANO WITHOUT LESSONS. AFTER MANY ODD JOBS, BECAME

Geo
LEE

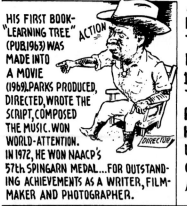

HIS FIRST BOOK- "LEARNING TREE" (PUB.1963) WAS MADE INTO A MOVIE (1969). PARKS PRODUCED, DIRECTED, WROTE THE SCRIPT, COMPOSED THE MUSIC. WON WORLD-ATTENTION. IN 1972, HE WON NAACP'S 57th SPINGARN MEDAL...FOR OUTSTANDING ACHIEVEMENTS AS A WRITER, FILM-MAKER AND PHOTOGRAPHER.

A WAITER ON THE NORTHERN PACIFIC R.R. BY CHANCE, LOOKED AT A MAGAZINE. THE PHOTOS SO IMPRESSED HIM THAT HE BOUGHT A 12.50 CAMERA. IT WAS 1937, BY 1942 HIS PHOTOS WON HIM THE FIRST ROSENWALD FELLOWSHIP IN PHOTOGRAPHY. HE GAINED MORE STUDY. HE BRILLIANTLY TOOK FASHIONS TO DOCUMENTARY. WORKED FOR OWI, STANDARD OIL CO. IN 1949 JOINED LIFE MAGAZINE AND STAYED OVER 20 YEARS.

A JAZZ PIONEER

LIONEL HAMPTON

INTERNATIONALLY FAMOUS KING OF THE VIBRAHARP HAS HAD A TREMENDOUS JAZZ CAREER. BORN IN LOUISVILLE, KY., IN 1913. EARLY EDUCATION IN CHICAGO... WHERE HE FIRST PLAYED THE BASS DRUM. AT 16 HE WENT TO LOS ANGELES. STUDIED MUSIC AT USC...SHOWED TALENT ON THE DRUMS. HE FIRST PLAYED WITH PAUL HOWARD'S BAND. THEN LES HITES BAND. FATE LED HIM TO LOUIS ARMSTRONG WHO WAS ON AN ENGAGEMENT DATE IN L.A. HAMP JOINED LOUIS AND IN A RECORDING SESSION HE CAME ACROSS A STUDIO VIBRAHARP HE TRIED IT AND LIKED IT. THEY MADE A RECORD WITH THE "VIBES" ...IT WAS A TOP SELLER. LOUIS WENT BACK EAST BUT HAMP STAYED AND TOOK A JOB AS A SINGLE IN A SMALL CAFE. BENNY GOODMAN HAPPENED BY AND HEARD HAMP ON THE "VIBES" AND ASKED HIM TO SIT IN WITH HIS TRIO IN A RECORDING DATE, THE IMPACT WAS GREAT AND THE TRIO BECAME A QUARTET...BENNY, CLARINET; TEDDY WILSON, PIANO; HAMP, VIBES; GENE KRUPA, DRUMS. THEY WERE GREAT! AFTER FOUR YEARS WITH BENNY, HAMP FORMED HIS OWN BAND (1940). WITH HIS WIFE GLADYS AS MANAGER. THEY FORMED LIONEL HAMPTON ENTERPRISES. THE BAND PLAYED AROUND THE WORLD. HAMP HAS DONE MUCH TO PROMOTE JAZZ AND STILL GOING STRONG!

1984 Geo L. Lee Feature Service

CLARA JONES

First Black President in the 100-year history of the American Library Assn (1976). A native of St. Louis and a graduate of Spelman College and the U of Mich. She started her library career at Dillard and Southern U in Louisiana. In 1944, Mrs. Jones a mother of three joined the Detroit Library System. In 1950 became head of the Connelly Br. Appointed the first Black director of the Detroit Public Library in 1970.

MARGARET HARRIS

Pianist, composer, conductor and musical director. The first Black woman to conduct more than 10 major orchestras. Born in Chicago she was a child prodigy. Made piano debut at 3. At 10 played a Mozart concerto with the Chicago Symphony. Won a scholarship to Curtis Insti. of Music (Phila.). A graduate of Juilliard School of Music. Started her career as conductor with the Broadway show "Hair" in 1970. Later musical director of "Raisin".

© 1977 George L. Lee Feature Service

BROWN BOMBER

PVT. JOE LOUIS BARROW

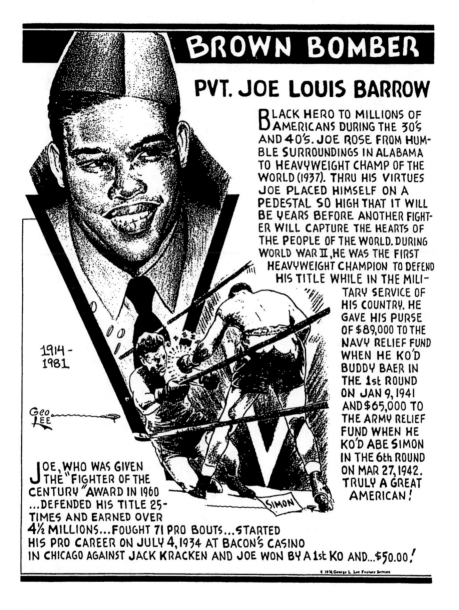

BLACK HERO TO MILLIONS OF AMERICANS DURING THE 30'S AND 40'S. JOE ROSE FROM HUMBLE SURROUNDINGS IN ALABAMA TO HEAVYWEIGHT CHAMP OF THE WORLD (1937). THRU HIS VIRTUES JOE PLACED HIMSELF ON A PEDESTAL SO HIGH THAT IT WILL BE YEARS BEFORE ANOTHER FIGHTER WILL CAPTURE THE HEARTS OF THE PEOPLE OF THE WORLD. DURING WORLD WAR II, HE WAS THE FIRST HEAVYWEIGHT CHAMPION TO DEFEND HIS TITLE WHILE IN THE MILITARY SERVICE OF HIS COUNTRY. HE GAVE HIS PURSE OF $89,000 TO THE NAVY RELIEF FUND WHEN HE KO'D BUDDY BAER IN THE 1st ROUND ON JAN 9, 1941 AND $65,000 TO THE ARMY RELIEF FUND WHEN HE KO'D ABE SIMON IN THE 6th ROUND ON MAR 27, 1942. TRULY A GREAT AMERICAN!

1914-1981

Geo LEE

SIMON

JOE, WHO WAS GIVEN THE "FIGHTER OF THE CENTURY" AWARD IN 1960 ...DEFENDED HIS TITLE 25-TIMES AND EARNED OVER 4½ MILLIONS...FOUGHT 71 PRO BOUTS...STARTED HIS PRO CAREER ON JULY 4, 1934 AT BACON'S CASINO IN CHICAGO AGAINST JACK KRACKEN AND JOE WON BY A 1st KO AND...$50.00!

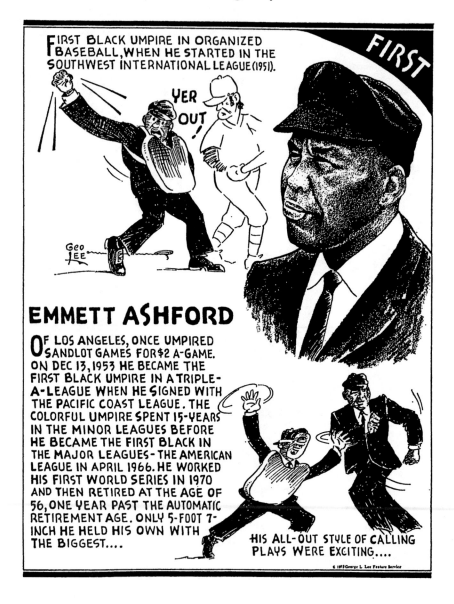

FIRST BLACK UMPIRE IN ORGANIZED BASEBALL, WHEN HE STARTED IN THE SOUTHWEST INTERNATIONAL LEAGUE (1951).

YER OUT!

FIRST

Geo LEE

EMMETT ASHFORD

OF LOS ANGELES, ONCE UMPIRED SANDLOT GAMES FOR $2 A-GAME. ON DEC 13, 1953 HE BECAME THE FIRST BLACK UMPIRE IN A TRIPLE-A-LEAGUE WHEN HE SIGNED WITH THE PACIFIC COAST LEAGUE. THE COLORFUL UMPIRE SPENT 15-YEARS IN THE MINOR LEAGUES BEFORE HE BECAME THE FIRST BLACK IN THE MAJOR LEAGUES - THE AMERICAN LEAGUE IN APRIL 1966. HE WORKED HIS FIRST WORLD SERIES IN 1970 AND THEN RETIRED AT THE AGE OF 56, ONE YEAR PAST THE AUTOMATIC RETIREMENT AGE. ONLY 5-FOOT 7-INCH HE HELD HIS OWN WITH THE BIGGEST....

HIS ALL-OUT STYLE OF CALLING PLAYS WERE EXCITING....

© 1973 George L. Lee Feature Service

92

DIRECTOR OF PEACE CORPS

DR. CAROLYN PAYTON

FIRST WOMAN DIRECTOR OF THE PEACE CORPS WHO WILL DIRECT OVER 6,000 VOLUNTEERS AND TRAINEES IN 62 DEVELOPING COUNTRIES AROUND THE WORLD. (1977) NATIVE OF NORFOLK, VA., DR. PAYTON EARNED HER PH.D IN PSYCHOLOGY AT COLUMBIA U. AND BECAME DIRECTOR OF COUNSELING AT HOWARD U. SHE LEFT HOWARD TO JOIN THE PEACE CORPS. FROM 1964 TO 1970 SERVED AS AN ADMINISTRATOR IN THE CARIBBEAN-LATIN AMERICA.

Geo LEE

FIRST BLACK WOMAN MAYOR

LELIA FOLEY

ON APRIL 3, 1973, MRS FOLEY WAS ELECTED MAYOR OF TAFT, OKLA., AN ALL-BLACK TOWN OF 600 POP. A HI-SCHOOL GRADUATE AND MOTHER OF 5, THE FIRST BLACK WOMAN... "MAYOR" IN THE U.S...WAS ONCE ON WELFARE!

© 1978 George L. Lee Feature Service

LADY DAY 🎵 🎶

BILLIE HOLIDAY
1915 - 1959

ONCE THE FIRST LADY OF SONG ON NEW YORK'S FAMED 52ND ST, AND THE HIGHEST PAID BEGAN HER SINGING CAREER AT THE AGE OF 15 AT JERRY PRESTON'S LOG CABIN CLUB IN NYC. BORN ELEANORA FAGAN ON APRIL 7, IN BALTIMORE, MD. THE ORIGINAL SONG STYLIST WAS KNOWN TO MILLIONS AS BILLIE HOLIDAY. DURING THE LATE THIRTIES SHE SANG WITH COUNT BASIE AND ARTIE SHAW. IN THE FORTIES SHE SANG SOLO IN NIGHTSPOTS THRU-OUT THE COUNTRY BUT MAINLY IN NYC. IN 1944 AND 1945 BILLIE WAS ESQUIRE'S TOP FEMALE VOCALIST. SHE RECORDED WITH

Geo LEE

GOD BLESS THE CHILD THATS GOT HIS OWN....

LESTER YOUNG NAMED HER — "LADY DAY". HER BEAUTIFUL DREAM WAS TO CARE FOR STRAY DOGS AND ORPHAN KIDS... BUT IT NEVER BECAME A REALITY....

BENNY GOODMAN, BASIE, SHAW, EDDIE HEYWOOD. HER RECORDING OF "LOVER MAN" AND "STRANGE FRUIT" SOLD OVER A MILLION COPIES. OTHER BIG HITS- I'LL GET BY, LOVER COME BACK TO ME AND GLOOMY SUNDAY. SHE CO-AUTHORED HER AUTOBIOGRAPHY - THE LADY SINGS THE BLUES, IN 1956. ONE OF THE TRULY GREAT VOCALISTS HER CAREER CAME TO A TRAGIC END DUE TO THE USE OF DRUGS.

KING of CHICAGO BLUES

1915
1983

Geo
LEE

MUDDY WATERS

THE LEGENDARY CHICAGO BLUES SING-ER, GUITARIST AND COMPOSER. WHO DEVELOPED THE URBAN BLUES SOUND. BORN McKINLEY MORGANFIELD, APRIL 4, 1915 IN ROLLING FORK, MISS. THE SON OF A SHARECROPPER. AS A CHILD HE PLAYED IN A MUDDY CREEK. HIS GRANDMOTHER CALLED HIM-MUDDY...IT STUCK. FRIENDS ADDED-WATERS. AT 13, PLAYED THE HAR-MONICA. LATER THE GUITAR. HE LEARN-ED THE DELTA SOUND. IN 1941 TWO FOLK SONG COLLECTORS OF THE LIBRARY OF CONGRESS WENT TO THE STOVALL PLANTATION WHERE MUDDY WAS WORKING AND RECORDED HIS MUSIC. HE WENT TO CHICAGO IN 1943. PLAYED SATURDAY NIGHT FISH-FRIES AND HE ELECTRONICALLY AMPLIFIED HIS BLUES AND A NEW SOUND EMERGED -THE CHICAGO BLUES. BEGAN RECORD-ING, 1950. TOURED EUROPE WITH HIS SMALL BAND, 1955. HIS BLUES SOUND INFLUENCED YOUNG WHITE ROCK MUSICIANS SUCH AS THE "ROLLING STONES" WHO TOOK THEIR NAME.... FROM MUDDY's SONG "ROLLIN' STONE". HE TRULY WAS KING OF CHICAGO BLUES.

1984 Geo L. Lee Feature Service

A FEW HITS!
SHE MOVES ME
ROLLIN' AND TUMBLIN'
I CAN'T BE SATISFIED
BABY PLEASE DON'T GO
ROLLIN' STONE
LONG DISTANCE CALL

HOOCHIE COOCHIE MAN
GOT MY MOJO WORKIN'
SHE LOVES ME

6 GRAMMY AWARDS!

95

POET LAUREATE of ILLINOIS

GWENDOLYN BROOKS

ONE OF AMERICA'S BEST POETS WAS NAMED AS SUCCESSOR TO THE LATE CARL SANDBURG AS "POET LAUREATE OF ILLINOIS"(1968). BORN IN TOPEKA, KAN., ON JUNE 17, 1917 AND RAISED IN CHICAGO. SHE STARTED RHYMING WORDS AT SEVEN. A GRADUATE OF ENGLEWOOD HIGH AND WILSON JUNIOR COLLEGE (1936). SHE ENROLLED IN A POETRY CLASS AT THE SOUTH SIDE COMMUNITY ART CENTER WHERE MANY BLACK ARTISTS STARTED. IN 1943 SHE WON HER FIRST PRIZE IN POETRY AND A NEW BLACK EXPERIENCE BEGAN. THE MIDWESTERN WRITER'S CONFER-

Geo LEE

MISS BROOKS TAUGHT CREATIVE WRITING IN COLUMBIA COLLEGE IN CHICAGO; NORTHEASTERN ILL STATE COLLEGE; CITY UNIVERSITY (N.Y.); U OF WISCONSIN

A NOVEL- "MAUDE MARTHA" 1953

"THE BEAN EATERS" 1960

"BRONZE-VILLE BOYS AND GIRLS" 1956

"JUMP BAD" "RIOT"

SELECTED POEMS 1963

AND— MANY MORE!

ENCE AWARDED PRIZES TO HER IN 1943-44-45. MADEMOISELLE MAGAZINE'S 1946 PICK AS ONE OF "10 WOMEN OF THE YEAR". WON A GUGGENHEIM FELLOWSHIP (1946). IN 1950 SHE BECAME THE FIRST BLACK TO WIN THE PULITZER PRIZE, FOR HER BOOK "ANNIE ALLEN". ONE OF THE MOST ACCLAIMED WOMEN WRITERS OF HER TIME!

1982 GEO L. LEE FEATURE SERVICE

Gwendolyn Brooks is the 30th poet since 1937 to be appointed the Library of Congress's Consultant in Poetry (1985–1986) — the first black woman, and the second black, to hold the post.

NEVER TOO LATE TO DREAM

ADELE CHILTON GAILLARD

WHOSE OIL PAINTINGS DISPLAY A DELIGHTFUL...HIDDEN TALENT THAT HAD BEEN WAITING A LIFETIME UNTIL RETIREMENT. MOTHER OF 3 AND GRANDMOTHER OF 6 CHILDREN. BORN AND REARED IN CHICAGO, THE DAUGHTER OF THE FIRST BLACK U.S. DEPUTY MARSHALL IN CHICAGO. ALWAYS A FLAIR FOR ART AND CRAFTS, ADELE BECAME A DRESS MODEL. AFTER MARRIAGE WAS ONE OF THE FIRST BLACK TELE-TYPIST AND NIGHT MANAGERS OF POSTAL TELEGRAPH. VERY ACTIVE IN THE SCHOOL'S P.T.A. A RECEPTIONIST

Geo LEE

-SECRETARY WITH THE LOCAL B'NAI B'RITH. A TEACHERS AIDE WITH THE CHICAGO BOARD OF EDUCATION WHEN SHE AND HER HUSBAND OF 40 YEARS RETIRED TO TORRANCE, CAL., IN 1976. BACK TO HER DREAM- PAINTING. SHE ENROLLED IN ART CLASSES. ADELE'S TALENT BLOSSOMED...SOON A DREAM CAME TRUE...SHE IS AN ARTIST!

HER BEAUTIFUL LANDSCAPES AND SEASCAPES WERE ADMIRED BY FRIENDS. SHE HAD A SUCCESSFUL SHOWING IN THE PREVIEW ROOM OF THE CENTURY PLAZA HOTEL, CENTURY CITY, CAL. IN MAY 1980 SHE HAD A CHICAGO SHOWING AT ST. BERNARD HOSPITAL'S 75th ANNIV. IT WAS GREAT.

1980 GEO L. LEE FEATURE SERVICE

HALL of FAME

ALONZO 'JAKE' SMITH GAITHER

ONE OF AMERICA'S BEST COLLEGE FOOTBALL COACHES. A NATIVE OF DAYTON, TENN. A GRADUATE OF KNOXVILLE COLLEGE (1927). BEGAN CAREER AS TEACHER-COACH AT HENDERSON INSTITUTE (N.C.) JOINED FLA., A&M AS ASS'T COACH (1937)—HEAD COACH, 1945 TO 1969 CONTINUED AS ATHLETIC DIRECTOR RETIRED 1973. ENTERED COLLEGE FOOTBALL "HALL of FAME" ON JAN 30, 1975.

HE DEVELOPED HUNDREDS OF FINE PLAYERS

203 WINS 36 LOSSES 4 TIES

HALL of FAME IN 25 SEASONS

FLORIDA A&M COACH

BOB FELIX
C. CHILDS
BOB PAREMORE
WILLIE GALIMORE
BOB HAYES
C. OATS
R. FLEMING
AL DENSON
H. DIXON
H. LEE
GENE THOMAS

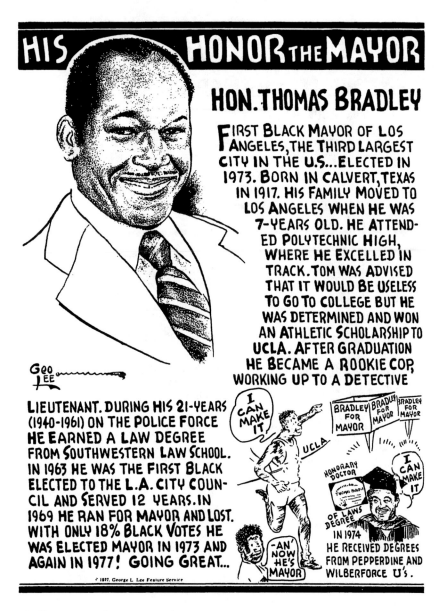

HIS HONOR THE MAYOR

HON. THOMAS BRADLEY

FIRST BLACK MAYOR OF LOS ANGELES, THE THIRD LARGEST CITY IN THE U.S...ELECTED IN 1973. BORN IN CALVERT, TEXAS IN 1917. HIS FAMILY MOVED TO LOS ANGELES WHEN HE WAS 7-YEARS OLD. HE ATTENDED POLYTECHNIC HIGH, WHERE HE EXCELLED IN TRACK. TOM WAS ADVISED THAT IT WOULD BE USELESS TO GO TO COLLEGE BUT HE WAS DETERMINED AND WON AN ATHLETIC SCHOLARSHIP TO UCLA. AFTER GRADUATION HE BECAME A ROOKIE COP, WORKING UP TO A DETECTIVE

Geo LEE

LIEUTENANT. DURING HIS 21-YEARS (1940-1961) ON THE POLICE FORCE HE EARNED A LAW DEGREE FROM SOUTHWESTERN LAW SCHOOL. IN 1963 HE WAS THE FIRST BLACK ELECTED TO THE L.A. CITY COUNCIL AND SERVED 12 YEARS. IN 1969 HE RAN FOR MAYOR AND LOST. WITH ONLY 18% BLACK VOTES HE WAS ELECTED MAYOR IN 1973 AND AGAIN IN 1977! GOING GREAT...

I CAN MAKE IT

UCLA

BRADLEY FOR MAYOR

BRADLEY FOR MAYOR

BRADLEY FOR MAYOR

HONORARY DOCTOR

I CAN MAKE IT

OF LAWS DEGREE

IN 1974 HE RECEIVED DEGREES FROM PEPPERDINE AND WILBERFORCE U'S.

-AN' NOW HE'S MAYOR

© 1977. George L. Lee Feature Service

Bradley was reelected for a fourth term in 1985, with the highest margin of victory in Los Angeles history. He had been only narrowly defeated for the governor's office in 1982—by less than 53,000 votes out of 7 million.

FREEDOM ALL THE WAY

FANNIE LOU HAMER

1917
1977

1. THE COURAGEOUS HEROINE OF SUNFLOWER COUNTY, MISS., WHO HAS RISEN FROM A SHARE-CROPPER TO FOUNDER AND VICE-CHAIRMAN OF THE MISSISSIPPI FREEDOM DEMOCRATIC PARTY. HER BATTLE CRY FOR FREE-DOM IS THE BALLOT BOX—REGISTER TO VOTE. BORN IN MONTGOMERY COUNTY, MISS., SHE WAS THE LAST OF 20 CHILDREN OF SHARECROPPER PARENTS. AT THE AGE OF 2 HER FAMILY MOVED

2. TO SUNFLOWER COUNTY. LIFE WAS MISERABLE. SHE WORKED IN THE COTTON FIELDS AND EDUCA-TION WAS A STRUGGLE. SHE LEARNED TO READ AND WRITE. AFTER HER MARRIAGE TO PERRY HAMER, THEY LIVED AND WORKED ON A PLANTATION IN SUNFLOWER COUNTY. BESIDES WORKING IN THE FIELDS SHE ACTED AS TIMEKEEPER,

3. RECORDING HOURS AND BALES PICKED. IN AUG 1962 SHE ATTEMPTED TO REGISTER TO VOTE, ONLY TO LOSE HER WORK AND SHE HAD TO LEAVE THE PLANTATION. AN ATTEMPT WAS MADE ON HER LIFE. SHE JOINED SNCC AND BECAME A FIELD SEC'Y. IN DEC 1962 SHE FINALLY WAS ABLE TO REGISTER. IN 1964 SHE LED THE BLACK DELEGATES TO THE NAT'L DEMOCRATIC CONVENTION FROM MISS. MRS. HAMER CONTINUED TO FIGHT FOR FREEDOM!

MISSISSIPPI FREEDOM DEMOCRATIC PARTY

1982 GEO L. LEE FEATURE SERVICE

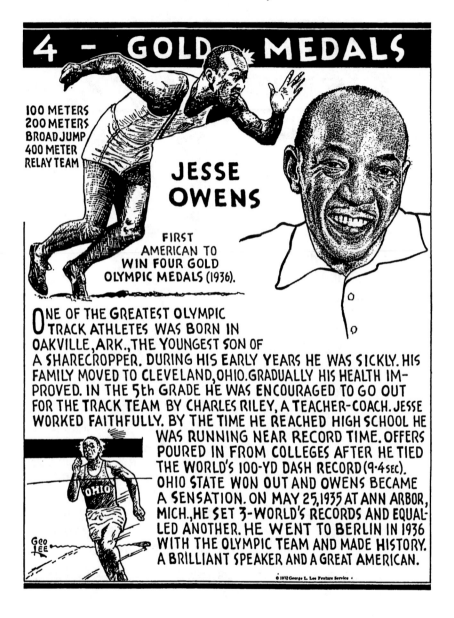

4 – GOLD MEDALS

100 METERS
200 METERS
BROAD JUMP
400 METER
RELAY TEAM

JESSE OWENS

FIRST
AMERICAN TO
WIN FOUR GOLD
OLYMPIC MEDALS (1936).

ONE OF THE GREATEST OLYMPIC TRACK ATHLETES WAS BORN IN OAKVILLE, ARK., THE YOUNGEST SON OF A SHARECROPPER. DURING HIS EARLY YEARS HE WAS SICKLY. HIS FAMILY MOVED TO CLEVELAND, OHIO. GRADUALLY HIS HEALTH IMPROVED. IN THE 5th GRADE HE WAS ENCOURAGED TO GO OUT FOR THE TRACK TEAM BY CHARLES RILEY, A TEACHER-COACH. JESSE WORKED FAITHFULLY. BY THE TIME HE REACHED HIGH SCHOOL HE WAS RUNNING NEAR RECORD TIME. OFFERS POURED IN FROM COLLEGES AFTER HE TIED THE WORLD'S 100-YD DASH RECORD (9·4sec). OHIO STATE WON OUT AND OWENS BECAME A SENSATION. ON MAY 25, 1935 AT ANN ARBOR, MICH., HE SET 3-WORLD'S RECORDS AND EQUALLED ANOTHER. HE WENT TO BERLIN IN 1936 WITH THE OLYMPIC TEAM AND MADE HISTORY. A BRILLIANT SPEAKER AND A GREAT AMERICAN.

Geo Lee

© 1972 George L. Lee Feature Service ·

NAACP's WOMAN CHAIRPERSON

MARGARET BUSH WILSON

THE VERY EFFICIENT, COMPETENT AND COURAGEOUS CHAIRPERSON OF THE NAACP BOARD. ELECTED IN 1975 THE FIRST WOMAN SINCE MARY W. OVINGTON (1919). SHE WAS THE FIRST WOMAN TO CHAIR THE ST. LOUIS BRANCH. IN 1978 RECEIVED THE "DEMOCRACY IN ACTION AWARD" OF THE AMERICAN JEWISH CONGRESS, ST. LOUIS COUNCIL..."FOR HER COURAGEOUS WORK ON THE BEHALF OF HUMAN AND CIVIL RIGHTS." BORN IN ST. LOUIS, MRS. WILSON ATTENDED THE PUBLIC SCHOOLS THERE AND GRADUATED FROM SUMNER HIGH WITH HONORS.

Geo LEE

THE CHAIR RECOGNIZES.....

YOU MEAN CHAIRPERSON!

SHE MAKES A GOOD CHAIRMAN

EARNED HER B.A. DEGREE (CUM LAUDE) IN ECONOMICS FROM TALLADEGA COLLEGE (ALA)... A LL.B DEGREE FROM LINCOLN UNIV., LAW SCHOOL IN 1943... A PRACTICING ATTORNEY IN ST. LOUIS. SHE IS A MEMBER OF THE MISSOURI BAR, ILLINOIS BAR AND ADMITTED TO PRACTICE BEFORE THE U.S. SUPREME COURT.

1979 GEO L. LEE FEATURE SERVICE

LENA HORNE, 44, YEARS IN SHO-BIZ

FIRST BIG BROADWAY ROLE WAS IN "JAMAICA" WITH RICARDO MONTALBAN (1957)

Geo Lee

LENA WAS BORN IN BROOKLYN, N.Y. IN 1917. AS A YOUNGSTER SHE HAD NO THOUGHT OF THE THEATRE. SHE ATTENDED THE PUBLIC SCHOOLS AND THE GIRLS' HIGH SCHOOL IN BROOKLYN. HER MOTHER ONCE AN ACTRESS WITH THE LAFAYETTE STOCK CO., IN HARLEM ENCOURAGED HER SINGING CAREER. AT 16 SHE STARTED AS A CHORUS GIRL AT THE FAMED COTTON CLUB IN 1933. SHE BECAME A SENSATION! LATER APPEARED WITH CHARLIE BARNETT'S ORCHESTRA AS A FEATURED SINGER OVER NBC RADIO. LENA WAS A NATURAL IN SHOW BUSINESS... A STAR OF CAFE SOCI-ETY, BROADWAY, RECORDINGS, MOVIES AND TELEVISION OF THE HIGHEST MAGNITUDE. LENA HORNE SEEMS AGELESS AS SHE CONTI-NUED TO SHINE IN 1977. NO STORMY WEATHER!

© 1977, George L. Lee Feature Service

Lena Horne received the Spingarn Medal—for "the highest or noblest achievement by an American Negro"—in 1983. In 1985 she received the Eubie Award from the New York chapter of the National Academy of Recording Arts and Sciences, for her contributions to entertainment.

FIRST BLACK WOMAN COMMERCIAL PILOT

WILLA BROWN
OF CHICAGO

PIONEER AVIATRIX WHO FOUGHT FOR BLACKS IN THE FIELD OF AVIATION. BORN IN KENTUCKY AND EDUCATED IN INDIANA... SHE ONCE TAUGHT SCHOOL IN GARY. STARTED FLYING IN THE CHICAGO AREA IN 1934 AND EARNED HER COMMERCIAL PILOTS LICENSE IN 1937. A FOUNDER AND DIRECTOR OF THE COFFEY SCHOOL OF AERONAUTICS (1938). THRU HER EFFORTS

OVER 1,000 HOURS

Geo LEE

© 1975 George L. Lee Feature Service

IN THE CIVILIAN PILOTS TRAINING PROGRAM (U.S.) IN 1941 BLACKS WERE INCLUDED...WHICH AIDED IN THE FORMATION OF THE FAMED 99th PURSUIT SQUADRON AT TUSKEGEE. THE COFFEY SCHOOL TRAINED OVER 200 PILOTS FROM 1938 to 1945 WHEN IT CLOSED. TODAY BLACKS HAVE MADE GREAT STRIDES IN AVIATION. IN 1972 SHE BECAME A MEMBER OF (WACO), THE FEDERAL AVIATION AGENCY'S WOMEN'S ADVISORY COMM., ON AVIATION THE FIRST BLACK WOMAN. MISS BROWN NOW MRS. CHAPPELL HAS MADE OUTSTANDING CONTRIBUTIONS IN HER FIELD!

FOUNDER of DUSABLE MUSEUM

DR. MARGARET BURROUGHS

A SCULPTOR, PAINTER, WRITER, POET, ART COLLECTOR AND LISTED IN "WHO'S WHO AMONG AMERICAN ARTISTS." A NATIVE OF ST. ROSE, LA.. AT 6, HER FAMILY MOVED TO CHICAGO. A PRODUCT OF THE PUBLIC SCHOOLS GRADUATING FROM CHICAGO NORMAL COLLEGE AS A TEACHER IN ART AND HUMANITIES. EARNED HER B.A. AND M.A. DEGREES IN ART EDUCATION AT THE ART INSTITUTE OF CHICAGO. TAUGHT IN THE PUBLIC SCHOOLS AND ART AT DUSABLE HIGH. FOUNDED THE SOUTHSIDE COMMUNITY ART CENTER IN 1940. STARTED "NEGRO HISTORY MUSEUM" IN HER GALLERY APARTMENT IN 1945.

DR. BURROUGHS THE EXECUTIVE DIRECTOR OF THE MUSEUM NAMED IN HONOR OF JEAN BAPTISTE POINTE DUSABLE A HAITIAN WHO IN 1772 SETTLED IN ILLINOIS ON THE SPOT NOW KNOWN AS THE CITY OF CHICAGO.

Jean Baptiste Pointe DuSable

IN A LARGER HOME SHE AND HER HUSBAND CHARLES, A CURATOR AND MORE ARTIFACTS OPENED THE "EBONY MUSEUM OF NEGRO HISTORY AND ART" IN 1961. BY 1972 MORE SPACE WAS NEEDED. THEY SOUGHT AN UNUSED BUILDING IN WASHINGTON PARK. THEY RAISED MONEY TO RENOVATE AND THE "DUSABLE MUSEUM OF AFRICAN-AMERICAN HISTORY"... WAS BORN!

Geo LEE

1983 Geo L. Lee Feature Service

PAINTER of AMERICA'S BLACK LIFE

CHARLES WHITE

1918
1979

INTERNATIONALLY FAMOUS ARTIST AND TEACHER. A MASTER POR-TRAYER OF BLACK ART. BORN AND REARED IN CHICAGO. HIS GOAL IN LIFE WAS SET WHEN HIS MOTHER BOUGHT HIM A SET OF OIL PAINTS FOR HIS 7th BIRTHDAY. BY 14 HE WAS A SIGN PAINTER. CHARLES WON A NATIONWIDE HI-SCHOOL PENCIL SKETCHING CONTEST AND WAS GRANTED A YEAR'S SCHOLARSHIP TO THE ART INSTITUTE IN CHICAGO. LATER HE STUDIED AT THE ART STUDENTS' LEAGUE (NYC) AND IN MEXICO. A JULIUS

Geo LEE

MR. WHITE'S WORK WAS DISPLAYED IN 49 MUSEUMS AROUND THE WORLD!

AMONG HIS MOST NOTED WORKS WAS A SERIES OF PORTRAITS THAT ILLUS-TRATED, HISTORIAN LERONE BENNETT'S BOOK-THE SHAPING OF BLACK AMERICA." HE WON 39 U.S. AND EUROPEAN AWARDS. 53 ONE-MAN SHOWS!

ROSENWALD GRANT OPENED THE DOOR FOR MORE STUDY. IN 1947, HIS FIRST ONE-MAN SHOW IN NEW YORK. WITH HIS WIFE HE TRAVELED THROUGHOUT EUROPE. IN 1952 HIS WORK WAS EXHIBITED BY THE METRO-POLITAN MUSEUM OF ART...WON 2-GOLD MEDALS OF THE INTERNAL., GRAPHIC SHOW AT LEIPZIG, GER., IN 1960 AND 1966. BEGAN TEACHING CAREER AT THE OTIS ART INSTITUTE OF L.A. COUNTY (1967-79).
(CALIF)

106

FIRST BLACK MAYOR of DETROIT

COLEMAN A. YOUNG

ON NOV 6, 1973 HE WAS ELECTED MAYOR OF DETROIT, THE NATION'S FIFTH LARGEST CITY AT THE AGE OF 55. BORN IN TUSCALOOSA, ALA., THE OLDEST OF 5-CHILDREN OF A TAILOR AND RAISED IN DETROIT SINCE AGE 5. STARTED WORKING AT A VERY EARLY AGE AND CONTINUED DOING ODD JOBS THROUGH HI-SCHOOL. HE WENT TO WORK AT THE FORD MOTOR CO. AFTER READING ABOUT A. PHILIP RANDOLPH AND UNIONS HE BECAME ACTIVE

IN ORGANIZING UNIONS. IN 1960 WAS ELECTED TO THE MICHIGAN CONSTITUTIONAL CONVENTION. LOST A BID FOR A SEAT..IN STATE HOUSE OF REPRESENTATIVES IN 1962...BUT WAS ELECTED IN 1964 AS A MICHIGAN STATE SENATOR. BECAME THE FIRST BLACK TO SERVE ON THE NAT'L DEMOCRATIC COMM., ON EQUAL RIGHTS IN 1968. MR. YOUNG HAS SERVED WELL AND IN 1977 WAS RE-ELCTED MAYOR!

WE'LL MAKE IT A GREAT CITY!

MAYOR YOUNG, WITH A DEGREE FROM THE..... SCHOOL OF HARD KNOCKS..HAS GREAT PLANS FOR DETROIT!

Geo LEE

1979 GEO L. LEE FEATURE SERVICE

In 1984, Coleman Young was named Mayor of the Year by the National Urban League.

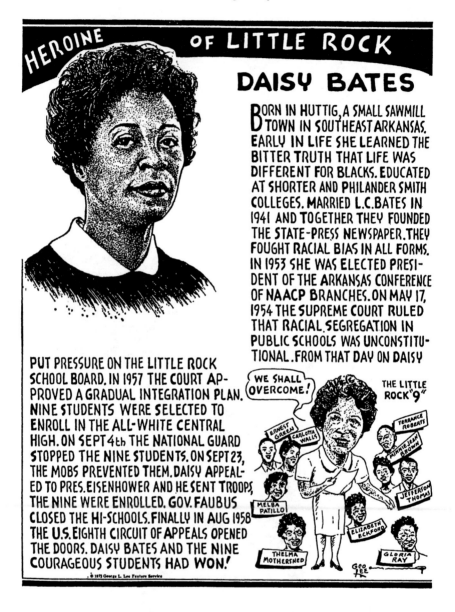

HEROINE OF LITTLE ROCK

DAISY BATES

BORN IN HUTTIG, A SMALL SAWMILL TOWN IN SOUTHEAST ARKANSAS. EARLY IN LIFE SHE LEARNED THE BITTER TRUTH THAT LIFE WAS DIFFERENT FOR BLACKS. EDUCATED AT SHORTER AND PHILANDER SMITH COLLEGES. MARRIED L.C. BATES IN 1941 AND TOGETHER THEY FOUNDED THE STATE-PRESS NEWSPAPER. THEY FOUGHT RACIAL BIAS IN ALL FORMS. IN 1953 SHE WAS ELECTED PRESIDENT OF THE ARKANSAS CONFERENCE OF NAACP BRANCHES. ON MAY 17, 1954 THE SUPREME COURT RULED THAT RACIAL SEGREGATION IN PUBLIC SCHOOLS WAS UNCONSTITUTIONAL. FROM THAT DAY ON DAISY PUT PRESSURE ON THE LITTLE ROCK SCHOOL BOARD. IN 1957 THE COURT APPROVED A GRADUAL INTEGRATION PLAN. NINE STUDENTS WERE SELECTED TO ENROLL IN THE ALL-WHITE CENTRAL HIGH. ON SEPT 4th THE NATIONAL GUARD STOPPED THE NINE STUDENTS. ON SEPT 23, THE MOBS PREVENTED THEM. DAISY APPEALED TO PRES. EISENHOWER AND HE SENT TROOPS, THE NINE WERE ENROLLED. GOV. FAUBUS CLOSED THE HI-SCHOOLS. FINALLY IN AUG 1958 THE U.S. EIGHTH CIRCUIT OF APPEALS OPENED THE DOORS. DAISY BATES AND THE NINE COURAGEOUS STUDENTS HAD WON!

WE SHALL OVERCOME!

THE LITTLE ROCK "9"

ERNEST GREEN
CARLOTTA WALLS
TERRANCE ROBERTS
MINNIE JEAN BROWN
JEFFERSON THOMAS
MELBA PATILLO
ELIZABETH ECKFORD
THELMA MOTHERSHED
GLORIA RAY

Geo LEE

© 1973 George L. Lee Feature Service

AUTHOR · CONSULTANT · PILOT

JOHN STEWARD SLOAN

OF CHICAGO, HAS HAD A VERY INTERESTING CAREER. BORN IN LOUISVILLE, KY., IN 1918. RECEIVED HIS B.A. DEGREE FROM KENTUCKY STATE U., EXTENSIVE GRADUATE STUDY IN PSYCHOLOGY AND INDUSTRIAL RELATIONS AT FISK U. (TENN) AND U OF CHICAGO. A TALENT FOR WRITING, HIS FIRST EFFORTS APPEARED IN THE KENTUCKY REPORTER WEEKLY. DURING WORLD WAR II... A FIGHTER-PILOT IN THE FAMOUS 99th FIGHTER SQUADRON AND EARNED A PURPLE HEART.

A PRIVATE PILOT SINCE 1962. HE HAS BEEN A SALESMAN, AN INDUSTRIAL RELATIONS CONSULTANT AND A RADIO D.J., THEN IN A STEEL FIRM MANAGEMENT. FROM KENTUCKY, HE LOVED HORSES SO TURNED AUTHOR AND WROTE A BRILLIANT BOOK ON HARNESS RACING "THE GAME PLAN FOR HANDICAPPING HARNESS RACES" (1975)

1979 GEO L. LEE FEATURE SERVICE

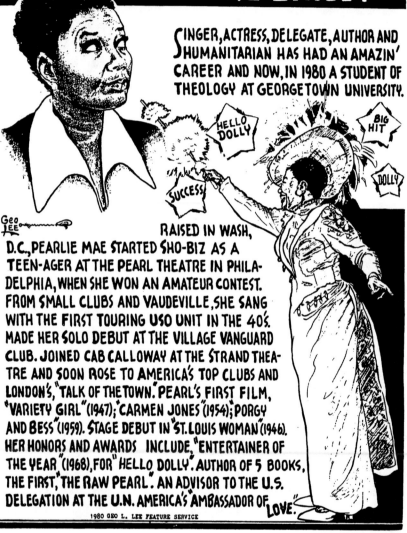

PEARL BAILEY

SINGER, ACTRESS, DELEGATE, AUTHOR AND **S**HUMANITARIAN HAS HAD AN AMAZIN' CAREER AND NOW, IN 1980 A STUDENT OF THEOLOGY AT GEORGETOWN UNIVERSITY.

HELLO DOLLY

BIG HIT

DOLLY

SUCCESS

Geo LEE

RAISED IN WASH, D.C., PEARLIE MAE STARTED SHO-BIZ AS A TEEN-AGER AT THE PEARL THEATRE IN PHILA-DELPHIA, WHEN SHE WON AN AMATEUR CONTEST. FROM SMALL CLUBS AND VAUDEVILLE, SHE SANG WITH THE FIRST TOURING USO UNIT IN THE 40'S. MADE HER SOLO DEBUT AT THE VILLAGE VANGUARD CLUB. JOINED CAB CALLOWAY AT THE STRAND THEA-TRE AND SOON ROSE TO AMERICA'S TOP CLUBS AND LONDON'S, "TALK OF THE TOWN." PEARL'S FIRST FILM, "VARIETY GIRL" (1947); "CARMEN JONES" (1954); "PORGY AND BESS" (1959). STAGE DEBUT IN "ST. LOUIS WOMAN" (1946). HER HONORS AND AWARDS INCLUDE, "ENTERTAINER OF THE YEAR" (1968), FOR "HELLO DOLLY." AUTHOR OF 5 BOOKS, THE FIRST, "THE RAW PEARL". AN ADVISOR TO THE U.S. DELEGATION AT THE U.N. AMERICA'S "AMBASSADOR OF LOVE."

1980 GEO L. LEE FEATURE SERVICE

FAMED TROUBADOUR

NAT "KING" COLE

1919
1965

A GIANT IN THE ENTERTAIN-MENT FIELD. ROSE FROM A 5.00-A-NIGHT JAZZ PIANIST TO A 25,000-A-WEEK ENTERTAINER - BORN IN MONTGOMERY, ALA., HIS FATHER A BAPTIST PREACHER AND A MUSICAL MOTHER WHO TAUGHT HIM PIANO. RAISED IN CHICAGO... HE PLAYED THE ORGAN IN HIS FATHER'S CHURCH AT 12.

HIS RECORDS SOLD OVER 25-MILLION!

Geo LEE

SWEET LORRAINE   UNFORGETTABLE
RAMBLING ROSE
BALLERINA   MONA LISA
NATURE BOY
TOO YOUNG
THE CHRISTMAS SONG

STARTED HIS CAREER IN HIS BROTHER'S BAND...THE ROGUES OF RHYTHM. JOINED "SHUFFLE ALONG" AND WENT TO CALIF. (1937). FORMED THE KING COLE TRIO (1938). RECORDED HIS OWN SONG "STRAIGHTEN UP AND FLY RIGHT" (1943). NAT WAS DESTINED TO BE A SINGER... SUCCESS CAME WITH HIS RECORDING OF THE CHRIST-MAS SONG "(1947)... ON TO THE TOP!

FIRST BLACK TV SHOW HOST ON NATIONWIDE NETWORK (1957). MADE 7-FILMS INCLUDING- ST. LOUIS BLUES AND CHINA GATE

© 1975 George L. Lee Feature Service

111

JAMES EDWARDS

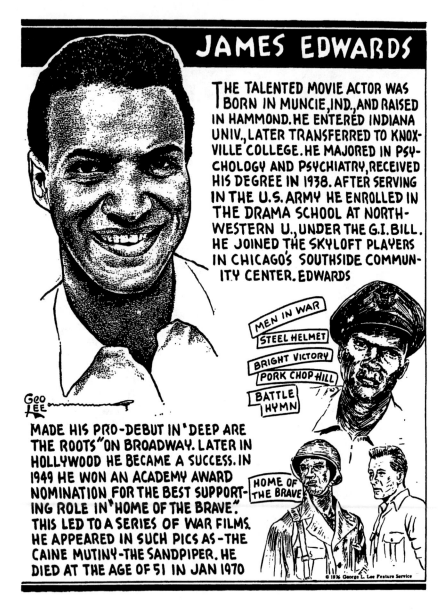

THE TALENTED MOVIE ACTOR WAS BORN IN MUNCIE, IND., AND RAISED IN HAMMOND. HE ENTERED INDIANA UNIV., LATER TRANSFERRED TO KNOXVILLE COLLEGE. HE MAJORED IN PSYCHOLOGY AND PSYCHIATRY, RECEIVED HIS DEGREE IN 1938. AFTER SERVING IN THE U.S. ARMY HE ENROLLED IN THE DRAMA SCHOOL AT NORTHWESTERN U., UNDER THE G.I. BILL. HE JOINED THE SKYLOFT PLAYERS IN CHICAGO'S SOUTHSIDE COMMUNITY CENTER. EDWARDS

MEN IN WAR

STEEL HELMET

BRIGHT VICTORY

PORK CHOP HILL

BATTLE HYMN

Geo LEE

MADE HIS PRO-DEBUT IN "DEEP ARE THE ROOTS" ON BROADWAY. LATER IN HOLLYWOOD HE BECAME A SUCCESS. IN 1949 HE WON AN ACADEMY AWARD NOMINATION FOR THE BEST SUPPORTING ROLE IN "HOME OF THE BRAVE". THIS LED TO A SERIES OF WAR FILMS. HE APPEARED IN SUCH PICS AS - THE CAINE MUTINY - THE SANDPIPER. HE DIED AT THE AGE OF 51 IN JAN 1970

HOME OF THE BRAVE

© 1976 George L. Lee Feature Service

FIRST WOMAN ASS'T SEC'Y OF STATE

BARBARA WATSON

1919
1983

FIRST WOMAN AND THE FIRST BLACK TO HOLD THE RANK OF ASS'T SECRETARY OF STATE IN THE U.S. SHE JOINED THE STATE DEPT., IN 1966 AS SPECIAL ASS'T TO THE DEPUTY UNDER-SEC'Y OF STATE. IN 1967 PRES. JOHNSON NAMED HER ACTING ADMINISTRATOR OF THE BUREAU OF SECURITY AND CONSULAR AFFAIRS (SCA)....SWORN IN AS ADMINISTRATOR AUG 1968. A NATIVE OF NYC, HER FATHER, JUDGE JAMES S. WATSON WAS THE FIRST ELECTED BLACK JUDGE IN NYC. EARNED BACHELOR'S DEGREE AT BARNARD COLLEGE. GRADUATED

ADMINISTRATOR OF BUREAU OF SECURITY AND CONSULAR AFFAIRS

BARBARA TOOK THE OATH OF OFFICE FROM HER BROTHER, U.S. CUSTOMS JUDGE JAMES L. WATSON AND SHE BECAME THE HIGHEST RANKING WOMAN IN THE U.S. STATE DEPT. 1968.

NYU LAW SCHOOL WITH HONORS. SHE LEFT THE STATE DEPT., IN NOV 1974 WHEN PRES. FORD ACCEPTED HER RESIGNATION. BECAME A LECTURER AT COLLEGES, 1975-77. PRES. CARTER NAMED HER ADMIN., OF (SCA) AGAIN IN 1977... SHE BECAME AMBASSADOR TO MALAYSIA -1980-81. HER LONG SERVICE IN CONSULAR AFFAIRS SHE CONTRIBUTED MUCH TO AMERICAN FOREIGN POLICY.

1985 GEO L. LEE FEATURE SERVICE

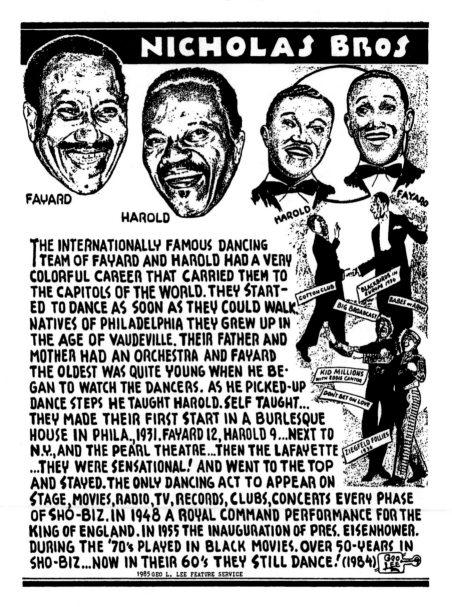

NICHOLAS BROS

FAYARD

HAROLD

HAROLD

FAYARD

THE INTERNATIONALLY FAMOUS DANCING TEAM OF FAYARD AND HAROLD HAD A VERY COLORFUL CAREER THAT CARRIED THEM TO THE CAPITOLS OF THE WORLD. THEY START- ED TO DANCE AS SOON AS THEY COULD WALK. NATIVES OF PHILADELPHIA THEY GREW UP IN THE AGE OF VAUDEVILLE. THEIR FATHER AND MOTHER HAD AN ORCHESTRA AND FAYARD THE OLDEST WAS QUITE YOUNG WHEN HE BE- GAN TO WATCH THE DANCERS. AS HE PICKED-UP DANCE STEPS HE TAUGHT HAROLD. SELF TAUGHT... THEY MADE THEIR FIRST START IN A BURLESQUE HOUSE IN PHILA., 1931. FAYARD 12, HAROLD 9...NEXT TO N.Y., AND THE PEARL THEATRE...THEN THE LAFAYETTE ...THEY WERE SENSATIONAL! AND WENT TO THE TOP AND STAYED. THE ONLY DANCING ACT TO APPEAR ON STAGE, MOVIES, RADIO, TV, RECORDS, CLUBS, CONCERTS EVERY PHASE OF SHO-BIZ. IN 1948 A ROYAL COMMAND PERFORMANCE FOR THE KING OF ENGLAND. IN 1955 THE INAUGURATION OF PRES. EISENHOWER. DURING THE '70's PLAYED IN BLACK MOVIES. OVER 50-YEARS IN SHO-BIZ...NOW IN THEIR 60's THEY STILL DANCE! (1984)

COTTON CLUB

BIG BROADCAST

BLACKBIRDS IN EUROPE 1936

BABES IN ARMS

KID MILLIONS WITH EDDIE CANTOR

DON'T BET ON LOVE

ZIEGFELD FOLLIES 1936

Goo LEE

1985 GEO L. LEE FEATURE SERVICE

CHARLIE PARKER

1920 - 1955

ONE OF THE MOST INFLUENTIAL FIGURES OF THE MODERN JAZZ MOVEMENT (BOP). A BRILLIANT ALTO SAXOPHONIST WHO WAS BORN IN KANSAS CITY, MO., WHERE HE ATTENDED SCHOOL. IN HIS EARLY HIGH SCHOOL DAYS HE PLAYED BARITONE HORN IN THE SCHOOL BAND. LATER HIS MOTHER BOUGHT HIM AN ALTO SAX, AND AT THE AGE OF 16 HE PLAYED PROFESSIONALLY WITH LAWRENCE KEYES' GROUP. IN KANSAS CITY. THEN WITH HARLAN LEONARD (1938-39); JOINED J. McSHANN (1940-41); EARL HINES (1942); BILLY ECKSTINE (1943-44). HE FORMED HIS OWN GROUP, FEATURING MILES DAVIS ON THE TRUMPET. HIS STYLE OF JAZZ RENDITIONS MADE HIM A LEGEND IN HIS OWN TIME. HE RECORDED WITH TINY GRIMES, RED NORVO, TRUMMY YOUNG AND JAY McSHANN. THE BIRD WAS GREAT.

WHAT'S A YARDBIRD?

SOOOOOO... THATS A YARDBIRD.

MAN... A "YARDBIRD" IS A COLORFUL SORT OF INDIVIDUAL WHOSE PERSONAL CHARACTERISTICS REMAIN ALMOST UNDESCRIBABLE AND, MORE IMPORTANT WHOSE NEXT MOVES ARE ENTIRELY UNPREDICTABLE... DIG!

U.S. SOLICITOR GENERAL

WADE HAMPTON McCREE

OUTSTANDING JUDGE WHO BELIEVES IN JUSTICE FOR ALL. IN FEB, 1977 PRES. JIMMY CARTER NOMINATED HIM AS THE 36th U.S. SOLICITOR GENERAL, THE THIRD HIGHEST POSITION IN THE JUSTICE DEPT. BORN IN DES MOINES, IA., ON JULY 3, 1920, WHERE HE RECEIVED HIS EARLY EDUCATION. A PHI BETA KAPPA GRADUATE OF FISK UNIV. SERVED 4-YEARS OF ACTIVE DUTY DURING WORLD WAR II. A HARVARD LAW SCHOOL GRADUATE. BEGAN LAW CAREER IN PRIVATE PRACTICE, SOON MOVED-UP TO

A SEMI-JUDICIAL POST OF MEMBER OF THE WORKMEN'S COMPENSATION COMM., OF MICH., FROM 1952-1954. GOV. WILLIAMS NAMED HIM CIRCUIT JUDGE OF WAYNE COUNTY (MICH). PRES. J.F. KENNEDY IN 1961 APPOINTED McCREE, U.S. DIST., COURT JUDGE...EASTERN DIST., OF MICH (DETROIT). ON SEPT 7, 1966, PRES. LYNDON JOHNSON NAMED HIM TO THE U.S. SIXTH CIRCUIT COURT OF APPEALS. A BRILLIANT CAREER!

1979 GEO L. LEE FEATURE SERVICE

WELL I'LL BE... I'M GOING TO FISK

SORRY, BUT THE DORMITORIES WITH DINING SERVICE ARE ALL WHITE BLAH... BLAH

IN APPLYING BY LETTER FOR A WAITER'S JOB AT THE U OF IOWA, A PICTURE WAS REQUIRED...THE REPLY WAS BITTER...NO! A LESSON LEARNED...HE WENT TO FISK, HIS MOTHER'S ALMA MATER........

116

HER FAITH IN GOD·REAFFIRMED

DELLA REESE

ON OCT. 3, 1979 SHE APPEARED ON A "TONIGHT SHOW" TAPING AT NBC STUDIOS IN BURBANK, CA SHE STARTED HER SECOND SONG "LITTLE BOY LOST" WHEN SHE SUDDENLY COLLAPSED. IN THE HOSPITAL SHE WAS TOLD SHE SUFFERED AN "ANEURYSM"... A BLOOD VESSEL HAD RUPTURED IN HER BRAIN NEAR HER OPTIC NERVE. DELLA A STRONGLY RELIGIOUS PERSON HAD FAITH. IT WAS SERIOUS AND THE SURGERY REQUIRED A SPECIALIST SHE WAS FLOWN TO LONDON, ONT., CANADA AFTER 2 OPERATIONS DELLA

Geo LEE

RECOVERED, HER FAITH IN GOD WAS REAFFIRMED. BORN IN DETROIT THE YOUNGEST OF SEVEN. AT 6 STARTED SINGING IN A CHURCH CHOIR. AT 13 AUDITIONED TO FILL A VACANCY WITH MAHALIA JACKSON TOUR AND WON. SHE TOURED DURING THE SUMMER. WENT 2-YEARS TO WAYNE UNIV., AS A PRE-MED STUDENT. HER BIG BREAK CAME AT 21 WHEN SHE WON FIRST PRIZE IN A SINGING CONTEST... A 1-WEEK ENGAGEMENT AT DETROIT'S FLAME SHOW AND STAYED 18-WEEKS. DELLA'S FAITH HAS CARRIED HER THROUGH YEARS OF A SUCCESSFUL CAREER OF ENTERTAINING!

AS A LEAD SINGER, DELLA TRAVELLED THE GOSPEL CIRCUIT SINGING IN NIGHT CLUBS, CHURCHES, THEATERS IN CONCERTS BEFORE SHE BECAME A BIG "NAME". ONCE A RADIO TALK SHOW HOST. AN ACTRESS ON TV AND IN MOVIES, A RECORDING ARTIST

©1993 GEO L. LEE FEATURE SERVICE

CANCER RESEARCHER

DR. JANE COOKE WRIGHT

OUTSTANDING DOCTOR IN THE FIELD OF CANCER CHEMOTHERAPY IS THE FIRST BLACK WOMAN TO BECOME AN ASSOCIATE DEAN OF A NATIONALLY KNOWN MEDICAL SCHOOL... THE NEW YORK MEDICAL COLLEGE (1967). BORN IN NEW YORK CITY AND EARLY EDUCATION AT THE ETHICAL CULTURE SCHOOLS. A GRADUATE OF SMITH COLLEGE IN 1942 IN A PRE-MED COURSE AND EARNED A 4-YEAR SCHOLARSHIP TO THE NEW YORK MEDICAL COLLEGE. SHE GRADUATED WITH HONORS (1945). SERVED INTERNSHIP AND RESIDENCY AT BELLEVUE AND HARLEM HOSPITALS. BECAME A SPECIALIST IN INTERNAL MEDICINE. HER FATHER (DR. LOUIS T. WRIGHT) THE NOTED SURGEON ENCOURAGED... CANCER RESEARCH. AT N.Y. UNIV., MEDICAL CENTER SHE WAS DIRECTOR OF CANCER-RESEARCH AND ASSOC., PROF., OF RESEARCH SURGERY. AFTER 22 YEARS, DR. WRIGHT RETURNED TO N.Y. MEDICAL COLLEGE-AS ASSOC., DEAN.

GEO LEE

1979 GEO L. LEE FEATURE SERVICE

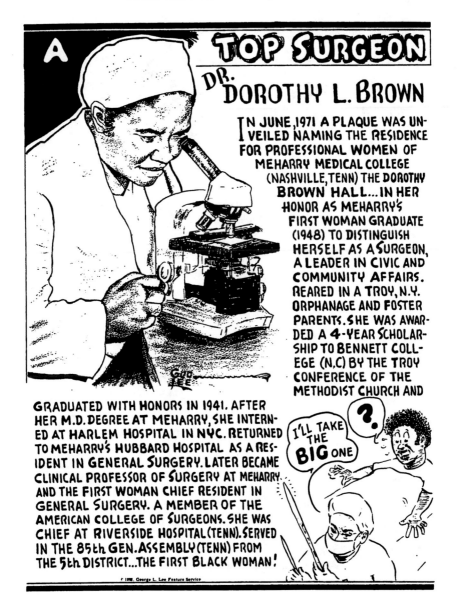

TOP SURGEON

DR. DOROTHY L. BROWN

IN JUNE, 1971 A PLAQUE WAS UNVEILED NAMING THE RESIDENCE FOR PROFESSIONAL WOMEN OF MEHARRY MEDICAL COLLEGE (NASHVILLE, TENN) THE DOROTHY BROWN HALL... IN HER HONOR AS MEHARRY'S FIRST WOMAN GRADUATE (1948) TO DISTINGUISH HERSELF AS A SURGEON, A LEADER IN CIVIC AND COMMUNITY AFFAIRS. REARED IN A TROY, N.Y. ORPHANAGE AND FOSTER PARENTS. SHE WAS AWARDED A 4-YEAR SCHOLARSHIP TO BENNETT COLLEGE (N.C) BY THE TROY CONFERENCE OF THE METHODIST CHURCH AND GRADUATED WITH HONORS IN 1941. AFTER HER M.D. DEGREE AT MEHARRY, SHE INTERNED AT HARLEM HOSPITAL IN NYC. RETURNED TO MEHARRY'S HUBBARD HOSPITAL AS A RESIDENT IN GENERAL SURGERY. LATER BECAME CLINICAL PROFESSOR OF SURGERY AT MEHARRY AND THE FIRST WOMAN CHIEF RESIDENT IN GENERAL SURGERY. A MEMBER OF THE AMERICAN COLLEGE OF SURGEONS. SHE WAS CHIEF AT RIVERSIDE HOSPITAL (TENN). SERVED IN THE 85th GEN. ASSEMBLY (TENN) FROM THE 5th DISTRICT... THE FIRST BLACK WOMAN!

I'LL TAKE THE BIG ONE

© 1978. George L. Lee Feature Service

119

BATTLE of CAMBRIDGE

GLORIA RICHARDSON

WHO LED THE PROTEST BATTLE IN CAMBRIDGE, MARYLAND DURING THE CIVIL RIGHTS MOVEMENT IN 1963. HER VIGOROUS EFFORTS FOCUSED NATIONAL ATTENTION WHEN THE NAT'L GUARD WAS CALLED-UP. MRS.RICHARDSON A SOCIOLOGY GRADUATE OF HOWARD UNIV.,(1941) WAS CHAIRMAN OF (CNAC) THE CAMBRIDGE NON-VIOLENT ACTION COMM. SHE FOUGHT FOR THE RIGHTS OF BLACK PEOPLE...THE FREEDOM OF EQUAL ACCESS TO PUBLIC ACCOMO- DATIONS. AT THE

WAKE UP CAMBRIDGE

HEIGHT OF THE DISCORD SHE CALLED ON PRES. KENNEDY TO "AVERT A CIVIL WAR." HER EFFORTS WITH ATTY.GENERAL ROBERT KENNEDY AND MAYOR OF CAMBRIDGE MADE IT POSSIBLE FOR BLACK PEOPLE TO WALK WITH DIGNITY. IN 1973 SHE BECAME AN ASS'T. DIRECTOR OF THE NAT'L COUNCIL OF NEGRO WOMEN IN N.Y.C... EQUITY FOR BLACK WOMEN!

120

'CHAPPIE'

FIRST BLACK 4-STAR GENERAL

AIR FORCE GEN. DANIEL (CHAPPIE) JAMES JR

DIED 1978

ON AUG 29, 1975 HE BE- CAME THE FIRST BLACK TO HOLD THE RANK OF FULL GENERAL. JAMES ASSUMED THE COMMAND OF THE NORTH AMERICAN AIR DEFENSE (NORAD). BORN IN PENSACOLA, FLA., IN 1920 HE RECEIVED HIS HIGHER EDUCATION AND FLYING TRAIN- ING AT TUSKEGEE INSTITUTE, GRADUATED IN 1942. COMMISSIONED A FIGHTER PILOT IN 1943. AND SERVED WITH DISTINCTION. HE ONCE COMMANDED THE WHEELING AIR FORCE BASE. IN 1970, NAMED DEPUTY ASS'T SECY FOR PUBLIC AFFAIRS. IN 1973 HELD THE HIGH PENTAGON POST OF DEP. ASS'T., SECRETARY OF DEFENSE. HE ROSE FROM BRIGADIER GEN., IN 1970 TO THE TOP, IN 1975. A VETERAN OF 31-YEARS IN 1974 HE WAS AWARDED THE DISTINGUISHED SERVICE MEDAL.

FLEW 101 COMBAT MISSIONS IN KOREA - 78 IN VIETNAM. HE WON THE DIS- TINGUISHED FLYING CROSS!

Geo Lee

© 1976 George L. Lee Feature Service

General James retired from the Air Force on Feb. 1, 1978, and died on Feb. 25. Defense Secretary Harold Brown praised him as "a fine man and a fine officer" who showed outstanding sensitivity to racial problems in the service.

FIRST BLACK NAVAL AVIATOR

ENSIGN JESSE BROWN

A NATIVE OF MISS-ISSIPPI BECAME THE NAVY'S FIRST BLACK AVIATOR IN 1948 WHEN HE RECEIVED HIS WINGS. HE SAW COMBAT SERVICE IN KOREA. HIS PLANE WAS SHOT DOWN ON HIS 21st MISSION IN NORTH KOREA WHILE GIVING AIR SUPPORT TO THE MARINES ON... DEC 5,1950. HE WAS THE FIRST BLACK NAVAL OFFICER KILLED IN THE KOREAN WAR. THE NAVY AWARDED HIM THE DISTINGUISHED FLYING CROSS AND THE AIR MEDAL. A DESTROYER-ESCORT WAS COMMISSIONED AND NAMED THE USS JESSE BROWN IN 1973... THE FIRST EVER NAMED FOR A BLACK NAVAL OFFICER.

GEO LEE

© 1976 George L. Lee Feature Service

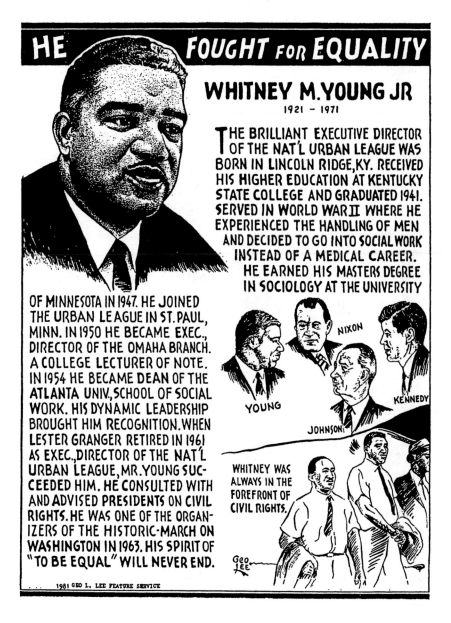

HE FOUGHT FOR EQUALITY

WHITNEY M. YOUNG JR
1921 – 1971

THE BRILLIANT EXECUTIVE DIRECTOR OF THE NAT'L URBAN LEAGUE WAS BORN IN LINCOLN RIDGE, KY. RECEIVED HIS HIGHER EDUCATION AT KENTUCKY STATE COLLEGE AND GRADUATED 1941. SERVED IN WORLD WAR II WHERE HE EXPERIENCED THE HANDLING OF MEN AND DECIDED TO GO INTO SOCIAL WORK INSTEAD OF A MEDICAL CAREER. HE EARNED HIS MASTERS DEGREE IN SOCIOLOGY AT THE UNIVERSITY OF MINNESOTA IN 1947. HE JOINED THE URBAN LEAGUE IN ST. PAUL, MINN. IN 1950 HE BECAME EXEC., DIRECTOR OF THE OMAHA BRANCH. A COLLEGE LECTURER OF NOTE. IN 1954 HE BECAME DEAN OF THE ATLANTA UNIV., SCHOOL OF SOCIAL WORK. HIS DYNAMIC LEADERSHIP BROUGHT HIM RECOGNITION. WHEN LESTER GRANGER RETIRED IN 1961 AS EXEC., DIRECTOR OF THE NAT'L URBAN LEAGUE, MR. YOUNG SUCCEEDED HIM. HE CONSULTED WITH AND ADVISED PRESIDENTS ON CIVIL RIGHTS. HE WAS ONE OF THE ORGANIZERS OF THE HISTORIC-MARCH ON WASHINGTON IN 1963. HIS SPIRIT OF "TO BE EQUAL" WILL NEVER END.

NIXON

YOUNG

KENNEDY

JOHNSON

WHITNEY WAS ALWAYS IN THE FOREFRONT OF CIVIL RIGHTS.

Geo Lee

CRUSADER FOR HUMAN RIGHTS

DOROTHY I. HEIGHT

ONE OF THE MOST POWERFUL AND HIGHLY RESPECTED BLACK WOMEN IN AMERICA. AS PRESIDENT OF THE NATIONAL COUNCIL OF NEGRO WOMEN SHE LEADS A FORCEFUL CRUSADE FOR HUMAN AND CIVIL RIGHTS OF OVER 4-MILLION WOMEN. SHE HEADS 27 AFFILIATES, 200 LOCAL SECTIONS EXTENDING TO AFRICA. IN HER YOUTH A SPEECH ON THE RECONSTRUCTION AMENDMENTS WON HER A SCHOLARSHIP TO N. Y. UNIV., ALSO EDUCATED AT COLUMBIA U. SHE SERVED WITH

Geo Lee

THE YWCA FROM 1944 TO 1957 AS AN EXECUTIVE DIRECTOR AND NATIONAL BOARD MEMBER. NAMED "WOMAN OF THE YEAR" IN 1974 BY THE LADIES HOME JOURNAL. SHE HAS RECEIVED 9 HONORARY DOCTORATE DEGREES. IN 1978 WAS THE FIRST WOMAN TO RECEIVE THE "DISTINGUISHED SERVICE AWARD" OF THE BLACK PRESS (NNPA). AN OUTSTANDING HUMANITARIAN!

SHE BECAME PRESIDENT OF NCNW IN 1958. NCNW WAS FOUNDED IN 1935 BY MARY BETHUNE WHO WAS ITS FIRST PRESIDENT UNTIL 1949 AND ACTIVE UNTIL HER DEATH IN 1955. MISS. HEIGHT HAS CARRIED ON THE DREAM AND PURPOSE OF NCNW-TO HARNESS BLACK WOMEN'S POWER.

1983 Geo L. Lee Feature Service

ALEX HALEY,

THE PULITZER PRIZE WIN-NING AUTHOR OF "ROOTS", THE BEST-SELLING BOOK WHICH TOOK 12-YEARS TO RESEARCH AND WRITE... HIS FAMILY'S AFRICAN (GAMBIA) HERITAGE. BORN IN ITHACA, N.Y.(1921), REARED IN HENNING, TENN., WITH HIS GRAND-MOTHER WHOSE STORIES OF SLAVES INSPIRED HIM LATER IN LIFE TO WRITE "ROOTS". A COLLEGE DROP-OUT, HE JOINED THE COAST GUARD AT 17 AS A MESSMAN. RETIRED AS CHIEF JOURNALIST (1958). BECAME A FREELANCE WRITER FOR TOP MAGAZINES. IN 1965 HIS BOOK "AUTOBIOGRAPHY OF MALCOLM X" WAS PUBLISHED...THEN STARTED "ROOTS". WINNER OF NAACP'S SPINGARN MEDAL (1977). HE FOUND HIS "ROOTS"... BRILLIANTLY.'

◄ 1980 George L. Lee Feature Service

FOUNDER of OIC

OPPORTUNITIES INDUSTRIALIZATION CENTERS (JAN 26, 1964)

REV. LEON H. SULLIVAN

PASTOR OF ZION BAPTIST CHURCH (PHILA.) AND A LEADING ACTIVIST FOR JOB TRAINING FOR BLACKS AND MINORITIES IN THE U.S. AND AFRICA. BORN IN CHARLESTON, W.VA., IN 1922. AS A BASKETBALL AND FOOTBALL STAR HE EARNED AN ATHLETIC SCHOLARSHIP TO W. VIRGINA STATE COLLEGE. AFTER GRADUATION HE WENT TO NEW YORK AND BECAME AN ASS'T MINISTER TO ADAM CLAYTON POWELL. RECEIVED HIS DIVINITY DEGREE FROM UNION THEOLOGICAL SEMINARY. HE WAS GREATLY INFLUENCED BY SUCH MEN AS, A. PHILIP RANDOLPH. IN PHILADELPHIA HE SOUGHT HIS GOAL FOR SELF-HELP FOR BLACKS AND FOUNDED THE OIC PROGRAM (1964). BY 1971 HE WAS CHAIRMAN OF 90 BRANCHES IN THE U.S. AND AFRICA... REV. SULLIVAN A BIG MAN WITH A TREMENDOUS IDEA!

1979 GEO L. LEE FEATURE SERVICE

WINNER OF THE NAACP's 56th SPINGARN MEDAL FOR HIS OUTSTANDING ACHIEVEMENT— OIC (1971)

MR. CHAIRMAN I SUGGEST....

REV. SULLIVAN IS THE FIRST BLACK TO BE ELECTED TO THE BOARD OF DIRECTORS OF GEN. MOTORS. (1971)

CHICAGO'S FIRST BLACK MAYOR

Geo
LEE

HAROLD WASHINGTON

PERHAPS A MAN OF DESTINY. HE MADE HISTORY AND NATIONAL IMPACT WHEN HE WAS ELECTED CHICAGO'S FIRST BLACK MAYOR ON APRIL 12,1983. A CONGRESS-MAN WHOSE RESOUNDING VICTORY BECAME MAYOR OF THE SECOND LARGEST U.S. CITY. A MAN OF CHARISMA, ELOQUENCE, ASTUTE-NESS AND CONFIDENCE. BORN IN CHICAGO ON APRIL 15,1922. HE ATTENDED THE PUBLIC SCHOOLS... GRADUATED DU SABLE HIGH(1940). DURING WORLD WAR II SERVED IN THE U.S. AIR FORCE ENGINEERS

AS FIRST SGT., (1942-46). GRADUATE OF ROOSEVELT U., IN POLITICAL SCI-ENCE ('49). NORTHWESTERN U., LAW SCHOOL('52). ASS'T. CORP, COUNSEL FOR CHICAGO ('54-'58). ARBITRATOR FOR ILL. INDUSTRIAL COMM., ('60-'64). ILL. STATE LEGISLATURE ('64-'76). ILL. STATE SENATOR('76-'80). U.S. CON-GRESS (ILL.) 1ST DIST ('80). REELECTED 1982. NOW HE'S READY FOR UNITY!

1983 Geo L. Lee Feature Service

In 1987, Washington was elected to a second term as mayor of Chicago, but he died of a heart attack later that same year.

HEADS CHICAGO DENTAL SOC.

DR. ROBERT L. KIMBROUGH

A FINE DENTIST WITH LEADER-SHIP QUALITIES. ON MAY 29, 1984 HE WAS INSTALLED AS PRESIDENT OF THE PRESTIGIOUS CHICAGO DENTAL SOCIETY - 8,000 MEMBERS (3800 CHICAGO AREA - 4200 WORLD-WIDE ASSOC., MEMBERS). SERVED AS SECRETARY BEFORE REACHING THE TOP. BORN IN BIRMINGHAM, ALA., ON AUG 20, 1922. SERVED IN U.S. ARMY AS STAFF SGT., (1943-46). WENT TO CHICAGO IN 1946. RECEIVED B.S. DEGREE FROM U OF ILLINOIS (1947); DDS DEGREE AT ILL. COLLEGE OF DENTISTRY (1951). BEGAN DENTAL CAREER IN ARMY DENTAL CORPS

Geo LEE

ON OCT 1, 1983 BOB WAS AWARDED A FELLOWSHIP IN THE AMERICAN COLLEGE OF DENTISTS... FOR THOSE WHO HAVE CONTRIBUTED TO THE ADVANCEMENT OF THE PROFESSION AND HUMANITY.....

GREAT

-BY INVITATION ONLY

(1950-53); WENT INTO PRIVATE PRACTICE IN CHICAGO. ACTIVE IN NAACP (1960-65); PRESIDENT OF SOUTH SIDE COMMUNITY ART CENTER (1975-80). HELD ALL ELECTED OFFICES OF KENWOOD -HYDE PK BRANCH (OF CDS)... PRESIDENT IN 1977-78. DR. KIMBROUGH HAS BEEN VERY ACTIVE IN DENTAL GROUPS. A MAN OF LEADER QUALITIES!

1984 Geo L. Lee Feature Service

128

"CARMEN JONES"

1924.
1965.

DOROTHY DANDRIDGE

BEAUTIFUL AND TALENTED ACTRESS AND NIGHT CLUB SINGER WHO PORTRAYED THE FIERY ROLE OF "CARMEN" IN THE FILM, "CARMEN JONES" WAS THE FIRST OPERATIC CARMEN THAT NEVER SANG A NOTE... HER VOICE WAS DUBBED WITH A TRAINED OPERATIC VOICE. BUT... HER EXCITING "CARMEN" WON AN ACADEMY AWARD NOMINATION FOR THE "BEST ACTRESS OF THE YEAR (1954)." SHE DID NOT WIN AN "OSCAR" BUT HER SUCCESS ZOOMED. BORN IN CLEVELAND, OHIO. AT AGE 5 HER CAREER STARTED IN A FAMILY ACT WITH HER SISTER, MOTHER AND AUNT THEY PERFORMED ON BOOK-SELLING TOURS FOR A PUBLISHING HOUSE. LATER COLLEGES AND VAUDEVILLE. AT 16, THE "COTTON CLUB." AFTER AN UNSUCCESSFUL MARRIAGE DOROTHY RETURNED TO THE NIGHT CLUBS. HOLLYWOOD OFFERED A FILMED CAREER... AND SUCCESS FOLLOWED. SHE MADE... "TARZAN'S PERIL," "BRIGHT ROAD," "SEE HOW THEY RUN," "PORGY AND BESS," "ISLAND IN THE SUN," "THE DECKS RAN RED" AMONG THEM. 1959-64 BEGAN A PERIOD OF DECLINE AND FALL. 1965 THE SKIES BRIGHTENED, THEN SUDDEN DEATH.

Geo
LEE

1978 GEO L.LEE FEATURE SERVICE

"PORTRAITS IN COLOR"

1924
1979

GWENDOLYN B. CHERRY

FIRST BLACK WOMAN ELECTED TO THE FLORIDA LEGISLATURE IN 1970. A MIAMI ATTORNEY FOR THE U.S. COAST GUARD SEVENTH DISTRICT IN ADMIRALTY LAW. BEFORE SHE MADE HISTORY SHE WAS A HIGH SCHOOL SCIENCE TEACHER, WHOSE STUDENTS WERE AMONG THE FIRST BLACKS TO WIN AWARDS IN NATIONAL SCIENCE COMPETITION. SHE WROTE "PORTRAITS IN COLOR" A BOOK ON BLACK WOMEN ACHIEVERS. DURING THE CIVIL-RIGHTS MOVEMENT THE U OF MIAMI OPENED ITS LAW AND MEDICAL SCHOOLS TO BLACKS.

AFTER TEACHING 18-YEARS IN THE DADE COUNTY SCHOOLS... SHE ENROLLED AND GRADUATED WITH A LLB LAW DEGREE. TAUGHT LAW CLASSES AT FLORIDA A&M COLLEGE. THEN TO THE U.S. COAST GUARD OFFICE. ENCOURAGED BY FRIENDS SHE RAN FOR THE STATE LEGISLATURE... AND WON! MRS. CHERRY WAS IN HER 4th TERM WHEN KILLED IN AN AUTO ACCIDENT. A VERY INTERESTING CAREER ENDED.

MRS. CHERRY RECEIVED A SPECIAL AWARD FROM WOMEN FOR POLITICAL PROGRESS FOR OUTSTANDING ACHIEVEMENT AS A POLITICAL ACTIVIST!

1982 GEO L. LEE FEATURE SERVICE

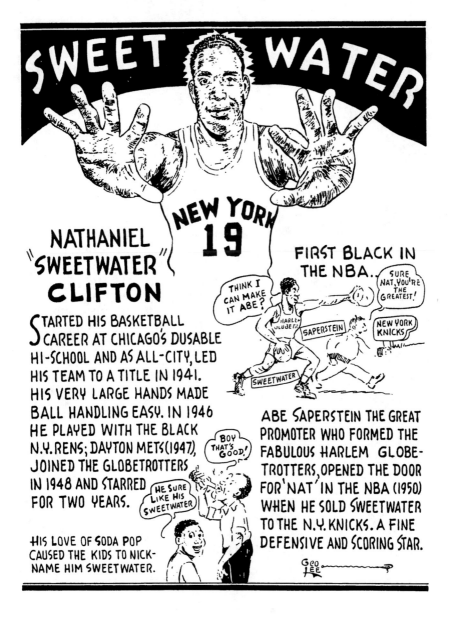

SWEET WATER

NATHANIEL "SWEETWATER" CLIFTON

NEW YORK 19

STARTED HIS BASKETBALL CAREER AT CHICAGO'S DUSABLE HI-SCHOOL AND AS ALL-CITY, LED HIS TEAM TO A TITLE IN 1941. HIS VERY LARGE HANDS MADE BALL HANDLING EASY. IN 1946 HE PLAYED WITH THE BLACK N.Y. RENS; DAYTON METS (1947), JOINED THE GLOBETROTTERS IN 1948 AND STARRED FOR TWO YEARS.

HIS LOVE OF SODA POP CAUSED THE KIDS TO NICK-NAME HIM SWEETWATER.

FIRST BLACK IN THE NBA...

THINK I CAN MAKE IT ABE?

HARLEM GLOBE...

SAPERSTEIN

SURE NAT, YOU'RE THE GREATEST!

NEW YORK KNICKS

SWEETWATER

BOY THAT'S GOOD!

HE SURE LIKE HIS SWEETWATER

ABE SAPERSTEIN THE GREAT PROMOTER WHO FORMED THE FABULOUS HARLEM GLOBE-TROTTERS, OPENED THE DOOR FOR 'NAT' IN THE NBA (1950) WHEN HE SOLD SWEETWATER TO THE N.Y. KNICKS. A FINE DEFENSIVE AND SCORING STAR.

GEO LEE

131

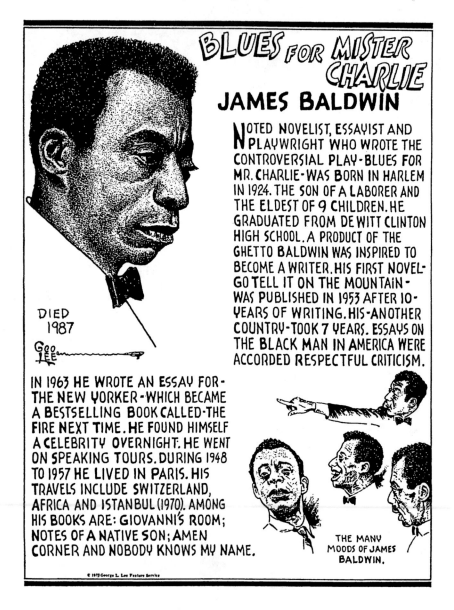

BLUES FOR MISTER CHARLIE

JAMES BALDWIN

NOTED NOVELIST, ESSAYIST AND PLAYWRIGHT WHO WROTE THE CONTROVERSIAL PLAY-BLUES FOR MR. CHARLIE-WAS BORN IN HARLEM IN 1924. THE SON OF A LABORER AND THE ELDEST OF 9 CHILDREN. HE GRADUATED FROM DE WITT CLINTON HIGH SCHOOL. A PRODUCT OF THE GHETTO BALDWIN WAS INSPIRED TO BECOME A WRITER. HIS FIRST NOVEL-GO TELL IT ON THE MOUNTAIN-WAS PUBLISHED IN 1953 AFTER 10-YEARS OF WRITING. HIS-ANOTHER COUNTRY-TOOK 7 YEARS. ESSAYS ON THE BLACK MAN IN AMERICA WERE ACCORDED RESPECTFUL CRITICISM.

DIED 1987

Geo Lee

IN 1963 HE WROTE AN ESSAY FOR-THE NEW YORKER-WHICH BECAME A BESTSELLING BOOK CALLED-THE FIRE NEXT TIME. HE FOUND HIMSELF A CELEBRITY OVERNIGHT. HE WENT ON SPEAKING TOURS. DURING 1948 TO 1957 HE LIVED IN PARIS. HIS TRAVELS INCLUDE SWITZERLAND, AFRICA AND ISTANBUL (1970). AMONG HIS BOOKS ARE: GIOVANNI'S ROOM; NOTES OF A NATIVE SON; AMEN CORNER AND NOBODY KNOWS MY NAME.

THE MANY MOODS OF JAMES BALDWIN.

COUNTRY CHARLEY PRIDE ♪

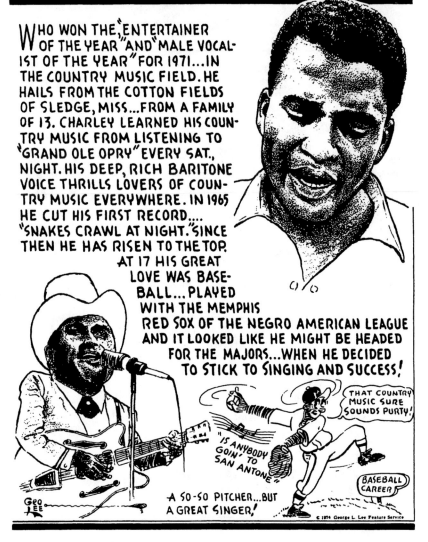

WHO WON THE "ENTERTAINER OF THE YEAR" AND "MALE VOCALIST OF THE YEAR" FOR 1971...IN THE COUNTRY MUSIC FIELD. HE HAILS FROM THE COTTON FIELDS OF SLEDGE, MISS...FROM A FAMILY OF 13. CHARLEY LEARNED HIS COUNTRY MUSIC FROM LISTENING TO "GRAND OLE OPRY" EVERY SAT., NIGHT. HIS DEEP, RICH BARITONE VOICE THRILLS LOVERS OF COUNTRY MUSIC EVERYWHERE. IN 1965 HE CUT HIS FIRST RECORD.... "SNAKES CRAWL AT NIGHT." SINCE THEN HE HAS RISEN TO THE TOP.

AT 17 HIS GREAT LOVE WAS BASEBALL... PLAYED WITH THE MEMPHIS RED SOX OF THE NEGRO AMERICAN LEAGUE AND IT LOOKED LIKE HE MIGHT BE HEADED FOR THE MAJORS...WHEN HE DECIDED TO STICK TO SINGING AND SUCCESS!

THAT COUNTRY MUSIC SURE SOUNDS PURTY!

"IS ANYBODY GOIN' TO SAN ANTONE"

BASEBALL CAREER

A SO-SO PITCHER...BUT A GREAT SINGER!

Geo Lee

© 1974 George L. Lee Feature Service

133

DIVINE SARAH

SARAH VAUGHAN

WHOSE UNIQUE STYLE OF FLAW-LESS JAZZ SINGING AND HER SUPERB IMPROVISATIONS... NEVER SINGING A SONG THE SAME WAY TWICE. A VOICE WITH 3-OCTAVES IN RANGE. BORN IN NEWARK, N.J., OF MUSICAL PARENTS. STUDIED THE PIANO AND ORGAN AT 8. PLAYED THE ORGAN FOR THE MT. ZION BAPTIST CHURCH IN NEWARK AT 12. LATER SANG IN THE CHOIR.

Geo LEE

AT 19 (1943) ENTERED A CONTEST AT HARLEM'S APOLLO THEATER AND WON. BILLY ECKSTINE DISCOVERED HER...SHE FIRST SANG WITH EARL HINES BAND. RECORDED FIRST IN 1944. HER REAL START CAME WITH MUSICRAFT RECORDS IN 1946. FROM THEN ON SUCCESS. AFTER 35 YEARS SHE CONTINUED TO CLIMB, MAINLY IN CONCERTS (1978). "THE DIVINE ONE."

KNOWN AS "SASSY" IN HER EARLY CAREER. WORKED WITH MUSIC GREATS, GILLESPIE, J.J. JOHNSON, MILES DAVIS, ADDERLEY, BASIE

"I'LL REMEMBER APRIL"

"IT'S MAGIC"

ACADEMY AWARDS WINNER

LOU GOSSETT Jr

HIS FINE PORTRAYAL OF THE TOUGH MARINE DRILL SGT. FOLEY IN "AN OFFICER AND A GENTLEMAN", WON HIM A 1983 "OSCAR" AS BEST "SUPPORTING ACTOR" AT THE 55th ANNUAL ACADEMY AWARDS. A NATIVE OF NEW YORK, LOU BEGAN ACTING AT 16. A STUDENT AT ABRAHAM LINCOLN HI IN BROOKLYN. A LEG INJURY FORCED HIM TO SIT OUT A BASKETBALL SEASON...HE ENTERED A DRAMA CLASS. THE TEACHER WAS IMPRESSED. HE BEAT OUT 400 FOR THE LEAD IN THE 1953 BROADWAY PLAY "TAKE A GIANT STEP" AND WON THE DONALDSON AWARD AS THE "BEST NEWCOMER" OF THE YEAR. FOR A ROLE IN THE BROADWAY PLAY "THE RIVER NIGER"...HAD TO SHAVE HIS HEAD...IT BOOSTED HIS CAREER! A PRE-MED GRADUATE OF NYU...BUT GOSSETT RETURNED TO BROADWAY. HE SOON LEARNED THAT HE SHOULD COMPETE FOR ANY ROLE. WON A TV "EMMY" AS "FIDDLER" IN ROOTS. PLAYED IN "BENNY'S PLACE," "THE DEEP," "SKIN GAME," "LAZARUS SYNDROME", "JAWS 3-D," "DON'T LOOK BACK" AMONG HIS MANY CREDITS!

AS- SGT. FOLEY IN "AN OFFICER AND A GENTLEMAN." A WINNING ROLE!

AS- ANWAR SADAT IN TV'S DOCU-DRAMA "SADAT" A FINE PORTRAYAL!

1984 Geo L. Lee Feature Service

Lou Gossett was honored with the Brotherhood Crusade's 1984 Walter Bremond Pioneer of Black Achievement Award, for his work as an actor and a humanitarian.

CALL ME MADAME SECRETARY

HON. VEL PHILLIPS

WISCONSIN'S FIRST WOMAN ELECTED SECRETARY OF STATE AND THE FIRST BLACK TO A STATE-WIDE CONSTITUTIONAL OFFICE (NOV '78). BORN IN MILWAUKEE AND A GRADUATE OF HOWARD UNIV. THE FIRST BLACK WOMAN TO RECEIVE A LAW DEGREE FROM THE UNIV. OF WISCONSIN. HER POLITICAL CAREER BEGAN IN 1956 WHEN SHE WAS ELECTED AS THE FIRST WOMAN AND THE FIRST BLACK TO SERVE AS AN ALDERMAN ON THE MILWAUKEE COMMON COUNCIL AND STAYED 16-YEARS. IN 1958 WAS THE FIRST BLACK WOMAN TO BE ELECTED TO SERVE ON THE DEMOCRATIC NATIONAL PARTY AS COMMITTEEWOMAN. MRS. PHILLIPS WAS APPOINTED AS COUNTY JUDGE IN 1971 AND THE FIRST BLACK. A CIVIL RIGHTS ACTIVIST AND A REAL ACHIEVER. HER CAREER IS VERY INTERESTING!

1982 GEO L. LEE FEATURE SERVICE

FIRST BLACK CONGRESSWOMAN

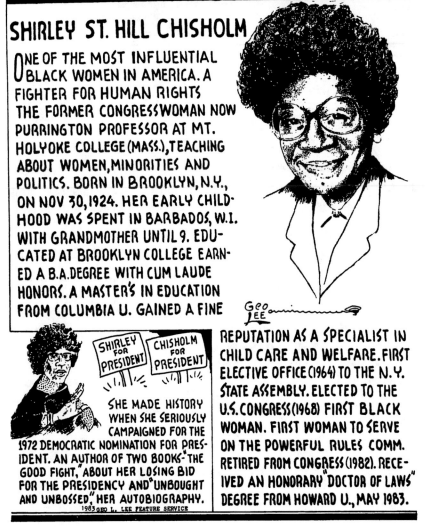

SHIRLEY ST. HILL CHISHOLM

ONE OF THE MOST INFLUENTIAL BLACK WOMEN IN AMERICA. A FIGHTER FOR HUMAN RIGHTS THE FORMER CONGRESSWOMAN NOW PURRINGTON PROFESSOR AT MT. HOLYOKE COLLEGE (MASS.), TEACHING ABOUT WOMEN, MINORITIES AND POLITICS. BORN IN BROOKLYN, N.Y., ON NOV 30, 1924. HER EARLY CHILDHOOD WAS SPENT IN BARBADOS, W.I. WITH GRANDMOTHER UNTIL 9. EDUCATED AT BROOKLYN COLLEGE EARNED A B.A. DEGREE WITH CUM LAUDE HONORS. A MASTER'S IN EDUCATION FROM COLUMBIA U. GAINED A FINE

Geo LEE

SHIRLEY FOR PRESIDENT   CHISHOLM FOR PRESIDENT

SHE MADE HISTORY WHEN SHE SERIOUSLY CAMPAIGNED FOR THE 1972 DEMOCRATIC NOMINATION FOR PRESIDENT. AN AUTHOR OF TWO BOOKS - THE GOOD FIGHT," ABOUT HER LOSING BID FOR THE PRESIDENCY AND "UNBOUGHT AND UNBOSSED," HER AUTOBIOGRAPHY.

1983 GEO L. LEE FEATURE SERVICE

REPUTATION AS A SPECIALIST IN CHILD CARE AND WELFARE. FIRST ELECTIVE OFFICE (1964) TO THE N.Y. STATE ASSEMBLY. ELECTED TO THE U.S. CONGRESS (1968) FIRST BLACK WOMAN. FIRST WOMAN TO SERVE ON THE POWERFUL RULES COMM. RETIRED FROM CONGRESS (1982). RECEIVED AN HONORARY "DOCTOR OF LAWS" DEGREE FROM HOWARD U., MAY 1983.

Shirley Chisholm retired from Congress in 1982 because she disagreed with President Reagan's policies. In 1984 she was named to head the Black Women's Political Caucus in Washington, D.C.

EVERY GOOD-BY ISN'T GONE

MALCOLM X
1925 - 1965

A MILITANT ADVOCATE OF BLACK PRIDE WAS BORN IN OMAHA, NEB., THE SON OF A BAPTIST MINISTER. HIS FAMILY MOVED TO MILWAUKEE, WIS. ONE OF 10 CHILDREN HIS FORMAL EDUCATION WAS LIMITED. WHILE LIVING IN LANSING, MICH., THE KKK BURNED DOWN THEIR HOME AND HIS FATHER WAS KILLED BY RACISTS. THE EVENTS HELPED TO INFLUENCE HIS ATTITUDE OF LIFE. DURING A TERM IN PRISON HE BECAME A DEVOUT READER OF SERIOUS BOOKS AND DEVELOPED HIS KEEN MIND. AFTER HIS RELEASE HE JOINED THE BLACK MUSLIMS HEADED BY ELIJAH MUHAMMAD. HIS LIFE CHANGED AND HIS RISE WAS RAPID. HE FOUNDED THE MUSLIM NEWSPAPER -MUHAMMAD SPEAKS. IN 1964 HE MADE A PILGRIMAGE TO THE HOLY CITIES OF MECCA AND MEDINA IN AFRICA. ON HIS RETURN HE HAD A CHANGE OF PHILOSOPHY AND BROKE WITH THE MUSLIMS AND FOUNDED THE ORGANIZATION FOR AFRO-AMERICAN UNITY. A BRILLIANT SPEAKER HE ENCOURAGED BLACK SELF-ASSERTION. MALCOLM WAS ASSASSINATED IN NYC AT THE AGE OF 39.

Geo LEE

WHAT'S MY NAME?

WHAT DOES HAJJ MEAN IN MALCOLM'S NEW NAME?

MALCOLM LITTLE
MALCOLM X
EL-HAJJ MALIK EL-SHABAZZ

IT MEANS HE HAS MADE A HOLY PILGRIMAGE TO MECCA AND SHABAZZ IS THE NAME OF THE CAPTIVE TRIBE OF AFRICANS BROUGHT TO AMERICA.

© 1979 George L. Lee Feature Service

NAACP EXECUTIVE DIRECTOR

BENJAMIN L. HOOKS

WHO OFTEN REFERS TO HIMSELF AS THE "POOR LITTLE 'OL COUNTRY PREACHER", TOOK ON THE TASK OF LEADING THE NAACP, THE NATIONS TOP CIVIL RIGHTS GROUP IN 1977. BORN IN MEMPHIS, TENN., ON JAN 31, 1925. HE ATTENDED PUBLIC SCHOOLS AND LE MOYNE COLLEGE. DRAFTED OUT OF COLLEGE HE SERVED IN WORLD WAR II. EARNED HIS LAW DEGREE AT DE PAUL UNIV., (1949). BECAME A PUBLIC DEFENDER. ENTERED POLITICS WITHOUT SUCCESS. FELT THE CALL TO "PREACH" IN 1955 AND BECAME PASTOR OF MEMPHIS' MIDDLE BAPTIST CHURCH. CO-FOUNDER AND V.P. OF THE MUTUAL FEDERAL SAVINGS AND LOAN ASSN. (1956-64). IN 1965 BECAME THE FIRST BLACK CRIMINAL COURT JUDGE IN TENN. IN 1972, THE FIRST BLACK MEMBER OF THE FEDERAL COMMUNICATIONS COMMISSION (FCC). SUCCEEDED ROY WILKINS AS EXECUTIVE DIRECTOR OF THE NAACP. A FINE ACHIEVER!

Geo Lee

ROY DID A GREAT JOB FOR 22-YEARS. I'LL DO MY BEST TO KEEP THE NAACP THE CIVIL RIGHTS CHAMPION!

WILKINS LEFT HIS IMPRINTS ON HISTORY

HOOKS

NAACP

1980 Geo. L. Lee Feature Service

FIRST BLACK WOMAN IN U.S. CABINET

PATRICIA R. HARRIS

1924-
1985

Geo
LEE

OUTSTANDING WASHINGTON ATTOR-
NEY WAS SECRETARY OF HOUSING
AND URBAN DEVELOPMENT (HUD),
THE FIRST BLACK WOMAN TO HOLD
A TOP CABINET POST (1977). APPOINTED
BY PRES. CARTER. BORN IN MATTOON,
ILL., THE DAUGHTER OF A DINING
CAR WAITER. A SUMMA CUM LAUDE
GRADUATE IN LIBERAL ARTS FROM
HOWARD U. (1945), M.A. FROM U OF
CHICAGO. A VERY INTERESTING
CAREER. A LATE STARTER IN LAW.
A GRADUATE OF GEORGE WASHING-
TON LAW SCHOOL (1960) WITH HONORS.
DEAN OF HOWARD'S LAW SCHOOL;

CHAIRPERSON, CREDENTIALS COMM., 1972
DEMOCRATIC NAT'L CONVENTION. LAW
JUDGE AT THE FEDERAL MARITIME
COMM. FIRST BLACK WOMAN TO HEAD A
AMERICAN EMBASSY AS AMBASSADOR TO
LUXEMBOURG (1965). CIVIL RIGHTS LOBBYIST.
A PARTNER IN A PRESTIGIOUS LAW FIRM.
IN 1978 WAS AMONG THE 25 MOST INFLU-
ENTIAL WOMEN BY WORLD'S ALMANAC'S
LIST.

IBM
CHASE MANHATTAN BANK
SCOTT PAPER CO
NATIONAL BANK OF WASH, D.C.

ATTY. HARRIS HAS SEATS
ON THE BOARD OF DIR-
ECTORS OF MAJOR FIRMS,
FIRST BLACK MEMBER OF
BOARD OF GEORGETOWN
UNIV.

1979 GEO L. LEE FEATURE SERVICE

SIDNEY POITIER

ACTOR! DIRECTOR! PRODUCER!
ONE OF AMERICA'S GREATEST!

ACADEMY AWARD WINNER FOR HIS ROLE IN "LILIES OF THE FIELD" (1963), WAS BORN FEB 20,1927 IN MIAMI, FLA.,THE LAST OF 8-CHILDREN. THE SON OF A WEST INDIAN TOMATO FARMER. AT 3-MONTHS HE WAS TAKEN TO THE FARM ON CAT ISLAND IN THE BAHAMAS. THERE WERE NO CARS, SCHOOLS, LIGHTS OR HOSPITALS. AT 11,HIS FAMILY MOVED TO NASSAU WHERE HE STARTED SCHOOL. LESS THAN 2-YEARS HE DROPPED-OUT TO HELP HIS FAMILY. IN 1943 HE WENT TO LIVE WITH A BROTHER IN

Geo LEE

MIAMI. AT 15 HE REALIZED IT WAS A TOUGH WORLD AND SAVED UNTIL HE HAD BUS FARE TO NEW YORK AND HARLEM. A COLD WINTER AND HE UPPED HIS AGE AND JOINED THE ARMY. A YEAR AND A HALF LATER HE RETURNED TO HARLEM. IN 1945 HE VISITED THE AMERICAN NEGRO THEATER,BUT SOON FOUND OUT HE WASN'T READY. 6-MONTHS LATER...BACK FOR ANOTHER TRY-OUT IN A PLAY "YOU CAN'T TAKE IT WITH YOU"BUT NO ONE NOTICED. THEN CAME "LYSISTRATA", "ANNA LUCASTA" AND THEN "NO WAY OUT"HE WAS NOTICED!

RED BALL EXPRESS
CRY,THE BELOVED COUNTRY
GO,MAN GO
BLACKBOARD JUNGLE
GOODBYE,MY LADY
EDGE OF THE CITY
BAND OF ANGELS
SOMETHING OF VALUE
PORGY AND BESS
MARK OF THE HAWK
THE DEFIANT ONES
A PATCH OF BLUE
IN THE HEAT OF THE NIGHT
TO SIR WITH LOVE
THEY CALL ME MISTER TIBBS
FOR THE LOVE OF IVY
WARM DECEMBER
LET'S DO IT AGAIN
BUCK AND THE PREACHER
UPTOWN SATURDAY NIGHT

"GUESS WHO'S COMING TO DINNER!"

SWEET SUCCESS

*1917. George L. Lee Feature Service

Sidney Poitier received the Urban League's 1982 Whitney M. Young award, for his contribution to the American film industry, his "conscientious effort . . . to help pave the way for the entry of other black actors and technical personnel."

WORLD RENOWNED SOPRANO

LEONTYNE PRICE

FAMOUS PRIMA DONNA OF GRAND OPERA. HER BEAUTIFUL RICH VOICE REMAINS UNBLEMISHED AFTER 27-YEARS SINCE HER AMERICAN OPERATIC DEBUT. BORN IN LAUREL, MISS., IN 1927 OF MUSICAL PARENTS. AT 9 SHE START-ED PLAYING THE PIANO AND SINGING IN THE CHURCH CHOIR. A GRADUATE OF CENTRAL STATE COLLEGE (OHIO) WHERE SHE SANG IN THE GLEE CLUB. IT SOON BECAME OBVIOUS THAT HER FUTURE LAY IN HER VOICE. SHE WON A SCHOLAR-SHIP TO JUILLIARD SCHOOL OF MUSIC (N.Y). WHILE THERE MADE HER FIRST OPERA DEBUT IN "FOUR SAINTS IN THREE ACTS". THEN TOURED WITH "PORGY AND BESS". IN 1955 MADE HER GRAND OPERA DE-BUT IN THE NBC-TV PRODUCTION "TOSCA". A TOUR TO EUROPE AND SANG WITH THE WORLD'S LEADING OPERA COMPANIES. LEONTYNE MADE HER METROPOLITAN OPERA DEBUT IN "IL TROVATORE" IN 1961.

AS LENORA, IN "IL TROVATORE"

THE FIRST BLACK TO OPEN A "MET" SEASON IN 1966. RECEIVED NAACP'S 50TH SPINGARN MEDAL - FOR HIGH ACHIEVEMENT IN 1965.

Geo LEE

1983 Geo L. Lee Feature Service

Leontyne Price bade farewell to the Met on January 3, 1985, with her dazzling performance in Verdi's "Aida." She was among 12 artists and patrons awarded the first National Medal of Arts by President Reagan in 1985.

FIRST AT WIMBLEDON 1957

ALTHEA GIBSON
OF NEW YORK CITY

ONE OF THE REAL GREAT WOMEN TENNIS CHAMPIONS. BORN IN SUMPTER, S.C., REARED IN NYC., WHERE SHE LEARNED TO PLAY PADDLE TENNIS ON THE PLAYGROUNDS OF HARLEM. WON HER FIRST TOURNAMENT, THE N.Y. STATE OPEN IN 1942. CRASHED RACIAL-BARRIERS OF BIG-TIME TENNIS IN 1950 WHEN SHE WAS

THE FIRST BLACK EVER ADMITTED TO THE U.S. LAWN ASSOC., CHAMPIONSHIPS AT FOREST HILLS, N.Y. (AUG 1950). AFTER SEVERAL YEARS OF MINOR SUCCESSES AND DISAPPOINTMENTS SHE ALMOST QUIT. HER COACH SIDNEY LLEWELLYN ENCOURAGED HER TO MAKE A FOREIGN TOUR. IT WAS THE TURNING POINT. SHE WON 18 TOURNAMENTS AND GAINED WORLD FAME. IN HER FIRST ATTEMPT AT WIMBLEDON, ENGLAND IN 1956 SHE FINISHED SECOND. IN 1957 AT THE AGE OF 29 SHE BEAT DARLENE HARD OF CALIF., TO WIN THE HIGHEST TENNIS HONOR FOR WOMEN AND THE FIRST BLACK. SHE WENT ON TO WIN THE U.S. TITLES. THE ONCE TENNIS QUEEN ENTERED THE NATIONAL LAWN TENNIS HALL OF FAME (N.Y) 1972.

Geo LEE

143

WE SHALL OVERCOME

RALPH DAVID ABERNATHY

TOP AIDE TO MARTIN LUTHER KING JR WHO FOUGHT WITH HIM EVERY STEP OF THE WAY FOR THE CIVIL RIGHTS OF BLACK PEOPLE WAS PASTOR OF THE FIRST BAPTIST CHURCH OF MONTGOMERY, ALA., WHEN IT WAS BOMBED BECAUSE OF HIS STAND IN SUPPORT OF THE MONTGOMERY BUS BOY-COTT (1955). BORN IN LINDEN, ALA...THE 10th CHILD OF AN ALABAMA FARMER. HE RE-CEIVED HIS SCHOOLING IN MAR-ENGO COUNTY. EARNED HIS BACCALAUAREATE DEGREE AT ALABAMA STATE COLLEGE IN 1950. HIS M.A. IN SOCIOLOGY AT ATLANTA UNIV. REV. ABERNATHY SUCCEEDED DR. KING AS PRESIDENT OF THE SOUTHERN CHRISTIAN LEADER-SHIP CONFERENCE (SCLC). A DYNAMIC SPEAKER HE CONTINUES HIS FIGHT FOR CIVIL RIGHTS!

WE SHALL OVERCOME!

RALPH   MARTIN

© 1975 George L. Lee Feature Service

Rev. Abernathy resigned from the SCLC in 1977 and now devotes his time to pastoring the West Hunter Street Baptist Church in Atlanta. He is also active with other groups. Rev. Abernathy was the first to receive the annual Martin Luther King Sr. Community Service Award in 1985.

REAR ADMIRAL

GERALD E. THOMAS

THE SECOND BLACK TO ACHIEVE THE HIGH RANK OF REAR ADMIRAL ON JAN 30, 1974... COMMANDING A FLEET OF A SIX DESTROYER SQUADRON, A MAJOR FLEET COMMAND OPERATING IN THE WESTERN PACIFIC. A NATIVE OF NATICK, MASS., HE SERVED IN THE NAVY STARTING AS ENSIGN AFTER GRADUATING FROM HARVARD UNIV., (1951). ADM. THOMAS EARNED A PH.D IN DIPLOMATIC HISTORY FROM YALE UNIV.,(1974). HE COMMANDED THE USS IMPERVIOUS (1962-63) AND THE USS BAUSELL (1966-68).

FIRST BLACK GRADUATE NURSE

MARY ELIZABETH MAHONEY

IN 1879 A LITTLE WOMAN OF ONLY FIVE FEET AND LESS THAN 100-POUNDS AND IN HER LATE 20's STEPPED-UP TO RECEIVE HER DIPLOMA FROM THE NEW ENGLAND HOSPITAL IN BOSTON. THE FIRST BLACK TRAINED NURSE. SHE SERVED EFFICIENTLY FOR OVER 40 YEARS. LATER BECAME A PRIVATE DUTY NURSE IN ROXBURY. SHE DIED IN 1926 AT AGE OF 80...IN THE SAME HOSPITAL.

Geo Lee

ARMY'S FIRST BLACK 4-STAR GENERAL

GEN. ROSCOE ROBINSON

THE COMMANDING LT. GEN. OF THE **U.S. ARMY'S IX CORPS** IN JAPAN HAS BEEN PROMOTED TO FULL GENERAL, THE FIRST BLACK 4-STAR GENERAL IN THE ARMY, SEPT '82. ROBINSON, 53, OF ST. LOUIS, MO., WAS ASSIGNED AS **U.S.** REPRESENTATIVE TO NATO's MILITARY COMM. A WEST POINT GRADUATE WITH A MILITARY ENGINEERING DEGREE AND A MASTER'S DEGREE FROM U. OF PITTSBURGH. HE ATTENDED THE NAT'L WAR COLLEGE AND THE ARMY'S COMMAND AND GENERAL STAFF COLLEGE. WON THE BRONZE STAR FOR BRAVERY IN KOREA. SILVER STAR FOR VALOR IN VIETNAM

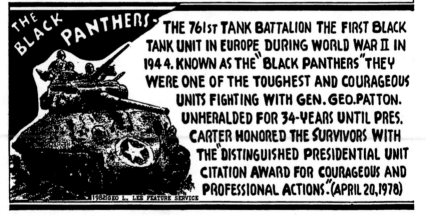

THE BLACK PANTHERS. THE 761st TANK BATTALION THE FIRST BLACK TANK UNIT IN EUROPE DURING WORLD WAR II IN 1944. KNOWN AS THE "BLACK PANTHERS" THEY WERE ONE OF THE TOUGHEST AND COURAGEOUS UNITS FIGHTING WITH GEN. GEO. PATTON. UNHERALDED FOR 34-YEARS UNTIL PRES. CARTER HONORED THE SURVIVORS WITH THE "DISTINGUISHED PRESIDENTIAL UNIT CITATION AWARD FOR COURAGEOUS AND PROFESSIONAL ACTIONS." (APRIL 20, 1978)

1982 GEO L. LEE FEATURE SERVICE

A FINE ACTOR

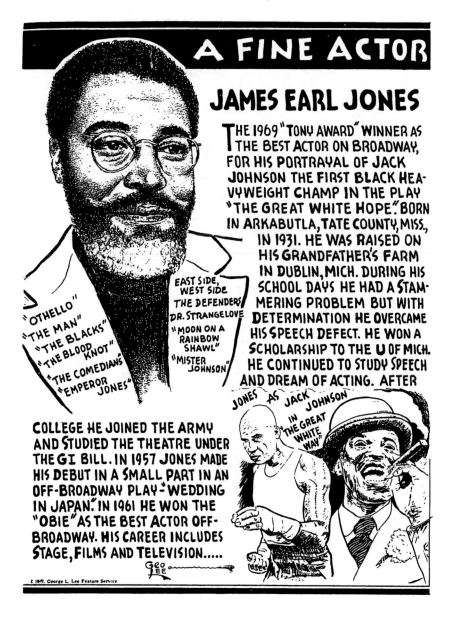

JAMES EARL JONES

THE 1969 "TONY AWARD" WINNER AS THE BEST ACTOR ON BROADWAY, FOR HIS PORTRAYAL OF JACK JOHNSON THE FIRST BLACK HEAVYWEIGHT CHAMP IN THE PLAY "THE GREAT WHITE HOPE." BORN IN ARKABUTLA, TATE COUNTY, MISS., IN 1931. HE WAS RAISED ON HIS GRANDFATHER'S FARM IN DUBLIN, MICH. DURING HIS SCHOOL DAYS HE HAD A STAMMERING PROBLEM BUT WITH DETERMINATION HE OVERCAME HIS SPEECH DEFECT. HE WON A SCHOLARSHIP TO THE U OF MICH. HE CONTINUED TO STUDY SPEECH AND DREAM OF ACTING. AFTER

"OTHELLO"
"THE MAN"
"THE BLACKS"
"THE BLOOD KNOT"
"THE COMEDIANS"
"EMPEROR JONES"

EAST SIDE, WEST SIDE
THE DEFENDERS
DR. STRANGELOVE
"MOON ON A RAINBOW SHAWL"
"MISTER JOHNSON"

JONES AS JACK JOHNSON IN "THE GREAT WHITE WAY"

COLLEGE HE JOINED THE ARMY AND STUDIED THE THEATRE UNDER THE GI BILL. IN 1957 JONES MADE HIS DEBUT IN A SMALL PART IN AN OFF-BROADWAY PLAY "WEDDING IN JAPAN." IN 1961 HE WON THE "OBIE" AS THE BEST ACTOR OFF-BROADWAY. HIS CAREER INCLUDES STAGE, FILMS AND TELEVISION.....

GEO LEE

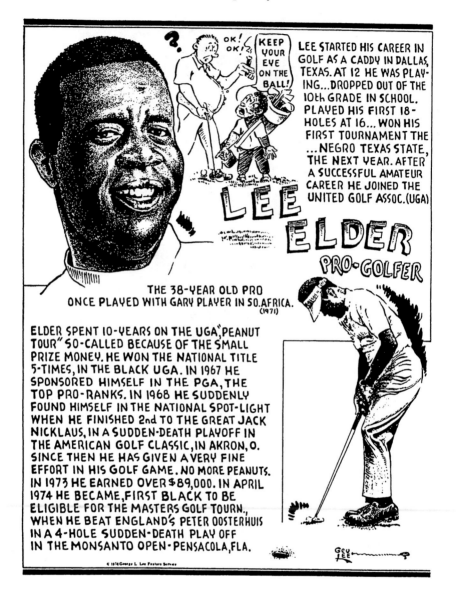

LEE STARTED HIS CAREER IN GOLF AS A CADDY IN DALLAS, TEXAS. AT 12 HE WAS PLAYING...DROPPED OUT OF THE 10th GRADE IN SCHOOL. PLAYED HIS FIRST 18-HOLES AT 16...WON HIS FIRST TOURNAMENT THE ...NEGRO TEXAS STATE, THE NEXT YEAR. AFTER A SUCCESSFUL AMATEUR CAREER HE JOINED THE UNITED GOLF ASSOC.(UGA)

LEE ELDER PRO-GOLFER

THE 38-YEAR OLD PRO ONCE PLAYED WITH GARY PLAYER IN SO.AFRICA. (1971)

ELDER SPENT 10-YEARS ON THE UGA "PEANUT TOUR" SO-CALLED BECAUSE OF THE SMALL PRIZE MONEY. HE WON THE NATIONAL TITLE 5-TIMES, IN THE BLACK UGA. IN 1967 HE SPONSORED HIMSELF IN THE PGA, THE TOP PRO-RANKS. IN 1968 HE SUDDENLY FOUND HIMSELF IN THE NATIONAL SPOT-LIGHT WHEN HE FINISHED 2nd TO THE GREAT JACK NICKLAUS, IN A SUDDEN-DEATH PLAYOFF IN THE AMERICAN GOLF CLASSIC, IN AKRON, O. SINCE THEN HE HAS GIVEN A VERY FINE EFFORT IN HIS GOLF GAME. NO MORE PEANUTS. IN 1973 HE EARNED OVER $89,000. IN APRIL 1974 HE BECAME, FIRST BLACK TO BE ELIGIBLE FOR THE MASTERS GOLF TOURN., WHEN HE BEAT ENGLAND'S PETER OOSTERHUIS IN A 4-HOLE SUDDEN-DEATH PLAY OFF IN THE MONSANTO OPEN-PENSACOLA, FLA.

148

FIRST BLACK MARINE FLYER

LT.COL. FRANK E. PETERSEN

OF THE **U.S.** MARINE CORPS IS THE HIGHEST RANKING BLACK OFFICER. A NATIVE OF TOPEKA, KANSAS. ON OCT 22, 1952 HE WAS AWARDED HIS COMMISSION AND WINGS AT PENSACOLA, FLA., TO BECOME THE FIRST BLACK FLYER IN THE HISTORY OF THE MARINE CORPS. HE RECEIVED TRAINING ALSO AT THE MARINE CORPS AIR STATION, EL TORO, CAL. PROMOTED TO 1st **LT.**, IN 1954 AND SERVED IN KOREA FLYING 64 COMBAT MISSIONS.

IN VIETNAM HE COMMANDED A FIGHTER SQUADRON FOR A YEAR AND WON THE DISTINGUISHED FLYING CROSS AND MANY OTHER MEDALS IN 31 COMBAT MISSIONS. IN 1973 HE ATTENDED THE NATIONAL WAR COLLEGE WHICH IS CONSIDERED A TRAINING GROUND FOR GENERALS.

© 1976 George L. Lee Feature Service

149

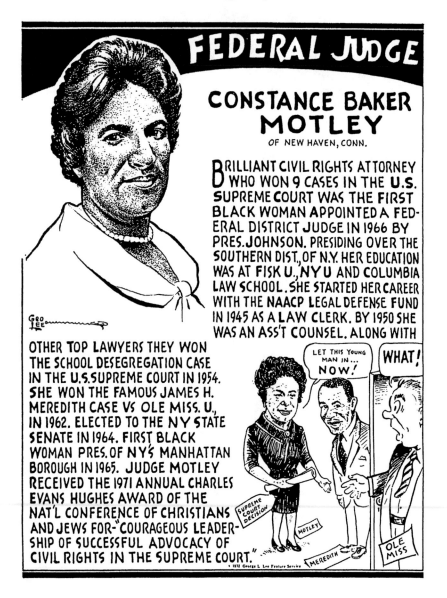

FEDERAL JUDGE

CONSTANCE BAKER MOTLEY
OF NEW HAVEN, CONN.

BRILLIANT CIVIL RIGHTS ATTORNEY WHO WON 9 CASES IN THE U.S. SUPREME COURT WAS THE FIRST BLACK WOMAN APPOINTED A FEDERAL DISTRICT JUDGE IN 1966 BY PRES. JOHNSON. PRESIDING OVER THE SOUTHERN DIST., OF N.Y. HER EDUCATION WAS AT FISK U., NYU AND COLUMBIA LAW SCHOOL. SHE STARTED HER CAREER WITH THE NAACP LEGAL DEFENSE FUND IN 1945 AS A LAW CLERK. BY 1950 SHE WAS AN ASS'T COUNSEL. ALONG WITH OTHER TOP LAWYERS THEY WON THE SCHOOL DESEGREGATION CASE IN THE U.S. SUPREME COURT IN 1954. SHE WON THE FAMOUS JAMES H. MEREDITH CASE VS OLE MISS. U., IN 1962. ELECTED TO THE NY STATE SENATE IN 1964. FIRST BLACK WOMAN PRES. OF NY'S MANHATTAN BOROUGH IN 1965. JUDGE MOTLEY RECEIVED THE 1971 ANNUAL CHARLES EVANS HUGHES AWARD OF THE NAT'L CONFERENCE OF CHRISTIANS AND JEWS FOR "COURAGEOUS LEADERSHIP OF SUCCESSFUL ADVOCACY OF CIVIL RIGHTS IN THE SUPREME COURT."

LET THIS YOUNG MAN IN... NOW!

WHAT!

SUPREME COURT DECISION

MOTLEY

MEREDITH

OLE MISS

© 1972 George L. Lee Feature Service

FOR SOCIAL CHANGE

CORETTA SCOTT KING

WIDOW OF THE PROPHET OF NON-VIOLENCE, MARTIN LUTHER KING, JR AND THE MOTHER OF FOUR, IS A BRILLIANT WOMAN. BORN IN MARION, ALA... GRADUATE OF ANTIOCH COLLEGE (OHIO), MAJORING IN MUSIC AND EDUCATION. EARNED A B.S. DEGREE IN MUSIC FROM THE NEW ENGLAND CONSERVA-TORY (BOS). GAVE UP A PROMISING CAREER AS A CONCERT PIANIST

-SINGER. A FINE SPEAKER. THE FIRST WOMAN TO DELIVER A COMMENCEMENT ADDRESS AT HARVARD (1968). THE FIRST WOMAN TO PREACH A STATUT-ORY SERVICE IN ST. PAUL'S CATH-EDRAL IN LONDON (1969). AUTHOR OF THE BEST SELLER-"MY LIFE WITH MARTIN LUTHER KING, JR." PUBLISHED IN 12-LANGU-AGES... WON MANY AWARDS!

© 1978 George L. Lee Feature Service

"WE SHALL OVERCOME"

CORETTA MARCHED WITH MARTIN FOR CIVIL RIGHTS. NOW IN 1978 SHE CONTINUES AS THE GUIDING FORCE IN THE KING CENTER FOR SOCIAL CHANGE

GEO LEE

U.N. AMBASSADOR

ANDREW YOUNG

AMERICA'S FIRST BLACK UNITED NATIONS AMBASSADOR. A NATIVE OF NEW ORLEANS AND A SON OF A PROSPEROUS DENTIST. AFTER HIS EARLY EDUCATION HE ATTENDED DILLARD U, AND RECEIVED HIS B.S.DEGREE FROM HOWARD U IN 1951. HE JOINED THE UNITED CHRISTIAN YOUTH MOVEMENT AT 19, THEIR PROGRAM "WINNING A MILLION YOUTH TO CHRIST". SO INSPIRED, ANDY DEDICATED HIS LIFE TO CHRIST AND ENROLLED IN THE HARTFORD (CONN) SEMINARY.... ORDAINED IN HIS HOME CHURCH, CENTRAL CONGREGATIONAL FEB 23, 1955. REV. YOUNG JOINED DR. MARTIN L. KING AND THE SCLC CIVIL RIGHTS MOVE-

MENT IN 1961 IN ATLANTA. AFTER KING'S DEATH IN 1968 HE TURNED TO POLITICS AND LOST HIS BID FOR U.S. CONGRESS FROM GEORGIA IN 1970. HE BECAME THE FIRST BLACK TO WIN A SEAT IN CONGRESS (1972) FROM GA., SINCE RECONSTRUCTION DAYS. LOOKING UP TO GREATER ACHIEVEMENTS!

WE HAVE RACISM HERE AT HOME!

TELL 'EM ANDY

WHEN OUTSPOKEN ANDY YOUNG SPEAKS EVERYONE LISTENS......

Geo LEE

© 1977, George L. Lee Feature Service

Andrew Young was inaugurated as the 55th mayor of Atlanta in January 1982 and began his second term in 1986.

152

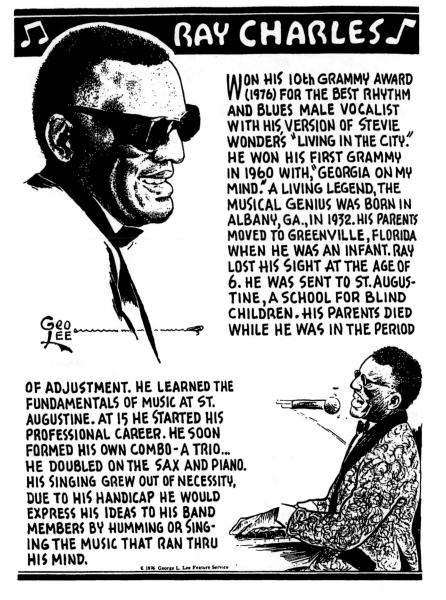

RAY CHARLES

WON HIS 10th GRAMMY AWARD (1976) FOR THE BEST RHYTHM AND BLUES MALE VOCALIST WITH HIS VERSION OF STEVIE WONDER'S "LIVING IN THE CITY." HE WON HIS FIRST GRAMMY IN 1960 WITH "GEORGIA ON MY MIND." A LIVING LEGEND, THE MUSICAL GENIUS WAS BORN IN ALBANY, GA., IN 1932. HIS PARENTS MOVED TO GREENVILLE, FLORIDA WHEN HE WAS AN INFANT. RAY LOST HIS SIGHT AT THE AGE OF 6. HE WAS SENT TO ST. AUGUS-TINE, A SCHOOL FOR BLIND CHILDREN. HIS PARENTS DIED WHILE HE WAS IN THE PERIOD

Geo Lee

OF ADJUSTMENT. HE LEARNED THE FUNDAMENTALS OF MUSIC AT ST. AUGUSTINE. AT 15 HE STARTED HIS PROFESSIONAL CAREER. HE SOON FORMED HIS OWN COMBO-A TRIO... HE DOUBLED ON THE SAX AND PIANO. HIS SINGING GREW OUT OF NECESSITY, DUE TO HIS HANDICAP HE WOULD EXPRESS HIS IDEAS TO HIS BAND MEMBERS BY HUMMING OR SING-ING THE MUSIC THAT RAN THRU HIS MIND.

© 1976 George L. Lee Feature Service

In 1986, Ray Charles received Stereo Review's annual Mable Mercer Award for his contributions to the quality of American life and music.

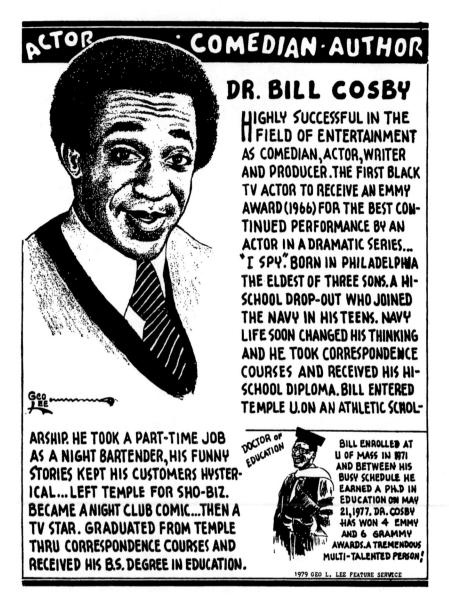

ACTOR · COMEDIAN · AUTHOR

DR. BILL COSBY

HIGHLY SUCCESSFUL IN THE FIELD OF ENTERTAINMENT AS COMEDIAN, ACTOR, WRITER AND PRODUCER. THE FIRST BLACK TV ACTOR TO RECEIVE AN EMMY AWARD (1966) FOR THE BEST CONTINUED PERFORMANCE BY AN ACTOR IN A DRAMATIC SERIES... "I SPY". BORN IN PHILADELPHIA THE ELDEST OF THREE SONS. A HI-SCHOOL DROP-OUT WHO JOINED THE NAVY IN HIS TEENS. NAVY LIFE SOON CHANGED HIS THINKING AND HE TOOK CORRESPONDENCE COURSES AND RECEIVED HIS HI-SCHOOL DIPLOMA. BILL ENTERED TEMPLE U. ON AN ATHLETIC SCHOL-ARSHIP. HE TOOK A PART-TIME JOB AS A NIGHT BARTENDER, HIS FUNNY STORIES KEPT HIS CUSTOMERS HYSTERICAL... LEFT TEMPLE FOR SHO-BIZ. BECAME A NIGHT CLUB COMIC... THEN A TV STAR. GRADUATED FROM TEMPLE THRU CORRESPONDENCE COURSES AND RECEIVED HIS B.S. DEGREE IN EDUCATION.

Geo LEE

DOCTOR OF EDUCATION

BILL ENROLLED AT U OF MASS IN 1971 AND BETWEEN HIS BUSY SCHEDULE HE EARNED A PH.D IN EDUCATION ON MAY 21, 1977. DR. COSBY HAS WON 4 EMMY AND 6 GRAMMY AWARDS. A TREMENDOUS MULTI-TALENTED PERSON!

1979 GEO L. LEE FEATURE SERVICE

Bill Cosby has recently been widely honored for his top-rated TV series, "The Cosby Show." His 1986 book, "Fatherhood," has sold over 1.5 million copies so far. He has received the NAACP's Medgar Evers Medal of Honor and the Spingarn Gold Medal.

MEDAL OF HONOR **HERO**

BRIG. GENERAL CHARLES C. ROGERS

CITED MAY 1970

THE HIGHEST-RANKING BLACK OFFICER TO RECEIVE THE "MEDAL OF HONOR" THE TOP U.S. ARMY AWARD. THE FORMER LT. COL., WHILE SERVING AS COMMANDING OFFICER OF THE 1st BATTALION, 5th ARTILLERY, 1st INF. DIV., DURING DEFENSE OF AN ARTILLERY BASE (VIETNAM) HE LED COUNTER ATTACKS AND DIRECTED HOWITZER FIRE ON THE ENEMY THO' WOUNDED.

FIRST BLACK WOMAN GENERAL

BRIG. GEN. HAZEL W. JOHNSON

AS COLONEL, WAS DIRECTOR OF THE WALTER REED INSTI., OF NURSING. AS BRIG. GEN., NOW HEADS THE U.S. ARMY NURSE CORPS. A NATIVE OF WEST CHESTER, PA., SHE HOLDS A BACHELOR AND MASTER'S DEGREE IN NURSING...SERVED AS CHIEF NURSE FOR THE ARMY MEDICAL COMMAND IN KOREA.

1979 GEO L. LEE FEATURE SERVICE

Hazel Johnson retired in 1983.

FIRST BLACK U.S. ARMY SEC'Y.

CLIFFORD ALEXANDER

BRILLIANT AND HIGHLY EDUCATED, MADE HISTORY WHEN PRESIDENT CARTER APPOINTED HIM THE FIRST BLACK SECRETARY OF THE ARMY. ...SWORN IN ON FEB 14, 1977. BORN IN HARLEM ON SEPT 21, 1933. EDUCATED IN PRIVATE SCHOOLS. GRADUATED CUM LAUDE FROM HARVARD AND EARNED A LAW DEGREE FROM YALE IN 1958. WHILE AT HARVARD HE WAS PRESIDENT OF STUDENT COUNCIL. BEGAN CAREER AS AN AIDE TO THE MANHATTAN DIST. ATTY IN 1961. MR. ALEXANDER WENT TO WASHINGTON IN 1963. UNDER PRES. KENNEDY WAS FOREIGN AFFAIRS OFFICER IN THE NAT'L SECURITY COUNCIL. CHAIRMAN OF EEOC FOR PRES. JOHNSON UNTIL 1969. HOSTED A D.C. TV-SHOW, "BLACK ON WHITE". ENTERED POLITICS ('74) FOR D.C. MAYOR ...LOST! ONCE A PRIVATE IN THE ARMY RESERVES FOR A 6-MOS HITCH (1959).

AS THE 13th SECRETARY HE HEADS A 1.3-MILLION ARMY OF REGULARS, RESERVES AND NAT'L GUARDSMEN AND 370,000 CIVILIAN EMPLOYEES!

$29 BILLION BUDGET

GEO LEE

1979 GEO L. LEE FEATURE SERVICE

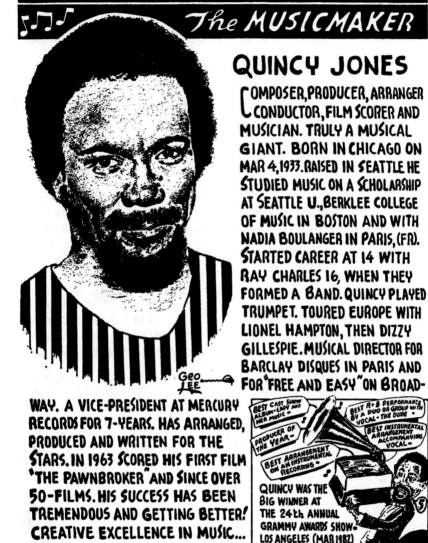

The MUSICMAKER

QUINCY JONES

COMPOSER, PRODUCER, ARRANGER CONDUCTOR, FILM SCORER AND MUSICIAN. TRULY A MUSICAL GIANT. BORN IN CHICAGO ON MAR 4, 1933. RAISED IN SEATTLE HE STUDIED MUSIC ON A SCHOLARSHIP AT SEATTLE U., BERKLEE COLLEGE OF MUSIC IN BOSTON AND WITH NADIA BOULANGER IN PARIS, (FR). STARTED CAREER AT 14 WITH RAY CHARLES 16, WHEN THEY FORMED A BAND. QUINCY PLAYED TRUMPET. TOURED EUROPE WITH LIONEL HAMPTON, THEN DIZZY GILLESPIE. MUSICAL DIRECTOR FOR BARCLAY DISQUES IN PARIS AND FOR "FREE AND EASY" ON BROAD-WAY. A VICE-PRESIDENT AT MERCURY RECORDS FOR 7-YEARS. HAS ARRANGED, PRODUCED AND WRITTEN FOR THE STARS. IN 1963 SCORED HIS FIRST FILM "THE PAWNBROKER" AND SINCE OVER 50-FILMS. HIS SUCCESS HAS BEEN TREMENDOUS AND GETTING BETTER! CREATIVE EXCELLENCE IN MUSIC...

Geo LEE

BEST CAST SHOW ALBUM-LADY AND HER MUSIC-

PRODUCER OF THE YEAR-

BEST ARRANGEMENT ON AN INSTRUMENTAL RECORDING-

BEST R+B PERFORMANCE BY A DUO OR GROUP WITH VOCAL-THE DUDE-

BEST INSTRUMENTAL ARRANGEMENT ACCOMPANYING VOCAL-

QUINCY WAS THE BIG WINNER AT THE 24th ANNUAL GRAMMY AWARDS SHOW- LOS ANGELES (MAR 1982)

1982 GEO L. LEE FEATURE SERVICE

DYNAMIC CONGRESSWOMAN

BARBARA JORDAN

U.S. REPRESENTATIVE (D) FROM TEXAS, THE FIRST BLACK WOMAN EVER ELECTED TO CONGRESS FROM THE SOUTH (1972) A NATIVE OF HOUSTON SHE WAS GRADUATED MAGNA CUM LAUDE FROM TEXAS SOUTHERN U. SHE RECEIVED HER LAW DEGREE FROM BOSTON U., IN 1959. PRATICED LAW IN HOUSTON. ENTERED POLITICS IN 1962 AND RAN FOR THE TEXAS HOUSE BUT LOST TWICE. IN 1966 RAN FOR STATE SENATE AND WON. A BRILLIANT CON-STITUTIONAL LAWMAKER REP. JORDAN WAS APPOINTED

Geo LEE

WHEN BARBARA JORDAN TALKS... EVERYONE LISTENS.

TO THE JUDICIARY COMM., AND LOOMS AS A POWERFUL INFLUENCE IN THE CAPITOL. A FINE ORATOR SHE WAS SELECTED AS KEYNOTER AT THE DEMOCRATIC CONVENTION IN 1976 IN MADISON SQUARE GARDEN. A CHAMPION OF CIVIL LIBERTIES AND FREEDOM!

© 1976 George L. Lee Feature Service

Barbara Jordan retired from Congress and returned to Texas in 1977. She became the Lyndon B. Johnson Public Service Professor at the L.B.J. School of Public Affairs (University of Texas). She was elected to the Orators Hall of Fame in 1984.

"A SONG OF VICTORY"

HE MADE HISTORY.

WORLD'S MIDDLEWEIGHT CHAMPION

5-TIMES CHAMP

IN DEFEAT LA MOTTA WAS A GAME CHAMP.

Geo LEE

'SUGAR' RAY ROBINSON

WON THE MIDDLEWEIGHT TITLE FROM JAKE LA MOTTA ON FEB 14,1951 ON A KO, WHEN REFEREE FRANK SIKORA STOPPED THE BOUT IN THE 13-RD. SUGAR LOST THE TITLE TO RANDY TURPIN IN LONDON ON JULY 10,1951. HE REGAINED IT ON SEPT 12,1951. RAY RETIRED, DEC 18,1952 AND GAVE UP THE TITLE. IN NOV,1954 HE RETURNED TO THE RING. ON DEC 9,1955 HE WON THE TITLE FROM BOBO OLSON. HE LOST IT TO GENE FULLMER ON JAN 2,1957. ON MAY 1, 1957 HE BEAT GENE FOR THE TITLE. LOST IT TO CARMEN BASILIO ON SEPT 23,1957. BEAT BASILIO ON MAR 25,1958 FOR HIS 5TH TITLE. GREAT!

159

James Meredith earned his law degree at Columbia University. In 1984 he became a visiting professor of Afro-American studies at the University of Cincinnati, teaching a course on "The Law and Black People."

𝒯𝒽𝑒 RIGHT TO READ

DR. RUTH LOVE

AN ASTUTE EDUCATOR. THE FIRST WOMAN AND FIRST BLACK SCHOOL SUPERINTENDENT IN THE CHICAGO SCHOOL SYSTEM. SHE IS MAKING FINE PROGRESS IN A TOUGH SITUATION. BORN IN LAWTON, OKLA., WHERE HER GRANDFATHER A RUNAWAY SLAVE, PERSEVERED FOR AN EDUCATION AND FOUNDED THE FIRST "SCHOOL FOR NEGROES." AT AGE TWO HER FAMILY MOVED TO BAKERSFIELD, CA. A FINE STUDENT SHE WENT ON TO SAN JOSE STATE

U., EARNING A BACHELOR'S DEGREE IN EDUCATION. THEN TO SAN FRANCISCO

STATE U., FOR MASTER'S IN GUIDANCE AND COUNSELING. HER DOCTORATE FROM U.S. INTERNATIONAL U., IN SAN DIEGO, CA., IN HUMAN BEHAVIOR. DR. LOVE'S TEACHING CAREER BEGAN IN OAKLAND. SHE HEADED

IN 1975 DR. LOVE BECAME THE FIRST WOMAN AND FIRST BLACK SUPERINTENDENT OF OAKLANDS SCHOOLS. AFTER 5-YEARS OF SUCCESS SHE ACCEPTED THE CHALLENGE OF THE CHICAGO SCHOOLS. (MAR '81)

THE CALIF., BUREAU OF COMPENSATORY EDUCATION FOR 6 YEARS. DIRECTED THE U.S. OFFICE OF EDUCATION'S "RIGHT TO READ" PROGRAM FROM 1971 TO 1975.

1982 GEO L. LEE FEATURE SERVICE

161

SECRETARY OF STATE - PENNSLYVANIA

HON. C. DELORES TUCKER

FIRST BLACK WOMAN TO BE APPOINTED TO THE CABINET OF THE COMMONWEALTH OF PENNSYLVANIA.. WHEN GOV. MILTON J. SHAPP, NAMED HER SECRETARY OF STATE IN JAN 1971. SHE WAS THE HIGHEST RANKING BLACK WOMAN ON THE STATE LEVEL.. ..AND THE THIRD HIGHEST OFFICIAL IN THE STATE. ACTIVE IN CIVIL RIGHTS... SHE WAS IN THE SELMA TO MONTGOMERY MARCH.(1965)

Geo. Lee

- MEMBER-BOARD OF PARDONS
- CHAIRMAN - STATE EMPLOYEES RETIREMENT BOARD
- MEMBER-BOARD OF PROPERTY
- BOARD OF FINANCE AND REVENUE
- STATE ATHLETIC COMMISSION
- KEEPER OF THE GREAT SEAL.

MY!

AMONG HER MANY OFFICIAL RESPONSIBILITIES.

A NATIVE OF PHILA., MRS. TUCKER IS A VERY BUSY PERSON IN COMMUNITY AFFAIRS...VICE PRES. OF THE STATE NAACP...VICE CHAIRMAN OF THE DEMOCRATIC STATE COMMITTEE. HAS HER OWN PUBLIC RELATIONS FIRM. A LADY ON THE MOVE!

© 1975 George L. Lee Feature Service

Delores Tucker left her Pennsylvania cabinet office in 1977. She later became chair of the Democratic Party Black Caucus. She was in 1961 the recipient of the NAACP Freedom Fund Award.

HIGHLY QUALIFIED JUDGE

AMAYLA KEARSE

THE FIRST WOMAN NAMED TO THE FEDERAL APPEALS COURT IN NEW YORK. IN 1979 PRES.CARTER NOMINATED HER TO THE SECOND U.S.CIRCUIT COURT OF APPEALS, CONSIDERED TO BE THE MOST IMPORTANT COMMERCIAL COURT, SECOND ONLY TO THE U.S.SUPREME COURT. A NATIVE OF VAUZHALL, N.J., A SECTION OF UNION CITY. HER FATHER WAS POSTMASTER OF VAUZHALL AND HER MOTHER A DOCTOR.SHE MAJORED IN PHILOSOPHY,STUDIED METAPHYSICS AND LOGIC AT WELLESLEY COLLEGE. EARNED HER LAW DEGREE AT U. OF MICHIGAN WHERE SHE HELD THE PRESTIGIOUS POSITION AS LAW REVIEW EDITOR. BEFORE HER JUDGESHIP SHE WAS AN ATTORNEY WITH THE WALL STREET FIRM OF HUGHES, HUBBARD AND REED FOR 17 YEARS, A PARTNER FOR NINE. A HUMANITARIAN ACTIVE IN CIVIL RIGHTS... THE HIGHEST BLACK WOMAN JUDGE.

MISS.KEARSE WAS NAT'L WOMEN'S PAIRS BRIDGE CHAMP IN 1971-72. SHE HAS SERVED ON THE NATL LAWS COMM.,OF THE AMERICAN CONTRACT BRIDGE LEAGUE.

HER MAIN HOBBY IS BRIDGE ALSO A MUSIC LOVER MOSTLY CLASSICAL.

1981 GEO L. LEE FEATURE SERVICE

SHE WRITES, BEST-SELLERS

TONI MORRISON

A VERY FINE AUTHOR WHO HAS REACHED THE TOP IN A RELATIVELY SHORT TIME. WROTE HER FIRST NOVEL, "THE BLUEST EYES"(1970). ROSE TO THE BEST-SELLER STATUS IN 7-YEARS WITH HER "SONG OF SOLOMON" PUBLISHED IN 1977. BORN IN LORAIN, OHIO. AS A YOUNG GIRL SHE WORKED IN THE LIBRARY AND LOVED TO READ. A GRADUATE OF HOWARD UNIV., SHE EARNED HER MASTER'S DEGREE FROM CORNELL U., IN 1953. TAUGHT ENGLISH AT TEXAS SOUTHERN U., RETURNED TO HOWARD AND TAUGHT FOR EIGHT YEARS...JOINED A WRITERS GROUP. HIGHLY ACCLAIMED BY THE CRITICS SHE ALSO WROTE "SULA" (1974). HER NOVEL "TAR BABY" (1981) WAS HIGH UP ON THE BEST-SELLER LISTS. FOR HER "SONG OF SOLOMON" TONI WON THE.... NATIONAL BOOK CRITIC'S CIRCLE AWARD AND THE AMERICAN ACADEMY AND INSTITUTE OF ARTS AND LETTERS AWARD. TRULY A BLACK ARTIST WHO WRITES BRILLIANTLY ABOUT BLACK LIVES AND LOVES!

Geo LEE

ANYWHERE WILLIE (I'VE GOT TO GET BACK TO MY NOVEL)

SENIOR EDITOR AT RANDOM HOUSE

LECTURER AT BARD COLLEGE

WHERE DO YOU WANT THESE MANUSCRIPTS?

OH NO

TONI MORRISON

A VERY BUSY LADY BUT MANAGES TO WRITE....BEST-SELLERS.

Toni Morrison won the 1988 Pulitzer Prize for Fiction for her novel "Beloved."

MICKI GRANT

OF NEW YORK CITY

WHO WROTE THE MUSIC AND LYRICS OF THE BROADWAY HIT MUSICAL "DON'T BOTHER ME I CAN'T COPE", WHICH OPENED IN N.Y. ON APR 19,1972... ONCE PLAYED THE PART OF PEGGY NOLAN A BLACK LAWYER IN TV'S SOAP OPERA-"ANOTHER WORLD". A NATIVE OF CHICAGO SHE STARTED HER BRILLIANT CAREER OF SINGER, ACTRESS, COMPOSER AND LYRICIST AT THE TENDER AGE OF SIX. WRITES MUSIC AND LYRICS FOR COMMERCIALS.

Geo.
LEE

NIKKI GIOVANNI

OF NEW YORK CITY

THE GIFTED POETESS WHO WROTE-GEMINI-MY HOUSE-BLACK FEELING BLACK AND SPIN A SOFT BLACK SONG AMONG HER BOOKS... WON THE 1973 "WOMAN OF THE YEAR" AWARD FROM THE LADIES HOME JOURNAL. IN 1972 NIKKI RECEIVED AN HONORARY DOCTORATE DEGREE FROM WILBERFORCE U. SHE ALSO RECORDS POETRY ALBUMS AND LECTURES AT COLLEGES.

Dr. *Samella S. Lewis*

OF LOS ANGELES, CALIF.

HIGHLY TALENTED ARTIST-TEACHER WHOSE WORKS ARE IN MANY COLLECTIONS, INCLUDING ATLANTA UNIV; BALTIMORE MUSEUM OF FINE ARTS; VIRGINIA MUSEUM OF FINE ARTS; HAMPTON UNIV., AND THE VIKTOR LOWENFELD MUSEUM GALLERY AT PENN STATE U. SHE IS A NATIVE OF NEW ORLEANS, LA.,

AND RECEIVED HER EDUCATION FROM HAMPTON U. (B.S.); MASTER'S IN SCULPTURE AND PH.D. IN PAINTING AND ART HISTORY FROM OHIO STATE; TUNG HAI U., IN TAIWAN; USC AND NYU. TAUGHT ART AT HAMPTON, MORGAN STATE COLLEGE, FLORIDA A+M AND RECENTLY CALIFORNIA STATE COLLEGE. (DOMINGUEZ HILLS). A BUSY LADY SHE IS CHAIRMAN OF THE BOARD OF DIRECTORS OF CONTEMPORARY CRAFTS, INC. (LA)

ACTRESS·DIRECTOR·MUSICAL CREATOR

VINNETTE CARROLL

WHOSE HIT GOSPEL MUSICAL,"YOUR ARMS TOO SHORT TO BOX WITH GOD,"GROSSED OVER 6½-MILLIONS IN 66-CITIES, HAS RETURNED TO BROADWAY (JUN'80). THE HIGHLY PROLIFIC CREATOR OF MUSICALS WAS BORN IN NEW YORK CITY AND SPENT MUCH OF HER EARLY YEARS IN JAMAICA WITH GRANDPARENTS. RETURNING TO NYC SHE FINISHED HISCHOOL AND EARNED HER DEGREE IN PSYCHOLOGY FROM LONG ISLAND U., A MASTERS FROM NYU. SHE FINISHED WORK ON A PH.D...THEN DECIDED ON... THE THEATRE. WITH A FULL SCHOLARSHIP SHE STUDIED UNDER EDWIN PISCATOR AT

THE NEW SCHOOL IN NYC. VINNETTE BEGAN DIRECTING PLAYS AT THE HARLEM YMCA. WON AN OBIE AWARD FOR HER ACTING IN,"MOON ON A RAINBOW SHAWL." BECAME CO-DIRECTOR OF THE INNER CITY REPERTORY CO., IN WATTS (L.A.); DIRECTOR OF THE GHETTO ARTS OF THE N.Y. STATE COUNCIL ON THE ARTS; FOUNDED THE URBAN ARTS CORP, A TRAINING PROGRAM FOR ASPIRING YOUNG ARTISTS.

1980 GEO L. LEE FEATURE SERVICE

DIRECTED
SLOW DANCE ON THE KILLING GROUND
A RAISIN IN THE SUN
THE FLIES
BLACK NATIVITY
THE PRODIGAL SON | BURY THE DEAD
BUT NEVER JAM TODAY
DARK OF THE MOON
WON EMMY FOR CBS-TV's: BEYOND THE BLUES
VERY NICE!
DON'T BOTHER ME, I CAN'T COPE
WHEN HELL FREEZES OVER, I'LL SKATE

ON STAGE·
MEMBER OF THE WEDDING
S.R.ALL WAR ON MURRAY HILL
JOLLY'S PROGRESS
IN FILMS
ONE POTATO, TWO POTATO
UP THE DOWN STAIRCASE

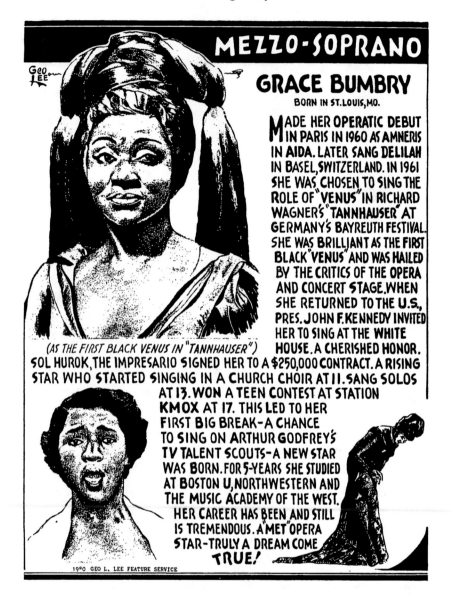

MEZZO-SOPRANO

GRACE BUMBRY
BORN IN ST. LOUIS, MO.

MADE HER OPERATIC DEBUT IN PARIS IN 1960 AS AMNERIS IN AIDA. LATER SANG DELILAH IN BASEL, SWITZERLAND. IN 1961 SHE WAS CHOSEN TO SING THE ROLE OF "VENUS" IN RICHARD WAGNER'S "TANNHAUSER" AT GERMANY'S BAYREUTH FESTIVAL. SHE WAS BRILLIANT AS THE FIRST "BLACK VENUS" AND WAS HAILED BY THE CRITICS OF THE OPERA AND CONCERT STAGE. WHEN SHE RETURNED TO THE U.S., PRES. JOHN F. KENNEDY INVITED HER TO SING AT THE WHITE HOUSE. A CHERISHED HONOR.

(AS THE FIRST BLACK VENUS IN "TANNHAUSER")

SOL HUROK, THE IMPRESARIO SIGNED HER TO A $250,000 CONTRACT. A RISING STAR WHO STARTED SINGING IN A CHURCH CHOIR AT 11. SANG SOLOS AT 13. WON A TEEN CONTEST AT STATION KMOX AT 17. THIS LED TO HER FIRST BIG BREAK-A CHANCE TO SING ON ARTHUR GODFREY'S TV TALENT SCOUTS-A NEW STAR WAS BORN. FOR 5-YEARS SHE STUDIED AT BOSTON U, NORTHWESTERN AND THE MUSIC ACADEMY OF THE WEST. HER CAREER HAS BEEN AND STILL IS TREMENDOUS. A MET OPERA STAR-TRULY A DREAM COME TRUE!

1970 GEO L. LEE FEATURE SERVICE

PULITZER PRIZE PLAY

CHARLES GORDONE

THE FIRST BLACK PLAYWRIGHT TO WIN THE COVETED PULITZER PRIZE FOR HIS PLAY "NO PLACE TO BE SOMEBODY" IN 1970. A NATIVE OF LOS ANGELES, CA., HE SPENT 7 YEARS IN WRITING THE BLACK COMEDY AND 3 YEARS FINDING SOMEONE TO PRODUCE IT!

The BLACK CAUCUS

REP. PARREN MITCHELL
OF BALTIMORE

THE FIRST BLACK CONGRESSMAN ELECTED FROM MARYLAND'S 7th DIST., (1970). ELECTED CHAIRMAN OF THE CONGRESSIONAL BLACK CAUCUS (1976). A SPECIALIST IN MINORITY BUSINESS AND A KEY SPOKESMAN OF THE CAUCUS. A MORGAN STATE COLLEGE GRADUATE. IN 1950 HE HAD TO BRING COURT ACTION AGAINST U OF MARYLAND TO BECOME THE FIRST BLACK GRADUATE STUDENT. EARNED HIS MASTERS DEGREE IN SOCIOLOGY AND JOINED MORGAN'S FACULTY AS A PROF. OF SOCIOLOGY. A SPLENDID ORATOR!

Geo Lee

© 1978 George L. Lee Feature Service

169

THE OWL AND THE PUSSYCAT

DIANA SANDS

1934
•
1973

Geo
LEE

WHO MADE A BIG HIT IN THE NON-RACIAL COMEDY, "THE OWL AND THE PUSSYCAT" ON BROADWAY WITH ALAN ALDA IN 1964-STARTED HER CAREER AS A DANCER. BORN IN NEW YORK CITY SHE GREW UP ON ST. NICHOLAS AVE IN HARLEM AND ATTENDED THE HIGH SCHOOL OF PERFORMING ARTS. IN HER EAGERNESS SHE FORMED AN ORIENTAL DANCE TEAM AND TRIED OUT IN CANADA. AFTER GRADUATING AS THE BEST ACTRESS IN HER CLASS SHE YEARNED FOR A DRAMATIC CAREER. WITH OFF-BROADWAY EXPERIENCE AND MORE SCHOOLING,

DIANA SCORED BIG IN A BROADWAY SUPPORTING ROLE AS THE IDEALISTIC SISTER OF SIDNEY POITIER IN "A RAISIN IN THE SUN" IN 1959. SHE WON THE OUTER CIRCLE AWARD AS THE BEST SUPPORTING ACTRESS. HER STAR SHONE ON BROADWAY IN "TIGER, TIGER, BURNING BRIGHT" AND "BLUES FOR MR. CHARLIE." IN 1967 SHE PLAYED SHAKESPEARE ROLES-LADY MACBETH TO CLEOPATRA..SHAW'S JOAN OF ARC.

THE LANDLORD · HONEYBABY, HONEYBABY · GEORGIA, GEORGIA · ?.?.? CLAUDINE ?.?. · A RAISIN IN THE SUN · THEY LOVE ME... · CAREER

HER FILMS WERE GOING GREAT....

THE TALENTS OF DIANA SANDS WERE CUT SHORT WHEN DEATH STEPPED IN AT THE AGE OF 39.

© 1977, George L. Lee Feature Service

I KNOW WHY THE CAGED BIRD SINGS

MAYA ANGELOU

A NATIVE OF ARKANSAS WHOSE REAL NAME IS MARGUERITE JOHNSON. SHE SPENT HER EARLY YEARS IN ST. LOUIS AND SAN FRANCISCO. A NOTED AUTHOR, SHE WAS THE FIRST BLACK WOMAN TO MAKE THE NON-FICTION BEST-SELLER LIST... HER AUTOBIOGRAPHY,"I KNOW WHY THE CAGED BIRD SINGS" (1970):"GATHER TOGETHER IN MY NAME(1973) AND"SINGIN' AND SWINGIN'AND GETTING MERRY LIKE CHRISTMAS"(1976). FIRST BLACK WOMAN TO HAVE AN ORIGINAL SCREENPLAY

GEO LEE

PRODUCED-"GEORGIA,GEORGIA"(1972) ALSO ITS DIRECTOR, ANOTHER FIRST! MAYA ROSE TO FAME AS A NIGHT CLUB SINGER AND DANCER OF CALYPSO MUSIC IN 1950'S. ACTIVE IN CIVIL RIGHTS IN 1960 -61, AS NORTHERN COORDINATOR OF THE SCLC. A DYNAMIC WOMAN OF MANY TALENTS. WHILE IN AFRICA SHE WAS AN ASSOCIATE EDITOR OF AN EGYPTIAN PU-BLICATION, A UNIV., LECTURER IN GHANA, WRITTEN POEMS,OFF-BROADWAY PLAYS AND HIT SONGS. THE BIRD IS FLYIN'HIGH!

THE TALL 6 FT ENTERTAINER MADE A STUNNING -APPEARANCE...

HANK AARON · HOME RUN KING

THIS IS IT!

ON APRIL 8, 1974 AARON SURPASSED BABE RUTH'S ALL-TIME RECORD OF 714 WHEN HE HIT 715! PLAYING FOR THE ATLANTA BRAVES. ..HE FINISHED THE 1974 SEASON WITH

NOT BAD 733!

AFTER A GREAT CAREER WITH THE ATLANTA BRAVES HE WAS TRADED TO THE MILWAUKEE BREWERS (AL) ON NOV 2, 1974... ON HIS OWN REQUEST. THE 40-YEAR SUPER-STAR WILL BE A DESIGNATED HITTER IN THE 1975 SEASON FOR THE BREWERS. HENRY STARTED HIS PLAYING DAYS IN MILWAUKEE (1954).

HIS NAT'L LEAGUE RECORDS: WON 4 HOME RUN TITLES; 4 RBI TITLES; BATTING CHAMP 1956-1959; MOST VALUABLE PLAYER AWARD 1957; 9th PLAYER IN HISTORY TO HIT 3000 HITS;

Geo Lee

© 1975 George L. Lee Feature Service

Hank Aaron was inducted into the Baseball Hall of Fame in 1982. He became director and vice president of player personnel for the Braves.

172

A SHINING STAR

DIAHANN CARROLL

THE GLAMOROUS SINGER, ACTRESS AND ONE OF THE WORLD'S MOST BEAUTIFUL AND TALENTED WOMEN. IN 1984 JOINED THE CAST OF TV's NIGHT-TIME SERIES-"DYNASTY" WITH OVER 35-MILLION VIEWERS... AS DOMINIQUE DEVERAUX, A VERY INTERESTING PART. ANOTHER BIG STEP IN HER CAREER. A NATIVE OF NYC AND HARLEM. DAUGHTER OF A SUBWAY CONDUCTOR AND A NURSE. AT 10, WON A MET OPERA SCHOLARSHIP BUT REALLY WANTED TO BE A ROLLER SKATE CHAMP. GRADUATE OF NY's HIGH SCHOOL OF PERFORMING ARTS, ENTERED NYU TO STUDY SOCIOLOGY. HER MIND WAS ON SHOW-BIZ. DURING HER FRESHMAN YEAR WON A TALENT CONTEST. SHE DROPPED OUT OF COLLEGE INTO A SINGING CAREER. AT 19, A HIT IN HER FIRST BROADWAY SHOW, "HOUSE OF FLOWERS" (1954). "PORGY AND BESS", MOVIE '59. SCORED BIG IN "NO STRINGS", '62 AND WON A TONY AWARD. HER OWN TV SERIES, "JULIA", 1968-71. AMONG HER CREDITS-PARIS BLUES! CARMEN JONES; THE SPLIT; HURRY SUNDOWN; AGNES OF GOD; SISTER, SISTER; AN OSCAR NOMINATION FOR "CLAUDINE"...

DIAHANN ROCKETED TO OVERNIGHT FAME AS THE NEW "CINDERELLA GIRL" OF N.Y.'s NIGHT CLUBS AFTER SHE WON TV's "CHANCE OF A LIFETIME" SHOW, JAN 8, 1954 FOR $1,000... AND THE NEXT 2-WEEKS. ONLY 18 SHE VAULTED INTO MANHATTAN'S SWANK CAFE SOCIETY AND LATIN QUARTER AND BIG TV SPOTS!

1985 GEO L. LEE FEATURE SERVICE

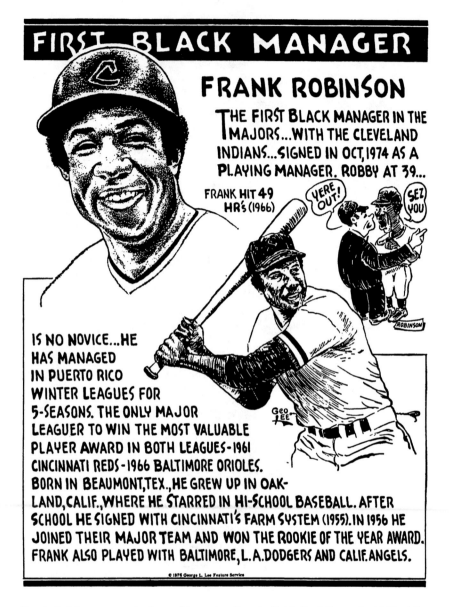

FIRST BLACK MANAGER

FRANK ROBINSON

THE FIRST BLACK MANAGER IN THE MAJORS...WITH THE CLEVELAND INDIANS...SIGNED IN OCT,1974 AS A PLAYING MANAGER. ROBBY AT 39...

FRANK HIT 49 HR'S (1966)

YERE OUT!

SEZ YOU

ROBINSON

IS NO NOVICE...HE HAS MANAGED IN PUERTO RICO WINTER LEAGUES FOR 5-SEASONS. THE ONLY MAJOR LEAGUER TO WIN THE MOST VALUABLE PLAYER AWARD IN BOTH LEAGUES-1961 CINCINNATI REDS-1966 BALTIMORE ORIOLES. BORN IN BEAUMONT,TEX., HE GREW UP IN OAK-LAND, CALIF.,WHERE HE STARRED IN HI-SCHOOL BASEBALL. AFTER SCHOOL HE SIGNED WITH CINCINNATI'S FARM SYSTEM (1955).IN 1956 HE JOINED THEIR MAJOR TEAM AND WON THE ROOKIE OF THE YEAR AWARD. FRANK ALSO PLAYED WITH BALTIMORE, L.A.DODGERS AND CALIF.ANGELS.

Geo LEE

© 1975 George L. Lee Feature Service

Frank Robinson was inducted into the Baseball Hall of Fame in 1982. Like Hank Aaron, he was one of only 13 men to win this honor in the first year of eligibility.

SHIRLEY VERRETT

INTERNATIONALLY FAMOUS MEZZO-SO-PRANO OF THE OPERA BEGAN SINGING AT 6. BORN IN NEW ORLEANS AND RAISED IN LOS ANGELES. SHE SANG IN THE 7th-DAY ADVENTIST CHOIR, SOON A SOLO-IST. STUDIED BUSINESS AT L.A. STATE COLLEGE, HER BIG LOVE-MUSIC. SHIRLEY COMPETED ON THE ARTHUR GODFREY TV TALENT SHOW AND WON TOP PRIZE. SHE WON A SCHOLARSHIP TO THE JULLIARD SCHOOL OF MUSIC WHERE SHE WAS AN OUTSTANDING STUDENT. SINGING CONCERTS BEFORE ENTERING OPERA. IN 1961 THE "MET" OPERA CO., ASKED HER TO JOIN THEM BUT SHE REFUSED UNLESS SHE COULD SING "CARMEN". FOR 7-YEARS SHE TOURED EUROPE SINGING THE ROLE SHE LOVED. IN 1968 MISS VERRETT MADE HER "MET" DEBUT SINGING THE GREATEST "CARMEN". IN 1977 SHE STILL EXCITED THE OPERATIC WORLD!

Geo LEE

© 1977 George L. Lee Feature Service

175

A LITTLE ROCK HERO MAKES GOOD

ERNEST GREEN

IN 1977 PRES. CARTER NOMINATED HIM TO BE ASS'T SEC. OF LABOR IN CHARGE OF EMPLOYMENT AND TRAINING. IN 1957, GOV. FAUBUS OF ARKANSAS CALLED OUT THE NAT'L GUARDS TO PREVENT "NINE BLACK YOUTHS" FROM INTEGRATING LITTLE ROCK'S CENTRAL HIGH SCHOOL... ERNEST WAS ONE OF THE "NINE". PRES. EISENHOWER FEDERALIZED THE GUARDS AND ORDERED THEM TO PROTECT THE "NINE". A YEAR LATER (1958) ERNEST WAS THE FIRST TO GRADUATE FROM CENTRAL HIGH. A HISTORIC INTEGRATION STEP. HE WENT ON TO MICH. STATE UNIV., AND EARNED

GEO LEE

APPLAUSE APPLAUSE APPLAUSE GRADUATION DAY - GREEN, OLDEST AND CALMEST, DISPLAYED DIGNITY AND COURAGE IN FACE OF CITYWIDE HATE... HE EMERGED A HERO! A 250-FORCE OF POLICE, GUARDS AND FBI AGENTS TO STOP VIOLENCE - BUT ONLY APPLAUSE!

HIS B.A. (1962) AND M.A. (1964) IN SOCIOLOGY. JOINED THE JOINT APPRENTICESHIP PROGRAM OF THE WORKERS DEFENSE LEAGUE (NOW RTP, INC) AS A FIELD REP., LATER EXEC. DIRECTOR. NOW A MEMBER OF GREEN, HERMAN & ASSOCIATES IN WASH, D.C. (1981).

1981 GEO L. LEE FEATURE SERVICE

AIN'T NO MOUNTAIN HIGH ENOUGH

Diana ROSS

THE HIGHLY TALENTED SUPER-STAR IN THE WORLD OF ENTERTAINMENT. A TOP NIGHTCLUB SINGER, RECORDING STAR AND FILM ACTRESS AND OWNS HER RECORD PRODUCTION FIRM. BORN IN DETROIT, MI... STUDIED DRESS DESIGN AND MODELNG IN CASS TECH HI-SCHOOL. BUT DIANA WANTED TO SING. AT 14 WITH SCHOOL FRIENDS FLORENCE BALLARD AND MARY WILSON THEY FORMED THE "PRIMETTES," SINGING AT PARTIES. A FRIEND SMOKEY ROBINSON GOT THEM AN AUDITION AT MOTOWN AND WERE

Geo
LEE.

TOLD TO FINISH SCHOOL THEN COME BACK...THEY DID! (1960). MOTOWN'S BERRY GORDY RENAMED THEM "THE SUPREMES," MUSICAL HISTORY WAS MADE! DIANA IN 1970 WENT SOLO AND CLIMBED ANOTHER MOUNTAIN...TV SPECIALS, 3-FILMS, VEGAS. IN 1981 AFTER 20-YEARS WITH MOTOWN SHE SIGNED WITH RCA FOR A REPORTED 20 MILLION. ANYMORE MOUNTAINS?

THE RISE OF THE ORIGINAL SUPREMES WAS PHENOMENAL. DIANA WAS THE FIRST AMERICAN ENTERTAINER TO BE INVITED TO JAPAN AND THE IMPERIAL PALACE. (1973)

1982 GEO L. LEE FEATURE SERVICE

Yes! In 1982, Diana Ross saw her star embedded in the Hollywood Walk of Fame. In 1985 she was honored by New York's Kaufman Astoria Studies for helping to revive the N.Y. film industry; the studio named a building after her.

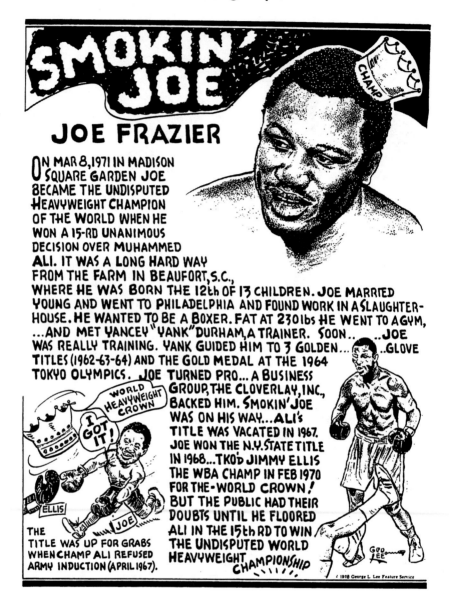

SMOKIN' JOE

JOE FRAZIER

ON MAR 8, 1971 IN MADISON SQUARE GARDEN JOE BECAME THE UNDISPUTED HEAVYWEIGHT CHAMPION OF THE WORLD WHEN HE WON A 15-RD UNANIMOUS DECISION OVER MUHAMMED ALI. IT WAS A LONG HARD WAY FROM THE FARM IN BEAUFORT, S.C., WHERE HE WAS BORN THE 12th OF 13 CHILDREN. JOE MARRIED YOUNG AND WENT TO PHILADELPHIA AND FOUND WORK IN A SLAUGHTER-HOUSE. HE WANTED TO BE A BOXER. FAT AT 230 lbs HE WENT TO A GYM, ...AND MET YANCEY "YANK" DURHAM, A TRAINER. SOON.. ..JOE WAS REALLY TRAINING. YANK GUIDED HIM TO 3 GOLDEN... ..GLOVE TITLES (1962-63-64) AND THE GOLD MEDAL AT THE 1964 TOKYO OLYMPICS. JOE TURNED PRO... A BUSINESS GROUP, THE CLOVERLAY, INC., BACKED HIM. SMOKIN' JOE WAS ON HIS WAY...ALI's TITLE WAS VACATED IN 1967. JOE WON THE N.Y. STATE TITLE IN 1968...TKO'D JIMMY ELLIS THE WBA CHAMP IN FEB 1970 FOR THE WORLD CROWN! BUT THE PUBLIC HAD THEIR DOUBTS UNTIL HE FLOORED ALI IN THE 15th RD TO WIN THE UNDISPUTED WORLD HEAVYWEIGHT CHAMPIONSHIP

WORLD HEAVYWEIGHT CROWN

I GOT IT!

ELLIS

JOE

THE TITLE WAS UP FOR GRABS WHEN CHAMP ALI REFUSED ARMY INDUCTION (APRIL 1967).

GEO LEE

© 1978 George L. Lee Feature Service

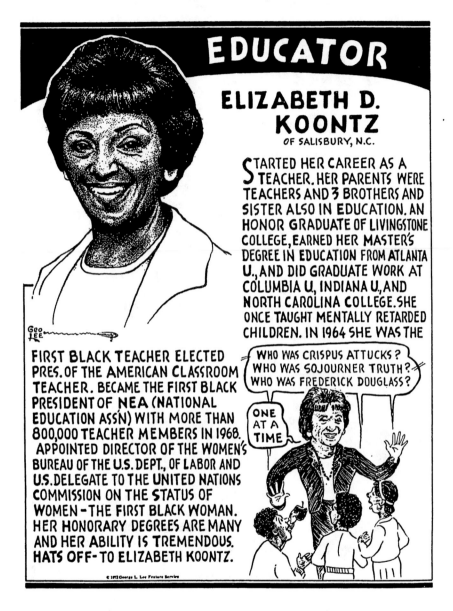

EDUCATOR

ELIZABETH D. KOONTZ
OF SALISBURY, N.C.

STARTED HER CAREER AS A TEACHER. HER PARENTS WERE TEACHERS AND 3 BROTHERS AND SISTER ALSO IN EDUCATION. AN HONOR GRADUATE OF LIVINGSTONE COLLEGE, EARNED HER MASTER'S DEGREE IN EDUCATION FROM ATLANTA U., AND DID GRADUATE WORK AT COLUMBIA U, INDIANA U., AND NORTH CAROLINA COLLEGE. SHE ONCE TAUGHT MENTALLY RETARDED CHILDREN. IN 1964 SHE WAS THE FIRST BLACK TEACHER ELECTED PRES. OF THE AMERICAN CLASSROOM TEACHER. BECAME THE FIRST BLACK PRESIDENT OF NEA (NATIONAL EDUCATION ASS'N) WITH MORE THAN 800,000 TEACHER MEMBERS IN 1968. APPOINTED DIRECTOR OF THE WOMEN'S BUREAU OF THE U.S. DEPT., OF LABOR AND U.S. DELEGATE TO THE UNITED NATIONS COMMISSION ON THE STATUS OF WOMEN — THE FIRST BLACK WOMAN. HER HONORARY DEGREES ARE MANY AND HER ABILITY IS TREMENDOUS. HATS OFF — TO ELIZABETH KOONTZ.

WHO WAS CRISPUS ATTUCKS? WHO WAS SOJOURNER TRUTH? WHO WAS FREDERICK DOUGLASS?

ONE AT A TIME

Geo Lee

© 1972 George L. Lee Feature Service

U.S. TREASURER

$$$

FIRST BLACK WOMAN TREASURER

AZIE TAYLOR MORTON

THE 36th TREASURER OF THE UNITED STATES AND THE FIRST BLACK WOMAN IN THE POSITION'S HISTORY. APPOINTED IN 1977, HER SIGNATURE APPEARS ON THE $1-$5 AND $10 BILLS. TREASURER MORTON'S $47,500-A-YEAR POST INCLUDES BEING THE NAT'L DIRECTOR OF THE U.S. SAVINGS BOND DIVISION AND SUPERVISES THE ACTIVITIES OF THE U.S. MINT. BORN IN DALE, TEXAS, SHE WAS ONCE A TEACHER. SERVED AS AN INVESTIGATOR WITH THE U.S. EQUAL EMPLOYMENT OPPORTUNITY COMM. SPECIAL ASS'T TO THE CHAIRMAN OF THE DEMO. NAT'L COMM. (1972-76). A HIGHLY QUALIFIED WOMAN WHO IS ON THE MONEY!

Geo LEE

1841 - 1898

BLANCHE KELSO BRUCE

THE FIRST BLACK TO BE APPOINTED REGISTER OF THE U.S. TREASURY AND SIGNED U.S. BONDS AND PAPER MONEY. APPOINTED BY PRES. GARFIELD IN 1881. BORN IN SLAVERY IN VIRGINIA, HE WAS THE FIRST BLACK U.S. SENATOR (MISS.) TO SERVE A FULL TERM (1875-1881). THE FIRST BLACK ON THE MONEY!

© 1977, George L. Lee Feature Service

180

DIRECTOR NAT'L URBAN LEAGUE

VERNON E. JORDAN JR.,

OUTSTANDING PERSONALITY WHO IS EMERGING AS A FORCEFUL LEADER IN THE CIVIL RIGHTS FIELD. NAMED DIRECTOR OF THE NATIONAL URBAN LEAGUE, AT THE AGE OF 36 (1971) THE YOUNGEST TO HEAD THE LEAGUE. BORN IN ATLANTA ON AUG 15, 1935 OF MIDDLE CLASS PARENTS. A GRADUATE OF DE PAUW U., (IND) WITH A B.A. DEGREE IN POLITICAL SCIENCE (1957). EARNED HIS LAW DEGREE FROM HOWARD U., (1960). BECAME VERY

ACTIVE IN CIVIL RIGHTS. TWO YEARS AS FIELD SECRETARY FOR GEORGIA'S NAACP. IN 1965, HEAD OF THE VOTER EDUCATION PROJECT OF THE SOUTHERN REGIONAL COUNCIL. ACCEPTED AN OFFER TO HEAD THE UNITED NEGRO COLLEGE FUND (1970). TRAGEDY BEFELL WHITNEY YOUNG THE LEAGUE'S HEAD IN MARCH 1971, HE MET AN UNTIMELY DEATH. JORDAN WAS SELECTED TO ASSUME LEADERSHIP... WITH MUCH SUCCESS...

1978 GEO L. LEE FEATURE SERVICE

After serving 10 years as the Urban League's director, Vernon Jordan resigned to join a prestigious law firm. He received the Fannie Lou Hamer Award from the National Conference of Black Mayors (1982) and the Distinguished Service Award from the Interracial Council for Business Opportunity (1983).

FAMED SCULPTOR

RICHARD HUNT

Geo.
LEE

ONE OF THE FOREMOST SCULPTORS IN AMERICA. HIS SKILL IN WELDING METAL INTO CREATIVE SMALL AND LARGE SCALE MONUMENTAL SCULPTURES IS AMAZING. A NATIVE OF CHICAGO'S SOUTHSIDE, HE GRADUATED FROM ENGLE-WOOD HIGH SCHOOL. WON A SCHOLARSHIP TO THE ART INSTITUTE OF CHICAGO...GRADUATED IN 1957. FIRST ONE-MAN SHOW AT 23. SUCCESS AND RECOGNITION WAS IMMEDIATE. HIS FIRST MAJOR MUSEUM EXHIBITION WAS IN 1971 AT THE MUSEUM OF MODERN ART IN N.Y. TODAY (1978), 42 YEAR OLD HUNT HAS NATIONAL PROMINENCE. HIS WORKS APPEARS IN SUCH COLLECTIONS AS: ART INSTITUTE OF CHICAGO, CLEVELAND MUSEUM, WHITNEY MUSEUM (NY), MUSEUM OF MODERN ART (NY), NAT'L MUSEUM OF ISRAEL. A GUGGENHEIM FELLOW.

WHAT BEAUTIFUL JUNK!

"FREEDOM HYBRID"
1976-

1979 GEO L. LEE FEATURE SERVICE

The Girl Who Upset 'BAMA

AUTHERINE LUCY

IN FEBRUARY 1956 THE U OF ALABAMA ADMITTED HER AS ITS FIRST BLACK STUDENT. IT CAUSED SUCH A TURMOIL FOR 3 DAYS THAT HER LIFE WAS THREATENED...THE SCHOOL SUSPENDED HER. IN THE AFTERMATH OVER 20 TEACHERS RESIGNED. A NATIVE OF SHILOH, ALA., SHE GRADUATED FROM MILES COLLEGE IN BIRMINGHAM. SHE WAS THE FIRST BLACK EVER ADMITTED TO A WHITE SCHOOL OR UNIVERSITY

Geo LEE

IN THE STATE. ALTHO MISS. LUCY NEVER RETURNED TO ALABAMA FOR HER GRADUATE DEGREE IN LIBRARY SCIENCE... SHE DID FOCUS ATTENTION, WHICH LATER OPENED THE DOORS TO BLACKS.

DARWIN T. TURNER

BRILLIANT STUDENT WHO IN 1947 BECAME THE YOUNGEST AT 15 TO MAKE THE PHI BETA KAPPA HONOR SOCIETY AT THE U OF CINCINNATI (OHIO) AND GRADUATED WITH AN A.B. DEGREE. STARTED NURSERY SCHOOL AT 2; FIRST GRADE AT 4; FOURTH GRADE AT 6; NINTH GRADE AT 9; GRADUATED FROM HI-SCHOOL AT 12; ENTERED U OF CINCINNATI AT 13 (1944). MAJOR- ENGLISH.

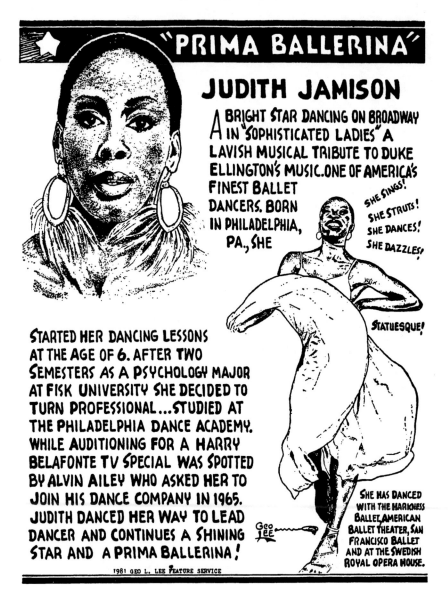

"PRIMA BALLERINA"

JUDITH JAMISON

A BRIGHT STAR DANCING ON BROADWAY IN "SOPHISTICATED LADIES" A LAVISH MUSICAL TRIBUTE TO DUKE ELLINGTON'S MUSIC. ONE OF AMERICA'S FINEST BALLET DANCERS. BORN IN PHILADELPHIA, PA., SHE

SHE SINGS!
SHE STRUTS!
SHE DANCES!
SHE DAZZLES!

STATUESQUE!

STARTED HER DANCING LESSONS AT THE AGE OF 6. AFTER TWO SEMESTERS AS A PSYCHOLOGY MAJOR AT FISK UNIVERSITY SHE DECIDED TO TURN PROFESSIONAL...STUDIED AT THE PHILADELPHIA DANCE ACADEMY. WHILE AUDITIONING FOR A HARRY BELAFONTE TV SPECIAL WAS SPOTTED BY ALVIN AILEY WHO ASKED HER TO JOIN HIS DANCE COMPANY IN 1965. JUDITH DANCED HER WAY TO LEAD DANCER AND CONTINUES A SHINING STAR AND A PRIMA BALLERINA!

GEO LEE

SHE HAS DANCED WITH THE HARKNESS BALLET, AMERICAN BALLET THEATER, SAN FRANCISCO BALLET AND AT THE SWEDISH ROYAL OPERA HOUSE.

1981 GEO L. LEE FEATURE SERVICE

FIRST BLACK TO WIN THE HEISMAN TROPHY!

1940 - 1963

ERNIE DAVIS
HALFBACK SYRACUSE U.(N.Y.)

WHO STEPPED INTO THE HALFBACK POSITION OF THE GREAT JIM BROWN AT SYRACUSE UNIV., AND WORE JIM'S No. 44...THEN WENT ON TO BREAK JIM'S COLLEGE RECORDS!

Geo Lee

ERNIE'S GREAT COLLEGE CAREER REACHED THE HEIGHTS WHEN HE WAS NAMED AS THE BEST COLLEGE "PLAYER OF THE YEAR"(1961)... AND WAS AWARDED THE "HEISMAN TROPHY" THE FIRST BLACK EVER IN ITS 27-YEAR HISTORY. HE FOLLOWED BROWN TO THE PROS... THE CLEVELAND BROWNS...BUT FATE THREW ERNIE FOR A LOSS..HE WENT DOWN WITH "LEUKEMIA" (DIED 1963).

© 1976 George L. Lee Feature Service

185

WILLYE WHITE in 5-OLYMPICS

HER OLYMPIC CAREER BEGAN AT 16 IN THE 1956 GAMES AT MELBOURNE, AUSTRALIA. AND WON A SILVER MEDAL IN THE LONG JUMP. THEN TO ROME, 1960. TOKYO IN 1964 WHERE WILLYE WON A SILVER MEDAL IN THE 400 METER RELAY. MEXICO CITY, 1968 AND MUNICH IN 1972. BORN ON A PLANTATION IN MONEY, MISS., GREW UP IN GREENWOOD. AT 10 CHOPPED COTTON. PLAYED HI-SCHOOL BASKETBALL IN THE FIFTH GRADE. AT 16 WAS RUNNING FOR TENNESSEE STATE. AN EXCELLENT ATHLETE SHE WAS THE ONLY AMERICAN FEMALE TO FINISH IN THE TOP 12 IN 5 OLYMPIADS. ON 39 INTERNATIONAL TEAMS AND TRAVELED TO 150 COUNTRIES. IN 1966, AWARDED THE FAIR PLAY MEDAL, THE WORLD'S HIGHEST SPORTSMANSHIP AWARD FOR 1965. SERVED AS A COACH IN 1979 AND 1981. FIRST BLACK WOMAN INDUCTED INTO THE MISS., HALL OF FAME - 1982. A DEGREE IN PUBLIC HEALTH ADMIN., FROM CHICAGO STATE U. IN 1983 A SUPERVISOR OF PHYSICAL FITNESS FOR THE CHICAGO DEPT. OF HEALTH. HER GREAT CAREER WILL ALWAYS INSPIRE OTHERS.

19' 11½"

1983 Geo L. Lee Feature Service

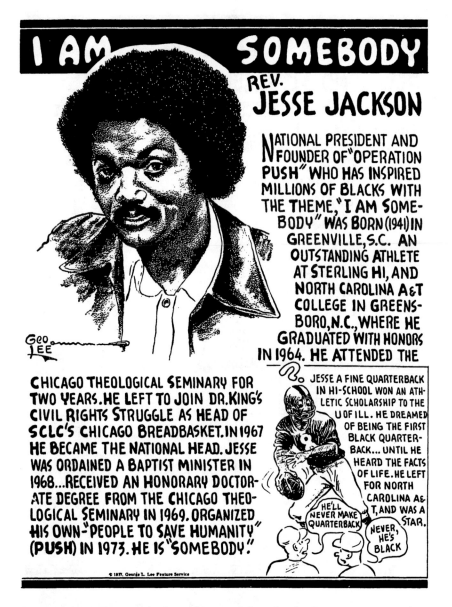

I AM SOMEBODY

REV. JESSE JACKSON

NATIONAL PRESIDENT AND FOUNDER OF "OPERATION PUSH" WHO HAS INSPIRED MILLIONS OF BLACKS WITH THE THEME, "I AM SOMEBODY" WAS BORN (1941) IN GREENVILLE, S.C. AN OUTSTANDING ATHLETE AT STERLING HI, AND NORTH CAROLINA A&T COLLEGE IN GREENSBORO, N.C., WHERE HE GRADUATED WITH HONORS IN 1964. HE ATTENDED THE

CHICAGO THEOLOGICAL SEMINARY FOR TWO YEARS. HE LEFT TO JOIN DR. KING'S CIVIL RIGHTS STRUGGLE AS HEAD OF SCLC'S CHICAGO BREADBASKET. IN 1967 HE BECAME THE NATIONAL HEAD. JESSE WAS ORDAINED A BAPTIST MINISTER IN 1968...RECEIVED AN HONORARY DOCTORATE DEGREE FROM THE CHICAGO THEOLOGICAL SEMINARY IN 1969. ORGANIZED HIS OWN "PEOPLE TO SAVE HUMANITY" (PUSH) IN 1973. HE IS "SOMEBODY."

JESSE A FINE QUARTERBACK IN HI-SCHOOL WON AN ATHLETIC SCHOLARSHIP TO THE U OF ILL. HE DREAMED OF BEING THE FIRST BLACK QUARTERBACK... UNTIL HE HEARD THE FACTS OF LIFE. HE LEFT FOR NORTH CAROLINA A&T, AND WAS A STAR.

HE'LL NEVER MAKE QUARTERBACK

NEVER, HE'S BLACK

© 1977, George L. Lee Feature Service

On Nov. 3, 1983, Jesse declared his candidacy for the Democratic Presidential nomination. He didn't win, but he gained international respect. On Oct. 10, 1987, he declared his candidacy for the 1988 race. He finished a tremendous second and his impact was felt in American politics!

187

The APOSTLE of HAPPINESS!

REVEREND AL GREEN

THE MASTER OF RHYTHM AND BLUES, THE PRINCE OF SOUL WHO SKYROCKETED TO FAME WITH 30-MILLION RECORD SALES IN 5-YEARS THEN TURNED TO THE PULPIT. BECAME AN ORDAINED MINISTER IN MEMPHIS. AL BOUGHT A CHURCH BUILDING IN 1976 AND STARTED HIS "FULL GOSPEL TABERNACLE" CHURCH. BORN IN FORREST CITY, ARK., A SON OF SOUTHERN BAPTIST PARENTS OF 10. AT 9, STARTED SINGING GOSPEL. AT 16, RHYTHM AND BLUES. HE FORMED A SINGING GROUP," THE CREATIONS," PLAYING SMALL CLUBS AND DEVELOPING A STYLE OF HIS OWN. HIS FIRST SINGLE, "BACK UP TRAIN" IN 1967 WAS A MILD HIT. IN 1971, HE

HIS SUCCESS CONTINUES IN SINGING GOSPEL ON BROADWAY IN "YOUR ARMS TOO SHORT TO BOX WITH GOD." (1982)

WROTE AND RECORDED HIS FIRST MILLION SELLER "TIRED OF BEING ALONE." AL WAS A BIG SUCCESS. HIS "LET'S STAY TOGETHER" SOLD OVER 2-MILLION. HE NEVER LOOKED BACK. ON STAGE HE IS "THE APOSTLE OF LOVE AND HAPPINESS !"

1983 Geo L. Lee Feature Service

188

FIRST BLACK AMERICAN in SPACE

LT.COL. GUION S. BLUFORD JR

WHEN THE SPACE SHUTTLE CHAL-LENGER, FLIGHT NO.8 LIFTED OFF ON ITS SKY-LIGHTING NIGHT LAUNCH FROM CAPE CANAVERAL, FLA., ON AUG 30, 1983-HISTORY WAS MADE! ASTRONAUT BLUFORD ONE OF A CREW OF 5 WENT INTO ORBIT. BORN IN PHILADELPHIA, PA., ON NOV 22, 1942. HIS MOTHER A TEACHER AND FATHER A MECHANICAL ENG-INEER. A GOOD MATH STUDENT. HE GRADUATED FROM PENN STATE U., IN 1964 AS A DISTINGUISHED AIR-FORCE ROTC GRADUATE AND A B.S. DEGREE IN AERO-SPACE ENGINEERING. IN 1965 RECEIVED HIS PILOT TRAINING AND HIS WINGS AT WILLIAMS AIR FORCE BASE IN ARIZONA. DURING THE VIETNAM WAR HE FLEW 144 COMBAT MISSIONS IN F-4 PHANTOM FIGHTER BOMBERS, 65 OVER NORTH VIETNAM(1966). AFTER HIS TOUR OF DUTY...AN AIR-FORCE JET PILOT INSTR-UCTOR. WITH A MASTER'S AND DOCTORATE IN AEROSPACE ENGINEERING AND SCIENCE, LASER EXPERT...NASA CHOSE HIM AN ASTRONAUT CANDI-DATE(1978). AS A "MISSION SCIENCE SPECIALIST...PERFORMED IN SPACE EXPERIMENTS ON THE SPACE-MEDICINE MACHINE TO AID IN DIABETES!

GEO LEE

189

U.S. CONGRESSWOMAN (D)

YVONNE B. BURKE

CALIFORNIA'S FIRST BLACK WOMAN ELECTED TO THE U.S. HOUSE OF REPRESENTATIVES IN NOV. 1972. A NATIVE OF LOS ANGELES, AND A GRADUATE OF UCLA. SHE EARNED HER LAW DEGREE FROM THE USC LAW SCHOOL AND A PRACTICING ATTORNEY FOR 10 YEARS. SERVED AS A DEPUTY CORPORATION COMMISSIONER AND A HEARING OFFICER FOR A POLICE COMMISSION. IN 1966 AFTER THE

WATTS RIOTS IN LOS ANGELES, COMMUNITY LEADERS DRAFTED HER TO RUN FOR THE STATE ASSEMBLY. SHE BEAT 3 MEN IN THE PRIMARIES AND A "JOHN BIRCHER" IN THE ELECTION TO BECOME THE FIRST BLACK..... ASSEMBLYWOMAN IN CALIFORNIA. MRS. BURKE, ROSE TO NATIONAL PROMINENCE WHEN SHE WAS VICE-CHAIRMAN OF THE DEMOCRATIC NATIONAL CONVENTION IN AUGUST, 1972. A VERY EXCITING PERSONALITY!

© 1976 George L. Lee Feature Service

Yvonne Burke was the first woman elected chair of the Congressional Black Caucus. Since leaving Congress in 1978 she has served on the Los Angeles County Board of Supervisors, the University of California Board of Regents, and the Olympic Organizing Committee.

SEARCHING FOR HIS ROOTS

SAM BOYNES

ASS'T MANAGER OF CHICAGO'S PLAY-BOY TOWERS HOTEL. BORN AND RAISED IN CHICAGO, A PRODUCT OF WENDELL PHILLIPS HIGH. HE OFTEN WONDERED WHY HIS NAME "BOYNES" WAS THE ONLY ONE IN THE PHONE BOOK. IN 1972 SAM WAS A MANAGER OF THE ROBERTS MOTEL. DURING THE NATIONAL BLACK CONV., HE MET A N.Y. DELEGATE NAMED... "BOYNES". THE DELEGATE TOLD HIM THAT HE WAS ORIGINALLY FROM ST. CROIX, VIRGIN ISLANDS WHERE MANY "BOYNESES" LIVED. SAM KNEW LITTLE ABOUT HIS ANCESTORS. HIS FATHER WAS BORN IN ILLINOIS. HIS GRANDFATHER

Geo LEE

DISAPPEARED SOON AFTER. IN 1975 SAM WENT TO ST. CROIX AND HE DID FIND HIS ROOTS...COUSINS. THEIR GREAT-GRANDFATHER, BOSS NISSON HAD BEEN BROUGHT TO ST. CROIX AS A SLAVE FROM HAITI. A BRICK-MASON HE EARNED HIS FREEDOM AND TOOK HIS FORMER OWNERS NAME "DE LA BOYNES."

1980 GEO L. LEE FEATURE SERVICE

SAM'S COUSINS BELIEVED THE BOYNES FAMILY CAME FROM HAITI...SO HE STARTED THERE IN 1978...THEN TO FRANCE IN 1979.

THE NAME IS THE SAME.

BOYNES

FRANCE

ILE DE BOYNES

INDIAN OCEAN

EAU DE BOYNES

HAITI

SAM MAKES NO CLAIM TO BLOOD LINES AND NOBILITY. HE LIKES TO.... TRAVEL!

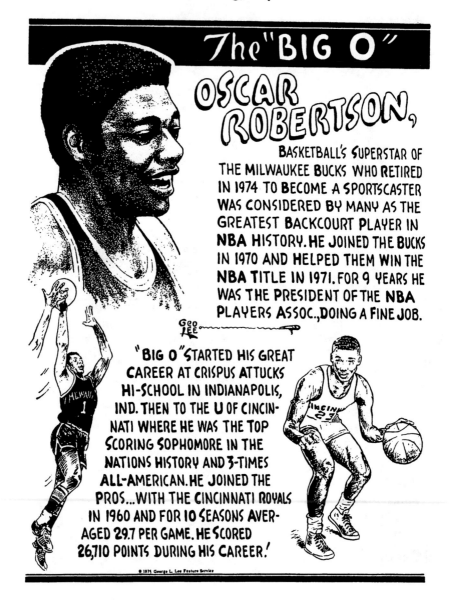

The "BIG O"

OSCAR ROBERTSON,

BASKETBALL'S SUPERSTAR OF THE MILWAUKEE BUCKS WHO RETIRED IN 1974 TO BECOME A SPORTSCASTER WAS CONSIDERED BY MANY AS THE GREATEST BACKCOURT PLAYER IN **NBA** HISTORY. HE JOINED THE BUCKS IN 1970 AND HELPED THEM WIN THE **NBA** TITLE IN 1971. FOR 9 YEARS HE WAS THE PRESIDENT OF THE **NBA** PLAYERS ASSOC., DOING A FINE JOB.

"BIG O" STARTED HIS GREAT CAREER AT CRISPUS ATTUCKS HI-SCHOOL IN INDIANAPOLIS, IND. THEN TO THE **U** OF CINCINNATI WHERE HE WAS THE TOP SCORING SOPHOMORE IN THE NATIONS HISTORY AND 3-TIMES ALL-AMERICAN. HE JOINED THE PROS... WITH THE CINCINNATI ROYALS IN 1960 AND FOR 10 SEASONS AVERAGED 29.7 PER GAME. HE SCORED 26,710 POINTS DURING HIS CAREER.'

HEADS AMERICA'S TEACHERS

MARY HATWOOD FUTRELL

A DEDICATED EDUCATOR AND SECRETARY-TREASURER OF THE NATIONAL EDUCATION ASSN. (NEA) AND THE ONLY CANDIDATE FOR PRESIDENT OF THE NEA. ON JULY 2, 1983 SHE WAS ELECTED HEAD OF THE 1.7-MILLION TEACHERS UNION. THE $71,000 A-YEAR PRESIDENT WAS BORN IN ALTA VISTA, VA., AND GREW UP IN LYNCHBURG, VA. GRADUATED FROM VIRGINIA STATE COLLEGE WITH A BUSINESS EDUCATION DEGREE. EARNED A MASTER'S DEGREE AT GEORGE WASHINGTON UNIV. HER TEACHING

Geo LEE

CAREER STARTED IN 1963 IN A HIGH SCHOOL IN ALEXANDRIA, VA., TEACHING BUSINESS. SHE BECAME INVOLVED IN THE EDUCATION ASSN. OF ALEXANDRIA (EAA) AND IN 1973-75 WAS ELECTED PRESIDENT. THE FIRST BLACK PRESIDENT OF VIRGINIA EDUCATION ASSN (VEA) 1976 AND 1978. WON A SEAT ON THE NEA BOARD, 1978. ELECTED SECRETARY-TREASURER, 1980. ...BEFORE REACHING THE TOP!

1984 Geo L. Lee Feature Service

"I WANT EVERY TEACHER IN THE CLASSROOM TO BE COMPETENT, LITERATE, VERY INTELLIGENT AND ABLE TO MOTIVATE STUDENTS."

MRS. FUTRELL EMERGES AS ONE OF THE MOST POWERFUL BLACK WOMEN IN AMERICA!

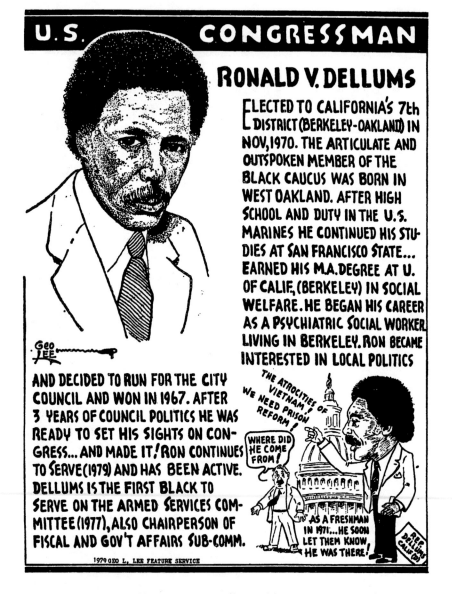

U.S. CONGRESSMAN

RONALD V. DELLUMS

ELECTED TO CALIFORNIA'S 7th DISTRICT (BERKELEY-OAKLAND) IN NOV, 1970. THE ARTICULATE AND OUTSPOKEN MEMBER OF THE BLACK CAUCUS WAS BORN IN WEST OAKLAND. AFTER HIGH SCHOOL AND DUTY IN THE U.S. MARINES HE CONTINUED HIS STUDIES AT SAN FRANCISCO STATE... EARNED HIS M.A. DEGREE AT U. OF CALIF., (BERKELEY) IN SOCIAL WELFARE. HE BEGAN HIS CAREER AS A PSYCHIATRIC SOCIAL WORKER LIVING IN BERKELEY. RON BECAME INTERESTED IN LOCAL POLITICS

AND DECIDED TO RUN FOR THE CITY COUNCIL AND WON IN 1967. AFTER 3 YEARS OF COUNCIL POLITICS HE WAS READY TO SET HIS SIGHTS ON CONGRESS... AND MADE IT! RON CONTINUES TO SERVE (1979) AND HAS BEEN ACTIVE. DELLUMS IS THE FIRST BLACK TO SERVE ON THE ARMED SERVICES COMMITTEE (1977), ALSO CHAIRPERSON OF FISCAL AND GOV'T AFFAIRS SUB-COMM.

THE ATROCITIES OF VIETNAM! WE NEED PRISON REFORM!

WHERE DID HE COME FROM!

AS A FRESHMAN IN 1971;...HE SOON LET THEM KNOW HE WAS THERE!

REP. DELLUMS CALIF (D)

GEO LEE

1979 GEO L. LEE FEATURE SERVICE

The year 1985 saw Dellums serving as chair of the Committee on the District of Columbia and of the House Armed Services Subcommittee on Military Construction, Installations and Facilities.

"I WILL NOT LET YOU FAIL"

MARVA COLLINS

Geo
LEE

HAILED A SUPER-TEACHER WHOSE LOVE, PATIENCE, UNDERSTANDING WITH CHILDREN GAINED HER NATIONAL RECOGNITION. AFTER 14 YEARS OF TEACHING IN CHICAGO PUBLIC SCHOOLS SHE DECIDED TO LEAVE THE SYSTEM. IN 1975 BEGAN HER WESTSIDE PREPARATORY SCHOOL IN HER HOME AND WENT BACK TO TEACHING THE BASICS... READING, WRITING AND ARITHMETIC, NO GIMMICKS. LOCATED ON CHICAGO'S WESTSIDE SHE STARTED WITH 6 SLOW LEARNING NEIGHBORHOOD CHILDREN. HER METHODS WERE AMAZING. BORN IN ATMORE, ALA.,

THE DAUGHTER OF A UNDERTAKER. A GOOD STUDENT AND AN AVID.... READER. A GRADUATE OF CLARK COLLEGE (ATLANTA) IN BUSINESS. RECEIVED HER TEACHING DEGREE FROM CHICAGO TEACHERS COLLEGE. HER SCHOOL HAS GROWN TO 200 PUPILS... 4 THRU 13, LEARNING THE BASICS TO SHAKESPEARE!

1981©Đ0 L. LEE FEATURE SERVICE

"YOU'RE GOING TO LEARN"

WINNER OF A $50,000. "ENDOW A DREAM" AWARD FROM MILLIONAIRE W. CLEMENT STONE OCT 1980.

"I WILL NOT LET YOU FAIL" JUNE 23, 1981 RECEIVED A JEFFERSON AWARD FROM THE AMERICAN INSTITUTE FOR PUBLIC SERVICE... FOR THE GREATEST PUBLIC SERVICE BENEFITING THE DISADVANTAGE."

195

PLANNED PARENTHOOD PRESIDENT

FAYE WATTLETON

THE FIRST WOMAN AND THE YOUNGEST PERSON (34) AND THE FIRST BLACK, APPOINTED NATIONAL PRESIDENT OF THE PLANNED PARENTHOOD FEDERATION OF AMERICA (JAN 1978), IN IT'S 62-YEAR HISTORY. FROM DAYTON, OHIO, SHE EARNED A M.A. DEGREE IN NURSING FROM COLUMBIA U. Ms. WATTLETON SERVED AS EXECUTIVE DIRECTOR OF PLANNED PARENTHOOD IN DAYTON FOR SEVEN YEARS.

Geo Lee

FIRST WOMAN LABOR EXEC.

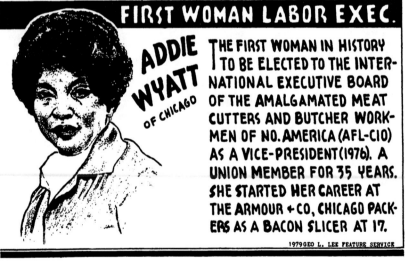

ADDIE WYATT OF CHICAGO

THE FIRST WOMAN IN HISTORY TO BE ELECTED TO THE INTERNATIONAL EXECUTIVE BOARD OF THE AMALGAMATED MEAT CUTTERS AND BUTCHER WORKMEN OF NO. AMERICA (AFL-CIO) AS A VICE-PRESIDENT (1976). A UNION MEMBER FOR 35 YEARS. SHE STARTED HER CAREER AT THE ARMOUR + CO, CHICAGO PACKERS AS A BACON SLICER AT 17.

1979 GEO L. LEE FEATURE SERVICE

196

A KNIGHT AND HER PIPS

GLADYS KNIGHT

THE DRAMATIC AND PENETRATING LEAD SINGER OF POP AND RHYTHM AND BLUES, HAS BEEN THE GUIDING LIGHT OF THE 'GLADYS KNIGHT AND THE PIPS' FOR 30 YEARS. BORN IN ATLANTA, GA., ON MAY 28, 1944. AT 4, SHE SANG HER FIRST RECITAL AT MT. MARIAH BAPTIST CHURCH. AT 7, AUDITIONED ON THE TED MACKS AMATEUR HOUR TV SHOW AND WON THE $2000. GRAND PRIZE. IN 1952 AT A FAMILY BIRTHDAY PARTY SHE, HER

BROTHER, MERALD AND COUSINS WILLIAM GUEST AND EDWARD PATTEN SANG AS A GROUP. THEY CREATED SO MUCH EXCITEMENT THAT COUSIN JAMES 'PIP' WOOD SUGGESTED THEY SHOULD FORM A QUARTET AND USE HIS NICKNAME - THE PIPS! THE ROAD WAS ROCKY BUT THEY ENDURED. RECORDED FIRST SINGLE, 1958. FIRST BIG HIT "EVERY BEAT OF MY HEART." (1960). STILL TREMENDOUS PERFORMERS!

1983 GEO L. LEE FEATURE SERVICE

THE PIPS

WILLIAM GUEST — EDWARD PATTEN

IN 1965 THE GROUP MADE IT TO MOTOWN AND THE GOLD RECORD CLASS. 30-YEARS OF EXCELLENCE!

MERALD "BUBBA" KNIGHT

Reggie left Oakland for Baltimore in 1976, then played for the New York Yankees, leading them to a World Series victory in 1977. He tied Babe Ruth's record for World Series single-game homers by hitting 3 in the sixth game. He won the Most Valuable Player–World Series Award. In 1987 he returned to Oakland.

SHE SINGS FOR HUMANITY

ROBERTA FLACK

GIFTED WITH MUSICAL TALENT SHE EXPRESSES HER FEELINGS FOR THE CAUSE OF HUMAN JUSTICE THROUGH HER LOVE SONGS.. BORN IN ASHE-VILLE, N.C., THE DAUGHTER OF MUS-ICAL PARENTS. GROWING UP IN VIRGINIA SHE STUDIED CLASSICAL MUSIC TO BE A CONCERT PIANIST. AT 15 ENTERED HOWARD U., ON A MUSIC SCHOLAR-SHIP EARNING A B.A. IN MUSIC. STARTED GRADUATE STUDY BUT.... WENT INTO TEACHING ENGLISH IN NO. CAROLINA AND TAUGHT IN WASH, D.C. DURING THAT TIME TOOK A PART-TIME JOB ACCOMPANYING OPERA SINGERS. ROBERTA LEFT TEACHING

AND BACK TO MUSIC AND "POP." HER CAREER STARTED IN MAY 1967 AT MR. HENRY'S PUB IN D.C., HER SOFT DELICATE STYLE SOON ATT-RACTED JAZZ PIANIST, LES McCANN WHO INTRODUCED HER TO ATLANTIC RECORDS AND HER FIRST ALBUM. SUCCESS, CONCERT TOURS ABROAD CONTINUES FOR A FINE ARTIST (1980).

WON GRAMMY AWARDS IN 1973 FOR FIRST TIME EVER "I SAW YOUR FACE" AND "WHERE IS THE LOVE." IN 1974 WITH-"KILLING ME SOFTLY WITH HIS SONG." VOTED NO.1 FEMALE VOCALIST BY DOWN BEAT POLL IN 1972. SANG IN YUGOSLAVIA, VENEZUELA, JAPAN, NEW ZEALAND IN 1980.

1980 GEO L. LEE FEATURE SERVICE

EMMY WINNER

CICELY TYSON

THE VERY FINE ACTRESS WHOSE PORTRAYAL, AS JANE PITTMAN WHO AGES TO 110-YEARS OLD, IN THE TELEVISION MOVIE..."THE AUTOBIOGRAPHY OF MISS JANE PITTMAN" WON THE EMMY AWARD IN 1974, AS THE "ACTRESS OF THE YEAR IN A SPECIAL". A NATIVE OF NEW YORK CITY'S EAST SIDE. AFTER HIGH SCHOOL SHE WAS A

CICELY AS JANE PITTMAN AT 110-YRS.

SECRETARY FOR THE RED CROSS POUNDING A TYPEWRITER...THEN TO MODELING. IN 1959 STARTED HER ACTING CAREER IN HARLEM. PLAYED OFF BROADWAY IN 1963...IN A MOVIE IN 1966. FIVE YEARS LATER HER BIG BREAK, THE PART OF REBECCA MORGAN IN "SOUNDER" THE HIGHLY SUCCESSFUL FILM. A BRIGHT SHINING STAR........

© 1976 George L. Lee Feature Service

ARTHUR ASHE OF RICHMOND, VA.

ARTHUR STARTED HIS GREAT CAREER AT 7. BY 12 HE WAS WINNING TOURNAMENTS. AT 17 HE WAS A U.S. JUNIOR CHAMP. HE WON THE NATIONAL CLAY COURTS CHAMPIONSHIPS IN CHICAGO AT THE AGE OF 20. WHILE HE ATTENDED UCLA HE WAS NO.1 PLAYER. THE TENNIS STAR GRADUATED IN 1966.

ASHE WAS THE FIRST TO WIN THE U.S. OPEN AT FOREST HILLS, N.Y. IN 1968. HIS TITLES ARE TOO NUMEROUS TO NAME. HE WON THE AUSTRALIAN OPEN (1970), THE PARIS INDOOR (1970) AND THE WORLD CHAMPIONSHIP TENNIS TITLE IN 1972. (RUNNER-UP IN 1973).

IN 1963 HE PLAYED AT WIMBLEDON, ENGLAND. ALTHO HE DID NOT WIN HE WAS NAMED TO THE U.S. DAVIS CUP TEAM, THE FIRST BLACK. HIS MOST DEADLY WEAPON IS HIS SERVE, WHICH HAS PUT HIM TO THE TOP WITH THE GREAT U.S. TENNIS PLAYERS. HIS PRO EARNINGS ARE HIGH. HE NETTED $141,000 IN 1970. A REAL SUPER STAR. A GREAT INSPIRATION TO THE BLACK YOUTH OF AMERICA.

Geo Lee

© 1973 George L. Lee Feature Service

201

FLYING HIGH

JILL BROWN

THE FIRST BLACK WOMAN TO RECEIVE HER WINGS AS A PILOT OF A MAJOR SCHEDULED AIRLINES WHEN SHE BECAME A FIRST OFFICER WITH THE TEXAS INTERNATIONAL AIRLINES IN 1978. THE 28-YEAR-OLD NATIVE OF MILLERSVILLE, MD., A GRADUATE OF UNIV. OF MARYLAND STARTED FLYING CAREER AT LEE-AIRPORT IN EDGEWATER, MD., IN 1974 THE NAVY ACCEPTED JILL AS THE FIRST BLACK WOMAN FOR PILOT TRAINING...BUT SHE LEFT FOR COMMERCIAL FLYING...HIGH!

Geo Lee

OTIS B. YOUNG

A FIRST OFFICER WITH THE PAN AM WORLD AIRWAYS WAS THE FIRST BLACK PILOT TO FLY THE 747 JUMBO JET. IN 1970 HE FLEW A 747 FROM LONDON TO LOS ANGELES ON ITS INAUGURAL NON-STOP FLIGHT...5,500 MI. A NATIVE OF WASH, D.C. AND A PILOT WITH PAN AM SINCE 1965, WHEN HE LEFT THE AIR-FORCE...

1979 GEO L. LEE FEATURE SERVICE

U.S. MEDAL of HONOR

PFC. MILTON L. OLIVE III

"*FOR CONSPICUOUS GALLANTRY AND INTREPIDITY IN ACTION AT THE RISK OF HIS LIFE ABOVE AND BEYOND THE CALL OF DUTY.*" THE CONGRESSIONAL MEDAL OF HONOR, WAS PRESENTED BY PRES. LYNDON B. JOHNSON... POSTHUMOUSLY TO PFC OLIVE OF CO. B, SECOND BATTALION (AIRBORNE) 503rd INFANTRY REGIMENT FIGHTING IN VIETNAM. ON OCT 22, 1965 HE HURLED HIMSELF ON A VIET CONG GRENADE AND SAVED

THE LIVES OF FOUR OF HIS COMRADES BUT GAVE UP HIS OWN. PFC. OLIVE OF CHICAGO WAS ONLY 19. HE WAS THE 3rd U.S. SOLDIER TO WIN THE HONOR IN THE VIETNAM WAR AND THE FIRST BLACK. A CHICAGO PARK AND COLLEGE WERE NAMED IN HIS HONOR.

© 1979 George L. Lee Feature Service

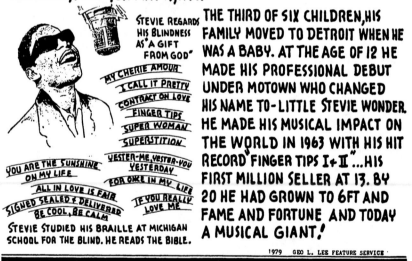

MUSICAL GENIUS

STEVIE WONDER

THE LITTLE BLIND PRODIGY WHO HAS BECOME A YOUNG MAN GENIUS OF THE MUSICAL WORLD IN SINGING AND COMPOSING. HIS ALBUM "SONGS IN THE KEY OF LIFE," WON 4 GRAMMYS AT THE 19th ANNUAL AWARDS ON FEB 19, 1977. IN 1978 HE RECEIVED THE HONORARY DOCTOR OF HUMANE LETTERS DEGREE FROM HOWARD U. BORN STEVEN JUDKINS, BLIND IN SAGINAW, MICH., ON MAY 13, 1950.

Geo
Lee

STEVIE REGARDS HIS BLINDNESS AS "A GIFT FROM GOD"

MY CHERIE AMOUR
I CALL IT PRETTY
CONTRACT ON LOVE
FINGER TIPS
SUPER WOMAN
SUPERSTITION
YESTER-ME, YESTER-YOU YESTERDAY
FOR ONCE IN MY LIFE
IF YOU REALLY LOVE ME

YOU ARE THE SUNSHINE ON MY LIFE
ALL IN LOVE IS FAIR
SIGNED SEALED & DELIVERED
BE COOL, BE CALM

STEVIE STUDIED HIS BRAILLE AT MICHIGAN SCHOOL FOR THE BLIND. HE READS THE BIBLE.

THE THIRD OF SIX CHILDREN, HIS FAMILY MOVED TO DETROIT WHEN HE WAS A BABY. AT THE AGE OF 12 HE MADE HIS PROFESSIONAL DEBUT UNDER MOTOWN WHO CHANGED HIS NAME TO- LITTLE STEVIE WONDER. HE MADE HIS MUSICAL IMPACT ON THE WORLD IN 1963 WITH HIS HIT RECORD "FINGER TIPS I + II"...HIS FIRST MILLION SELLER AT 13. BY 20 HE HAD GROWN TO 6FT AND FAME AND FORTUNE AND TODAY A MUSICAL GIANT!

1979   GEO L. LEE FEATURE SERVICE

In 1985, Stevie Wonder was awarded the Oscar for the best movie song, "I Just Called to Say I Love You." He accepted the award "in the name of Nelson Mandela," the best-known black prisoner of South Africa's apartheid system of white minority rule. Stevie's songs were banned by the South African state-owned radio station.

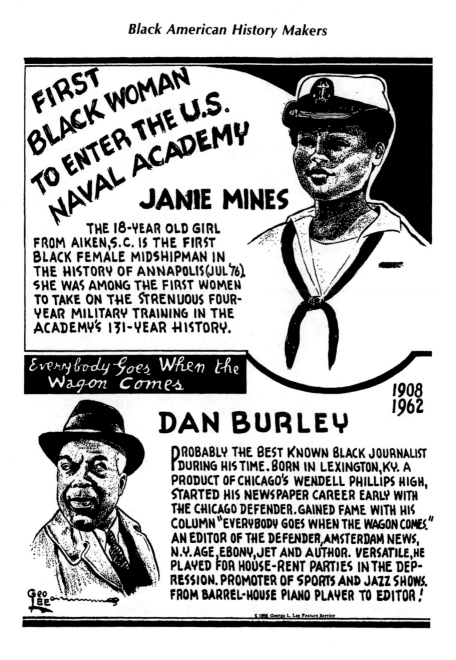

FIRST BLACK WOMAN TO ENTER THE U.S. NAVAL ACADEMY

JANIE MINES

THE 18-YEAR OLD GIRL FROM AIKEN, S.C. IS THE FIRST BLACK FEMALE MIDSHIPMAN IN THE HISTORY OF ANNAPOLIS (JUL '76). SHE WAS AMONG THE FIRST WOMEN TO TAKE ON THE STRENUOUS FOUR-YEAR MILITARY TRAINING IN THE ACADEMY'S 131-YEAR HISTORY.

Everybody Goes When the Wagon Comes

1908
1962

DAN BURLEY

PROBABLY THE BEST KNOWN BLACK JOURNALIST DURING HIS TIME. BORN IN LEXINGTON, KY. A PRODUCT OF CHICAGO'S WENDELL PHILLIPS HIGH, STARTED HIS NEWSPAPER CAREER EARLY WITH THE CHICAGO DEFENDER. GAINED FAME WITH HIS COLUMN "EVERYBODY GOES WHEN THE WAGON COMES." AN EDITOR OF THE DEFENDER, AMSTERDAM NEWS, N.Y. AGE, EBONY, JET AND AUTHOR. VERSATILE, HE PLAYED FOR HOUSE-RENT PARTIES IN THE DEPRESSION. PROMOTER OF SPORTS AND JAZZ SHOWS. FROM BARREL-HOUSE PIANO PLAYER TO EDITOR!

Geo Lee

© 1978 George L. Lee Feature Service

HE DREW SPORTS AND PEOPLE

GEORGE L. LEE

HE ARRIVED IN CHICAGO SEPT, 1927 FROM SEATTLE. A GAR- FIELD HIGH (1925) GRADUATE. A BIG CITY OFFERED SO MUCH... NEGRO NEWSPAPERS. HE WENT TO THE CHICAGO DEFENDER TO SEE MR. ABB- OTT... NO JOB... BUT SOME WORDS OF WISDOM." WHAT HAVE YOU DONE FOR YOUR -SELF?" IN 1928 A MESSEN- GER FOR... PURE OIL CO. 1930 MADE CONTACT WITH 'BANG'

A BOXING MAGAZINE AND CHICA- GO AMERICAN. 1934 CREATED 'SPORTING AROUND' FOR DEFEN- DER... ALSO 'YOUR HISTORY' FOR PITTSBURGH COURIER BY J.A. ROG- ERS. IN 1945-48 CREATED HIS OWN FEATURE INTERESTING PEOPLE. IN 1950's DREW BOXING-PUBLICITY FOR THE IBC (CHGO-STADIUM). RETIR- ED FROM POSTAL SER. (69). RE-CREAT- ED INTERESTING PEOPLE. RET. 80 YR's

JUL 31,1986

GEO LEE

About the Author

George L. Lee was born in Jamestown, N.Y., on July 27, 1906, and raised in the state of Washington in Spokane, Wenatchee and Seattle. As he was growing up he worked in the fruit orchards, shined shoes, and read Horatio Alger books with the positive attitudes of "Sink or Swim" and "Do or Die." He shipped out on the boats to California and Alaska from Seattle.

Lee graduated from Garfield High School in the class of 1925. It was here that he began his venture in drawing, though he had very little formal training. He drew his first sports cartoon in 1926. Deciding to go to Chicago, he saved $150 and arrived in September 1927. It certainly wasn't easy, but it was exciting, even in the Depression. His first sports cartoon was published in May 1930 in *Bang*, a boxing magazine. Sports drawing in those days was a big thing. Lee met Eddie Geiger, sports editor of the *Chicago American*, an evening paper. Geiger gave him the opportunity to publish a drawing that appeared on August 26, 1930. By 1933 Lee had drawn 15 cartoons on a free-lance basis. But then some one began asking, who is George Lee? The sports editor said he was a Negro, and that was the end. Lee then began drawing for the *Chicago Defender*. In 1934 he created the format and illustrations for a history feature for the *Pittsburgh Courier* by J.A. Rogers, noted historian. The feature was called "Your History."

Also in 1934, Lee drew publicity for Joe Louis's first pro fight in Chicago and was paid $50. Joe himself was paid $50 for the fight . . . that was as close as Lee ever got to the great Joe Louis! He married in 1936 and entered the Postal Service in 1937, the same year his son was born. He drew a weekly feature for the black press from 1945 to 1948, but the feature was discontinued because of a wartime newsprint shortage. He returned to sports and drew cartoons and publicity for the International Boxing Club during the fifties. He retired from the Postal Service in 1969 and recreated his feature in 1970. He continued the feature until he retired in 1986 at the age of 80!

Index

Aaron, Hank 172
Abbott, Robert S. 26
Abernathy, Ralph David 144
Alexander, Clifford 156
Alexander, Sadie Tanner 59
Alston, Charles 79
Angelou, Maya 171
Armstrong, Louis 66
Ashe, Arthur 201
Ashford, Emmett 92

Bailey, Pearl 110
Baldwin, James 132
Barnett, Ida B. Wells 19
Basie, Count 75
Basie, William see Basie, Count
Bates, Clayton "Peg Leg" 63
Bates, Daisy 108
Baumfree, Isabella 2
The Black Panthers 146
Bluford, Guion S., Jr. 189
Bojangles see Robinson, Bill
Bolin, Jane M. 44
Boynes, Sam 191
Bradley, Thomas 99
Brooks, Gwendolyn 96
Brown, Dorothy L. 119
Brown, Jesse 122
Brown, Jill 202
Brown, Willa 104
Brown, William W. 4
Bruce, Blanche Kelso 180
Bumbry, Grace 168
Bunche, Ralph J. 72
Burke, Yvonne B. 190
Burley, Dan 205

Burnett, Chester see Howlin' Wolf
Burroughs, Margaret 105

Carney, William H. 11
Carroll, Diahann 173
Carroll, Vinnette 167
Carver, George Washington 20
Catlett, Elizabeth 79
Charles, Ray 153
Cherry, Gwendolyn B. 130
Chisholm, Shirley St. Hill 137
Clifton, Nathaniel "Sweetwater" 131
Cole, Nat "King" 111
Coleman, Bessie 41
Collins, Marva 195
Cooper, Anna Julia 17
Coppin, Fanny L. Jackson 9
Cosby, Bill 154

Dandridge, Dorothy 129
Davis, Ernie 185
Deadwood Dick see Love, Nat
Dellums, Robert V. 194
Denison, Elizabeth Forth 1
Dolby, Mattie Cunningham 30
Dorsey, Thomas A. 65
Douglass, Frederick 5
Drew, Charles R. 71
Dunham, Katherine 84

Edwards, James 112
Elder, Lee 148
Ellington, Duke 67

Fields, Mary 8
Flack, Roberta 199
Foley, Lelia 93
Foster, Andrew (Rube) 31
Frazier, Joe 178
Futrell, Mary Hatwood 193

Gaillard, Adele Chilton 97
Gaither, Alonzo Smith "Jake" 98
Gibson, Althea 143
Giovanni, Nikki 165
Goldman, Martha Barksdale 55
Gordon, Odetta Felious see Odetta
Gordone, Charles 169
Gossett, Lou, Jr. 135
Grant, Micki 165
Green, Al 188
Green, Ernest 176

Haley, Alex 125
Hall, Juanita 68
Hamer, Fannie Lou 100
Hampton, Lionel 89
Handy, W.C. 76
Harper, Frances E. 7
Harris, Catherine 3
Harris, Margaret 90
Harris, Patricia R. 140
Hastie, William H. 74
Height, Dorothy I. 124
Henson, Matthew A. 57
Holiday, Billie 94
Hooks, Benjamin L. 139
Horne, Lena 103
Houston, Charles H. 46
Houston, Jessie "Ma" 64
Howlin' Wolf 85
Hughes, Langston 70

Index

Hunt, Richard 182
Hunter, Alberta 47
Hunter, Jane Edna 33

Jackson, Jesse 187
Jackson, Mahalia 86
Jackson, Reggie 198
James, Daniel "Chappie,"
  Jr. 121
Jamison, Judith 184
Johnson, Hazel W. 155
Johnson, James Weldon 27
Jones, Clara 90
Jones, James Earl 147
Jones, Lois Mailou 78
Jones, Quincy 157
Jones, Sadie Waterford 39
Joplin, Scott 23
Jordan, Barbara 158
Jordan, Vernon E., Jr. 181
Joyner, Marjorie S. 52
Julian, Percy L. 61

Kearse, Amayla 163
Kimbrough, Robert L. 128
King, Coretta Scott 151
King, Martin L., Sr. 62
Knight, Gladys 197
Koontz, Elizabeth D. 179

Lampkin, Daisy 34
Latimer, Lewis H. 13
Lawson, John S. 11
Lee, George 206–207
Lewis, Edmonia 12
Lewis, Samella S. 166
Lewis, William H. 22
Little, Malcolm see Mal-
  colm X
Louis, Joe 91
Love, Nat 14
Love, Ruth 161
Lucy, Autherine 183

Mabley, Jackie (Moms) 56
McCree, Wade Hampton
  116
McGee, Henry W. 73
McKinley, Ada S. 25
Mahoney, Mary Elizabeth
  145
Malcolm X 138
Marshall, Thurgood 80
Meredith, James H. 160
Metcalfe, Ralph 81

Michaux, Solomon L. 36
Mines, Janie 205
Mitchell, Arthur W. 37
Mitchell, Clarence 87
Mitchell, Parren 169
Mollison, Irvin C. 60
Morganfield, McKinley
  see Waters, Muddy
Morrison, Toni 164
Morton, Azie Taylor 180
Motley, Constance Baker
  150
Murphy, Isaac 37
Murray, Pauli 83

Nicholas Brothers 114

Odetta 85
Olive, Milton L., III 203
Owens, Jesse 101

Parker, Charlie 115
Parks, Gordon, Sr. 88
Parks, Rosa 7
Parsons, James B. 76
Payton, Carolyn 93
Petersen, Frank E. 149
Phillips, Vel 136
Pickett, Bill 18
Poitier, Sidney 141
Porter, James A. 77
Price, Leontyne 142
Pride, Charley 133

Rapier, James T. 10
Razaf, Andy 49
Reese, Della 117
Rhea, La Julia 69
Richardson, Gloria 120
Robertson, Oscar 192
Robeson, Eslanda Goode
  53
Robeson, Paul 57
Robinson, Bill 29
Robinson, Frank 174
Robinson, Jackie 6
Robinson, Roscoe 146
Robinson, "Sugar" Ray 159
Rogers, Charles C. 155
Ross, Diana 177

Salisbury, R.J. 35
Sampson, Edith 22
Sands, Diana 170
Savage, Augusta 42

Scott, William E. 7
Sloan, John Steward 109
Smalls, Robert 10
Smith, Bessie 48
Spears, Doris E. 19
Spingarn, Joel E. 24
Stevens, Grace Lee 43
Still, William Grant 50
Sullivan, Leon H. 126

Thomas, Gerald E. 145
Trotter, William Monroe
  28
Truth, Sojourner see
  Baumfree, Isabella
Tubman, Harriet 6
Tucker, C. Delores 162
Turner, Darwin T. 183
Tyson, Cicely 200

Van Der Zee, James 38
Vaughan, Sarah 134
Verrett, Shirley 175

Walker, C.J. 21
Walker, William O. 51
Washington, Harold 127
Washington, Sara S. 32
Waters, Muddy 95
Watson, Barbara 113
Wattleton, Faye 196
West, Harriet M. 44
White, Charles 106
White, Willye 186
Williams, Daniel H. 16
Williams, Helen E. vi
Williams, Mary Lou 82
Williams, Paul R. 45
Wilson, Edith 54
Wilson, Margaret Bush 102
Witherspoon, Fredda 58
Wonder, Stevie 204
Wright, Jane Cooke 118
Wright, Louis T. 40
Wright, Richard R. 15
Wyatt, Addie 196

Yerby, Frank 21
Young, Andrew 152
Young, Coleman A. 107
Young, Otis B. 202
Young, Whitney M., Jr.
  123